Pearl Harbor Jazz

Pearl Harbor Jazz

Change in Popular Music in the Early 1940s

Peter Townsend

University Press of Mississippi / Jackson

www.upress.state.ms.us

The University Press of Mississippi is a member of the
Association of American University Presses.

Copyright © 2007 by University Press of Mississippi
All rights reserved
Manufactured in the United States of America

First edition 2007
∞
Library of Congress Cataloging-in-Publication Data

Townsend, Peter, 1948–
    Pearl Harbor jazz : change in popular music in the early 1940s / Peter Townsend. — 1st ed.
        p. cm.
    Includes bibliographical references and index.
    ISBN-13: 978-1-57806-924-8 (cloth : alk. paper)
    ISBN-10: 1-57806-924-6 (cloth : alk. paper) 1. Jazz—1941–1950—History and criticism.
2. Jazz—Social aspects—United States. I. Title.
    ML3918. J39.T7 2007
    781.650973'09044—dc22

                                                                    2006012430

British Library Cataloging-in-Publication Data available

To Sue Clarke (1949–2002)

Contents

Acknowledgments

My thanks go to staff of libraries and archives, specifically the Archives Center in the Museum of American History at the Smithsonian, Washington, D.C.; the National Newspaper Library in Colindale, United Kingdom; and the National Jazz Archive, Loughton, England. I began the research that eventually produced this book when invited to contribute to the Duke Ellington Centenary Conference in Washington, D.C., in 1999. Sections of the book have been the subject of postgraduate and research seminars at Leeds College of Music and the School of Music at the University of Huddersfield, England.

I extend my thanks also to friends, family, and colleagues: Diane and Andrew Turnbull; Chris and Geraldine Baker and family; Les Berry; Alf and Liz Louvre, for their support and encouragement at a crucial time; Jim Burns, for help with obscure material from the period; and Santi Sillitto and Yvonne Kohler of Il Glicine, Sicily, where parts of this book were written. I especially thank Seetha Srinivasan and Walter Biggins at the University Press of Mississippi.

Pearl Harbor Jazz

Introduction

The sudden, if not completely unexpected, movement of the United States into war in December 1941 initiated a period of precipitate change in American society, culture, and music. A Department of Agriculture official told John Dos Passos, "Looks like the war has speeded up every kind of process, good or bad, in this country" (1945: 70). The war changed the social and economic conditions, and the music business and particular styles of music were quickly and materially affected.

World War II provoked the largest demographic shift experienced by American society since the original settlement of the land. This migration produced results that were unpredictable in relation to prewar musical culture. The defense construction boom moved the Alabama honky-tonk singer Hank Williams, who made his first amateur recording in May 1942, to the shipyards on the Gulf of Mexico and later to the yards in the Pacific Northwest. From the first months of the war, the same economic pull moved hundreds of thousands of black and white Southerners to California, leading to the growth of musical cultures such as the one that developed in the 1940s around Central Avenue in Los Angeles.

Even without the war, life had been getting tough for the territory bands that had been crisscrossing the United States, especially the Midwest, since the 1920s. George Simon's study (1974a) of the big bands listed 439 orchestras, of which about 90 percent were operating at the time of Pearl Harbor. The histories of jazz and popular music have preserved the names of a relatively small proportion of these. Others have been missed because they were ephemeral, never made it to a sufficient level of recognition, or their musical styles have passed out of fashion. Bands like those of Kay Kyser, Horace Heidt, Alvino Rey, and others were massively present in the average citizen's experience of contemporary music. All of them, however, are little remembered today, and historians of American popular music continue to show little interest in them.

Beyond this circle of the historically disadvantaged and beyond the reach of Simon's list, there were musical organizations all over the United States that survive only in passing references in the press or because their paths crossed with those of performers whose names are still known. The list of bands practicing their trade in the United States in December 1941 includes Bill Sawyer and his orchestra, playing the Michigan Union Ball in Ann Arbor; the band of Bob Hutsell on station WHAS from the Iroquois Amphitheatre in Louisville; Emil Flindt at the Merry Garden Ballroom in Chicago; the Buddy Johnston Band playing at "Cincinnati's most terrific show spot," the Casa Grande; the Buddy Arnold band of Bridgeport, Connecticut; Jimmy Parette of Scranton, Pennsylvania; Glenn Williams of Macon, Georgia; Charlie Baker of Jackson, Tennessee; Johnny McGee of Springfield, Illinois; Frank Lombardo of Wilkes-Barre, Pennsylvania; John Henry Morris of Shreveport, Louisiana; and Barron Elliot of Pittsburgh, "the Steel City's favorite."

A comprehensive picture of American popular music at the time of Pearl Harbor would include this layer of artists and performers and the full range of musical idioms that were played, listened to, or danced to. Bill Malone expressed the same sense of a large personnel of unknown and unrecorded country music artists, "The entire aggregate of hillbilly performers, ranging from the professionals to the amateurs who struggled for success in the honky-tonks or on obscure radio barn-dances, must have been enormous. Of the total, only a small percentage did well enough financially to warrant independent professional careers; most could not 'give up their day jobs'" (Malone 1987: 186). Country music, too, had territory bands who were making a precarious living. These were the "generations of sleep-deprived fiddlers and guitar players" (Davidoff 1998: 106) who traveled the South and Southwest in the same kinds of buses and converted limousines as the jazz and swing bands.

This nationwide population of people working in music depended upon a network of places. Bars, honky-tonks, nightclubs, ballrooms, juke joints, colleges, hotels, movie theaters, dance pavilions, county fairs, armories, ice rinks, sports arenas, warehouses, and a wide range of unofficial and occasional locations, from department stores to private parties, provided spaces for the performances. These spaces became the most important channels, together with radio, through which Americans received music at the beginning of World War II.

A ballroom in a town provided live music to a public who did not and could not make the same distinctions of category as are usual today. If the Rink Ballroom in Waukegan, Illinois, presented one week Duke Ellington (known as one of the greatest figures of an important culture, "jazz") and the next week the orchestra of Phil Levant, the only clear constant was the venue itself, the Rink Ballroom. For many of the public, Ellington and Levant fell into the pragmatic category of "what's playing at the Rink." As I note throughout the book, in the early 1940s American popular music had not yet been corralled into its separate narratives, categories, and spaces.

The places of American popular music fell into the same hierarchy as the acts that played in them. At the top, with a symbolic precedence that haunted popular musicians, was Carnegie Hall and its equivalents. Next were the metropolitan theaters and ballrooms, some of which were well known across the nation, including the Savoy in Harlem, Roseland on Broadway, and other venues in New York, Chicago, and Los Angeles. For black musicians, the Apollo Theatre in Harlem had a special status. Then there were theaters on the name-band circuits, such as the Howard in Washington, D.C.; the Paradise in Detroit; the Oriental in Los Angeles; and the Regal in Chicago. Among ballrooms, the Glen Island Casino in New Rochelle, New York, and the Meadowbrook, in Cedar Grove, New Jersey, were prime eastern locations with national reputations and networked radio hookups.

Other towns and cities had theaters, ballrooms, and nightclubs and their own local or national access to radio. Theaters like the Adams in Newark, the Palace in Columbus, Ohio; the Michigan in Detroit; and the State in Hartford, Connecticut, ranked somewhere in the hierarchy of places, as did ballrooms like the Valencia in York, Pennsylvania; the Modernistic in Milwaukee; the Uptown in Portland, Oregon; the Meadow

Acre in Topeka; the Val Air in Des Moines; and the King's Ballroom in Lincoln, Nebraska, among many others.

Some of these, such as the Adams, might attract name bands most of the time, whereas others had name bands only part of the time or occasionally. Some venues were identifiably black or white in their clientele and featured performers. From a distance of more than half a century, it is difficult to assess the character of many of these places of music. Research needs to be done on all the local memories, records, and images of the network of venues that covered the United States. This book is in part an attempt to mobilize some of that dormant information, to use material concerning the day-to-day movement and activity of musicians to ground popular music in the period.

Histories of American music for the period covered by this book have been concerned primarily with jazz. This leaves a large gap in the record. Popular music comes into the historians' sight only with the arrival of Elvis Presley in the 1950s, and there is an apparent assumption that mainstream popular music before that time contained little that is of interest, historically or aesthetically. Histories of jazz—and later those of blues and country music—have skirted around the large abandoned territory of 1940s popular music.

If one took a survey of the music that Americans were listening to in the early 1940s, given the assumptions of later orthodoxies, they were by and large wasting their time on popular trash. A considerable number were listening to jazz, blues, or country music, and our twenty-first-century perspective grants them some respect: these are accredited authentic musical traditions in which we are interested. But the millions of listeners to the bands of Vaughn Monroe, Les Brown, and Kay Kyser and to singers such as Connee Boswell and Dinah Shore are seen as associating with musical subcategories whose memory is not preserved and whose history is not worth writing. There was a large audience for popular song genres that are now dismissed as "sentimental." In the early 1940s, however, these styles were still powerful, and they formed part of the substrata of American musical taste. They were a surprisingly large element in the musical culture of many singers and players, even of some of the most "authentic."

The history of jazz has been written in a linear way, either in biographical accounts or in full-length histories of the music. Both of these modes have tended to isolate, separating the career of an individual musician from the complex context in which it occurred, or, in the full-scale histories, separating lines of development from other factors less easily woven into the narrative. The result of the separation assumed in most historical accounts of jazz (or of other "authentic" modes) is a sense of abstraction, music that existed in a contextual vacuum. The connections of jazz with the rest of American music are suppressed in favor of the narrative thread of what is essential to "jazz itself." Its connections with a broader context are suppressed or cursorily sketched in: media of performance, economic drives and constraints, other organizations producing music, other contemporary artistic expressions—in short, all of the rest of contemporary American life.

This book sets out an alternative to the linearity and the abstraction of the jazz narrative from a cultural and social context. To use a term from linguistics, most histories of jazz and comparable forms have been *diachronic*, dealing with a narrative chain of events. This book sets out to be synchronic, to show the concrete details of how American music operated as a system at a particular moment: not separating out individual narratives of jazz, swing, country, and popular music and relating each one in a horizontal way, but looking vertically at the fabric of American music at this time.

This book is about a moment in the history of popular musical forms. It covers a critical period of a little over one year, from the announcement of the Pearl Harbor attack in December 1941 to two events of the winter of 1942–1943: the sensational appearances made by Frank Sinatra at the Paramount Theater in New York and the premiere of Duke Ellington's "Black, Brown, and Beige" at Carnegie Hall three weeks later. The conjunction of Sinatra and Ellington—something that occurred three more times during the period—provides an example of ways in which the categories and separations of later narrative-making distort the real context in which musicians worked. As Ellington's new composition was being presented in January 1943, Sinatra was performing only twelve blocks away. Sinatra was part of Ellington's context just as Ellington was of Sinatra's. Despite being confined to separate historical narratives, the two men met and interacted, as did many other theoretically unlikely pairings.

Forms of music that conventional histories presented as successive were actually concurrent. Styles of music represented as distinct or antithetical were actually in contact or were impossible to distinguish from one another. People mixed, and the modes of simultaneity and copresence went even further than the meeting of parallel styles of music. Musicians, no more than anyone else, have a history abstracted from social matrices. In 1942 music was being played, recorded, and broadcast all over the United States all of the time. As accounts of the "Pearl Harbor moment" in chapter 1 show, to stop the clock on American music at any point catches people in different locations, different routines, different sectors of the network—a vertical slice through musical activity that was all happening at one time, rather than separate musical existences strung out along their own separate narratives: Duke Ellington in Oregon; Tommy Dorsey in Hollywood; Artie Shaw in Providence; Glenn Miller in New York; Andy Kirk in St. Louis; the radio playing Shostakovitch, Xavier Cugat, and Bunny Berigan; the Andrews Sisters in Cincinnati; and Count Basie in Wichita. Aside from the circumstance of Pearl Harbor, this dispersion, this spread of music, place, and occasion was entirely typical of the reality of musical culture: continuous, undesigned, and embedded in a real rather than an ideal context, a context made up of theater lines, hotels, radio stations, buses, salaries, audiences, routines, accidents, illnesses, towns, cities, newspapers, and critics.

The period centering on the year of 1942 was a time of instability and accelerated change in the United States. The music historian Colin Escott (2002: 45) referred to it as "one of those moments when all the cards are in the air." It was wartime, and the effects of a war economy on the business of music were felt with increasing force. The war limited movement and shut down possibilities for musicians in the poorer sectors of the market. It caused musicians to be inducted into the service and shifted large sections of the population to new centers, creating boomtown economies in unexpected places. Musicians were party to these global shifts as well as the ebbs and flows of their professional world. Dexter Gordon, the saxophonist touring the United States with the Les Hite band, connected the radical mobility of the times with the music, "It was a time of change because it was wartime and people were moving back and forth all over the United States and constantly traveling—armies, war jobs, defense jobs. And it was a time of change, and the music was reflecting this" (Gitler 1985: 311).

Historians of the music of this time have offered conflicting assessments of this reflection. Gunther Schuller (1989: 398) suggested that by

1942, in "parallel to the mounting pitch of war frenzy, . . . decibel levels in jazz had risen considerably." For others, there were contradictory signs of "a cooler romanticism" replacing "the excesses of the late thirties jitterbug" (Robertson 2000: 3), while for Gene Fernett (1970: 112), surveying the black swing bands, "the tempo of the music, and the era, was slowing." These contrary estimates are typical of music writers offering casual sociological opinions. Given the pervasive instability, however, it is possible that the contrary signs were actually visible.

In 1942 and the period surrounding it, musical styles were both coming together and breaking apart. In Scott DeVeaux's *The Birth of Bebop* (1997), 1942 was taken as the point of origin of the new jazz, the moment in which all its necessary factors were brought together. The year 1942 was also one of revivalism, the year of the literal rediscovery of the mythic traditional jazz player Bunk Johnson and of Hugues Panassié's book *The Real Jazz*, which gave a rationale to the search for a lost "authenticity." The year 1942 heard music that, in the recordings of Louis Jordan, Lucky Millinder, and Lionel Hampton, sounded like what was to be called "rhythm-and-blues." At the same time there were signs in some New York clubs and in the ambitions of the emergent Stan Kenton band of the progressivism that would eventually lead to a very different result. For some critics, jazz was on the threshold of a higher evolutionary level, while from others one can get "the impression that jazz died around 1942" (Schuller 1989: 844).

As a traveling bandleader and recording artist, Duke Ellington covered as broad a range of contexts as any American musician. The Ellington band played all grades of venues from high school gyms to Carnegie Hall. Its musicians knew the nation's highways and railroads through continuous traveling. They were immersed in the economic pressures of road tours and one-nighters, and yet they had aspirations to serious works for the concert hall. Ellington and his band, black artists and performers, also confronted the racial status quo of 1940s America. In this respect, the period is bounded by A. Phillips Randolph's threatened 1941 march on Washington and riots in Harlem and Detroit in the summer of 1943. Performers like Ellington were accustomed to moving back and forth across the racial partitions of their audience, playing in black theaters such as the Howard in Washington, D.C., and the white dance halls of New England and the Midwest. Ellington knew the racial geography as thoroughly as the railroad system.

Duke Ellington's position within the musical culture provides a special focus upon musical styles and how Americans thought of them, both in the early 1940s and afterward. Although he radically resisted all forms of categorization, Ellington is regarded as a jazz musician, perhaps the jazz musician *par excellence*. His work in 1942 and 1943, as we shall see later, was enlisted into the effort of repositioning jazz as a serious art form, with Ellington himself as its exemplar. But during these years, Ellington also moved through contexts that were not those of the art composer-musician. His experience contained tensions that bear upon the assumptions of jazz writers and theorists over the past half-century. These assumptions have affected the character of jazz as it has come down to the present generation: the way it is presented, even the way it is performed, as well as the way that people think of jazz. During 1942–1943, Ellington's place in this process was indicative of the ideological changes that were getting underway. Between Pearl Harbor and the Paramount was a turning point in American music, when some musical styles and the ways of conceiving of them were reconfigured along lines that were to set parameters for two generations ahead.

In chapter 1 I discuss where popular American musicians were on December 7, 1941, the day of the Japanese attack on Pearl Harbor. The following chapters refer to a combination of times and places: "The War" recounts the early response of the music business to the new situation; "The Alley" presents a broader picture of the songwriting and exploitation business at the time; and "The Avenue" and "The Street," referring to Central Avenue in Los Angeles and 52nd Street in New York, focus primarily on the East and West Coast scenes at various times in 1942. "The Road" refers more straightforwardly to *the road*, a generic fact of American life and music and of American life in music. "Disorder at the Border," which takes its title from an early bebop recording, refers to the energy being expended on setting up and maintaining the boundaries between "jazz" and other forms at this time. Each of these topographical and cultural features of the landscape reflects the same dynamics of change and acceleration of development as can be seen in musical styles themselves. Together with long-term effects of some social and cultural undercurrents that were already in motion, the war changed them all.

Chapter 1

Sunday Matinee
in St. Louis

We had the radio on, probably listening to Glenn Miller or
Benny Goodman. It didn't really mean a thing for a while.

—DENNIS KEEGAN (Terkel 2001: 25)

On the Sunday afternoon of December 7, 1941, many Americans were occupying themselves with music. The first radio announcement of an attack on Pearl Harbor, a little after two o'clock in the afternoon, cut into a WABC broadcast of Shostakovich's "First Symphony," being played by the New York Philharmonic. Another sector of the radio audience was at that moment listening to the Latin orchestra of Xavier Cugat broadcasting on WNEW. News bulletins for the rest of the day were heard among the music of Bunny Berigan, Judy Garland, the cowboy singer Gene Autry, Dinah Shore, and Phil Spitalny's All-Girl Orchestra—musicians who played different styles of music, all scheduled to be on network radio during the peak hours of that evening.

The clarinetist Mezz Mezzrow heard the news while in prison on Hart's Island, New York, "December 7th 1941: we're listening to some hot records over the radio, news flash comes through telling about Pearl Harbor"

(Mezzrow and Wolfe 1961: 308). In Lowell, Massachusetts, a college football player and aspiring jazz writer, Jack Kerouac, heard the news from a newspaper seller as he left a showing of Orson Welles's new film *Citizen Kane*. The singer Woody Guthrie was performing in New York at a concert urging U.S. involvement in the war; the word of Pearl Harbor, arriving in the middle of the concert, made the organizers' point. The music critic of the *Providence Journal* had spent that afternoon at a classical concert in the city. His review in the following day's edition contained this thought, "When we came into the office after the concert, we heard for the first time that the country was at war. Making music and listening to it seemed extremely trivial pursuits" (*PJ* 12.8.41: 15).

Professional musicians remembered where they were on December 7, 1941, by the jobs they were playing at that moment. The Benny Goodman band, with their new vocalist Peggy Lee, heard the news of Pearl Harbor while relaxing in a coffee bar in Passaic, New Jersey. Maxine Andrews, one of the singing sisters then at the height of their success, heard the news at a theater in Cincinnati. The Andrews Sisters were doing record-breaking business, and even in the depths of that winter, there had been lines outside the theater. According to Maxine, "This Sunday morning, I walked over and there were no lines. I thought, Now, this is funny. I walked on to the stage, which was very dark. The doorman and the stagehands were sitting around the radio. They had just one light on. They were talking about Pearl Harbor being bombed" (Terkel 2001: 295).

Musicians in the big traveling bands, which were the staple of popular music, were scattered across the continent. For them, that Sunday was one afternoon out of years of traveling the roads in buses, one-night stands in theaters and ballrooms, town after town, city after city. The Count Basie band was on a circuit through the Midwest, and Pearl Harbor Sunday marked one of the limits of their travels, "I don't remember all of the places we hit on that string of one-nighters," Basie wrote, "but I do know that we went out west as far as Wichita because that was where I was on December 7. Somebody woke me up that Sunday . . . because the news on the radio was about Pearl Harbor" (Basie and Murray 1987: 318).

The Andy Kirk band was in St. Louis, playing the Tune Town Ballroom. "It was a Sunday matinee dance," Kirk remembered, "and loaded with GI's from the camp near there." The soldiers in the ballroom audience had been reminiscing with him about earlier meetings on road tours. They were expecting soon to complete their peacetime duties and to be sent home. Instead, it was Kirk's duty at the Sunday matinee to announce that, because of what had just occurred at Pearl Harbor, the GIs had orders to return to camp (Kirk and Lee 1989: 105).

The Artie Shaw band was also on the road, in New England. According to the trumpeter Max Kaminsky, during that tour in the fall of 1941, "Artie was bigger than ever. People followed his bus and swarmed in to collect autographs wherever it stopped" (Kaminsky and Hughes 1965: 125). Shaw's band operated in a higher market than Kirk's—Kaminsky's weekly salary was $175, six times the income of the average American. The Artie Shaw band traveled as a unit of thirty musicians, the big band augmented with a string section. This nationally rated enterprise also experienced the same disruptive moment, "We were playing a Sunday afternoon show at a theatre in Providence on December 7, 1941, when the manager interrupted the performance to announce that the Japanese had bombed Pearl Harbor" (1965: 127). For the Lucky Millinder band, there is recorded evidence of the abrupt arrival of the news. The band were performing at the Savoy Ballroom in Harlem on the afternoon of December 7, and on a recording of "Let Me off Uptown" from the broadcast of that session, there is an Associated Press newsflash announcing an emergency meeting called by President Roosevelt.

The Millinder band made a recording a few weeks later of one of the anti-Japanese songs produced in the first flush of wartime. "We're Gonna Have to Slap the Dirty Little Jap," by the country songwriter Carson Robison, was one of the flood of songs that in early 1942 quickly exhausted the rhyming possibilities of the word *Jap*. The country artist Denver Darling is credited with the first recording to comment explicitly on the events of December 7, the song "Cowards over Pearl Harbor," composed by the phenomenally successful country performer Roy Acuff and recorded fifteen days after the attack. The swing orchestras of Teddy Powell and Dick Robertson, however, had already tied for the first war song of the conflict, both recording "Goodbye Mama (I'm off to Yokohama)" on December 16 in New York.

The Hawaii-based bandleader Giggie Royce was stranded in Los Angeles by the emergency, with no early prospect of a boat back to Honolulu. The band of Billy MacDonald was even more closely affected, having survived the air-raid during a residency at the Lau Yee Chai restaurant in Hawaii (*DB* 1.1.42: 8).[1] One of the major bandleaders, Jimmy Dorsey, broadcasting on December 7 on WNEW from the Meadowbrook Ballroom in New Jersey, suffered forty-two interruptions for news bulletins during a one-hour program, six of them during his solo feature "Fingerbustin'." Dorsey finally dealt with the delay by breaking into an impromptu version of "The Star Spangled Banner," which caused the station to hold off further interruptions and the Meadowbrook audience to join in singing with the band.

For the members of Lionel Hampton's new big band, that Sunday held a journey between gigs, across New York City, just after the announcement of the attack, "We were in Jersey at the time and had to catch the subway for our engagement at the Strand Theater in Brooklyn," the saxophonist Marshall Royal recalled. "I was with Hamp's band at the Brooklyn Strand when Roosevelt went on the air and declared war—Pearl Harbor" (Royal and Gordon 1996: 74). The picture is of interruption, a sudden change of life and career prospects. Royal noted that with Pearl Harbor came summonses to draft boards and the expectation of a halt to his life in music.

A similar sense of personal consequences affected the musicians of the Stan Kenton band, who had spent 1941 on an upward curve of success on the West Coast, "I woke up Sunday and heard the newscast," said the bassist Howard Rumsey, "and I felt that somebody had pulled the ladder to success right out from under me. . . . I took it as a personal affront" (Easton 1973: 68). As *Down Beat* put it in the first editorial of 1942, "To every musician war is a personal puzzle. Will I lose my job? Shall I sell my horn? How long will it last? Will it end my career?" (*DB* 1.1.42: 1).

But as well as this radical disruption, there was also an automatic continuity. Stalled for a moment by the immediate shock, musicians carried on their professional commitments. Billie Holiday, ending a run at the Apollo Theatre in Harlem, was due to open four days later at the Famous Door on 52nd Street. Fats Waller was leading an aggregation of musicians and entertainers on a tour of the Midwest and looking forward to a speculative (and in the event unsuccessful) engagement at Carnegie Hall six weeks later. The Duke Ellington orchestra was continuing a series of dates on the West Coast, despite power blackouts that affected southern California in the first days after the declaration of war.

In the cities, the swing bands were playing as usual in ballrooms, theaters, and nightclubs. On the weekend of Pearl Harbor, the Woody Herman band was at the Strand Theater on 47th Street in Manhattan, coupled on the bill with a Western movie, *They Died with Their Boots On*. On 128th Street in Harlem, Café Society's uptown branch presented the violinist Eddie South, the John Kirby group, and the Golden Gate Quartet, while downtown had Teddy Wilson, the singer Helen Humes, and the boogie piano of Pete Johnson and Albert Ammons.

Across New York, the name bands were in residence in the high-profile locations. Benny Goodman was at the New Yorker Hotel, and Harry James was at the Lincoln. Artie Shaw's band was playing at the State Theater, while Muggsy Spanier's new band was breaking attendance records at the Arcadia on Broadway. The Charlie Barnet band was featured at the Flatbush in Brooklyn and Claude Thornhill's at the Glen Island Casino in New Rochelle. Albany had the Cab Calloway orchestra at the New Kenmore. Fletcher Henderson and his band were at one of Chicago's prime locations, the Grand Terrace Café, broadcasting every evening on WBBM. Jimmie Lunceford's dynamic band was at the Palace Theater in Akron, Ohio. On the West Coast, Bob Crosby's Dixieland-styled orchestra was playing at the Trianon Ballroom in Southgate and Tommy Dorsey at the MGM Theatre in Hollywood. The orchestra of Duke Ellington was playing a college prom on December 7, 1941, in Eugene, Oregon.

After the attack on Pearl Harbor, the recording industry proceeded without an immediate disturbance, although this was to change dramatically over the following year—and not only because of the war. In Chicago in the last months of 1941, despite a decline in the popularity of blues, the Blue Bird and Okeh companies were running sessions by the likes of Jazz Gillum, Sonny Boy Williamson, Memphis Minnie, and Big Bill Broonzy. The subjects of some late-1941 blues already reflected war-mindedness. On the Tuesday before Pearl Harbor, Broonzy recorded "In the Army Now," and on Friday, December 5, Jazz Gillum recorded "War Time Blues."

Despite the declaration of war, the recording of jazz and popular music went on as planned. By the Thursday following the United States' entry into war, the top-ranking big bands of Glenn Miller, Benny Goodman, and Harry James had been in the New York studios. Before the end of the month they were followed by Jimmy Dorsey, Tommy Dorsey, Woody Herman, Cab

Calloway, Jimmy Lunceford, Artie Shaw, Gene Krupa, Lionel Hampton, Les Brown, Horace Heidt, Charlie Spivak, Tony Pastor, Guy Lombardo, Bob Chester, and others. Popular singers were also in the studios in those first weeks of wartime: Lena Horne; the Andrews Sisters; Carmen Miranda, representing wartime spirit in "Thank You, North America"; and Frank Sinatra, still a band vocalist with Tommy Dorsey, recording on December 22 "How About You," a song from the movie *Babes on Broadway* that premiered over the Christmas season.

Some important recordings were produced in these first weeks, such as Jimmy Dorsey's best-selling "Tangerine" and several competing versions of "Blues in the Night," a song that was already a hit for Woody Herman. In late 1941, no band in the United States was more popular than Glenn Miller's. The band was in the Victor studios in New York the day after Pearl Harbor, recording a number that had been in their repertoire for months under the title "This Is Where We Came In," but that Monday was retitled "Keep 'Em Flying." The Miller band was heard on eight network radio spots in the week before Pearl Harbor, broadcasting from its winter location at the Café Rouge in the Hotel Pennsylvania. On Monday, December 8, Miller did the usual evening broadcast on the NBC-Blue network, though the week's run of radio shows was curtailed to seven. The Tuesday night program sponsored by Chesterfield cigarettes gave way to President Roosevelt's first fireside chat of wartime.

Chapter 2

The War

Let it suffice that the war is in full swing—and people have to do
something or else.

—*Amsterdam News*, February 28, 1942

The attack on Pearl Harbor unexpectedly changed the plans of many
in the music business. The saxophonist Coleman Hawkins had a
Chicago-based band on tour in late 1941, with the hope that the band might
eventually make it to New York, the ultimate destination of all rising bands
and performers. Pearl Harbor came upon Hawkins's band in Indianapolis,
and, in the words of one of Hawkins's sidemen, "That ended the tour and
all of Hawk's plans; he told us all to go back home" (Chilton 1990: 193). In
New York, the impresario Ernie Anderson had gambled on filling Carnegie
Hall for a concert by the pianist and entertainer Fats Waller, to take place
in January 1942. In his regular checks of the ticket racks in the box office,
Anderson "was just beginning to see some small sale starting, when we
were hit by a devastating blow. The Japs bombed Pearl Harbor and the
entire United States of America went to war. Ticket sales for everything
froze up. The papers were chockablock with grim news. Nobody wanted to
know about jazz concerts" (Wright 1992: 379).

17

Bands with stable personnel or a run of forward bookings weathered the difficulties of the first weeks, but as Barney Bigard, a long-time member of Duke Ellington's orchestra, wrote, "I had never seen anything like the change that World War II brought about in the world" (Bigard and Martyn 1985: 75). Ellington's musicians had heard about Pearl Harbor at a railroad station in Eugene, Oregon, where the band was due to play a college prom on the night of December 7. The Eugene show was the first date of a Pacific Northwest tour. Arriving in late afternoon from Los Angeles, the Ellington musicians knew nothing of the attack until they heard the news as they pulled into the Oregon college town. Ellington's band had been on the West Coast for the second half of 1941, following the premiere of his show "Jump for Joy" in Los Angeles. The planned opening of a lavishly refurbished Los Angeles venue, the Trocadero, promised a major showcase for the Ellington band, but the renovations had not materialized by December. The Trocadero was an early casualty of wartime, its redesign scaled down through building restrictions and finally cancelled altogether.

The band that Ellington had during 1940–1941 is widely considered his best ever. One of its strengths was the innovative work of a young bass player, Jimmy Blanton. In the words of another great bassist, Milt Hinton, "He revolutionized bass playing, and Duke was just the man to know how to use his talent" (Gitler 1985: 44). It was during the months on the West Coast that Blanton began to show symptoms of tuberculosis. Hinton gave this account of his condition in late 1941: Blanton was a weak kid. He might get on the bus soaking wet after a gig and drive two or three hundred miles like that while his clothes dried on him. Eventually he got tuberculosis, and of course we had no penicillin or sulfa drugs then. The only treatment was to go to bed and rest. So he got sick in California" (Gitler 1985: 44). The Ellington band was heading back East, and in 1942 the band would cover at least 30,000 miles in its traveling schedule. For a while a second bassist, Junior Raglin, shadowed the ailing Blanton in band performances, and when the band caught the train out of Los Angeles at the end of 1941, Blanton was left behind in a treatment clinic.

Measured by income, exposure, and the end-of-year polls in music magazines such as *Down Beat* and *Metronome*, the Ellington orchestra was maintaining a strong position in the market, especially among "colored" bands. Ahead of Ellington in popularity were white bands such as those of Benny Goodman, Artie Shaw, and Glenn Miller (in ascending order of popularity at the time). Other bands of the same configuration but offering distinctive approaches were coming through, most notably the Harry James orchestra. Late that fall, the James band arrived at the Brooklyn Paramount at 8:00 a.m. after having driven all night from a date in Pittsburgh. Fans were lined up around the block waiting for the first show. As James remembered, when he got off the bus, "I thought there had been an accident or a fire or something because we hadn't seen a big crowd since we started the band. So I walked up and asked somebody, 'What's wrong?' and the guy said, 'We're waiting to see Harry James'" (Levinson 1999: 103).

The career of James and his band might have suffered from the timing of its breakthrough a matter of days before the war, but the orchestra continued to increase in popularity through the next two years. Its recording of the old song "You Made Me Love You" was already a success, and on the Thursday after Pearl Harbor, the band recorded a new song with a special resonance, Frank Loesser's "I Don't Want to Walk Without You," containing a yearningly emotional performance by the singer Helen Forrest.

Other bands were making breakthroughs at this historically disadvantageous moment. An engagement at a major New York venue represented the threshold of success for Lionel Hampton's band. As reported the day before Pearl Harbor, "Not since Jimmie Lunceford made his New York debut as a bandleader has Harlem been so set back on its haunches as has the mad, super-talented aggregation headed by Lionel Hampton heard in the Apollo this week" (*AN* 12.6.41: 20). (At this time of writing *Harlem* was either a definite location, or, more commonly, a metonym for *black*.) Another band growing in acclaim in its constituency was Lucky Millinder's, already a fixture at the Savoy Ballroom but broadening its appeal through record sales, "Remember a couple of years or so back when most everyone thought Lucky was on the way out as a band leader? Remember how folks passed him on the street without recognition? It's all changed now. Luck, with several nightly chain broadcasts from the Savoy, his recordings zooming sky high, including 'Big Fat Mama,' can't walk down B'way without propositions from songwriters, publishers, etc." (*AN* 1.24.42: 14).

Publicity and out-of-town reputation preceded the arrival in New York of two bands that were indicative of stylistic changes. One was the Californian orchestra of Stan Kenton, which had gathered a following at the Rendezvous Ballroom at Balboa Beach and the Palladium in Los Angeles. A one-night performance at the Glendale Auditorium resulted in "a wild, chaotic mob scene, with the auditorium jammed beyond its two thousand capacity and nearly twice that number lined up around the block" (Easton 1973: 67). Even at this early stage, the Kenton orchestra was creating a polarization of opinion that it was never able completely to transcend. With its "sharp, offbeat syncopation, improvised solos and frequent, screaming brass fanfares," it reached beyond contemporary styles into a realm that came to be called "progressivism." The orchestra's New York opening promised to challenge both critical opinion and the reactions of the dancers.

In November 1941, the Jay McShann orchestra, out of Kansas City, was reported breaking attendance records at the Civic Auditorium in Houston, Texas, and at venues across the country. There was a flurry of competition among the agencies to sign McShann, who had already made successful recordings, to a new contract. The William Morris agency was reported angling for the band, but eventually a deal was made with Moe Gale, a controller of major venues in Harlem, who booked McShann's orchestra for a date in the Savoy early in 1942. The band's popularity was based on straightforward big-band arrangements of the blues, but among its personnel as the band approached New York City was a young saxophonist named Charlie Parker.

These new presences would have to make their way not only through the usual vicissitudes of the business but also the unpredictable circumstances of a wartime economy. Conditions in the music business at the end of 1941 were unstable even without the additional confusion of the onset of war. There were some promising signs, however. After a prolonged slump, record sales had been climbing back to the same level as in the last peak year of 1928. Mannie Sachs, president of Columbia Records, was able to predict that total sales for 1941 would reach 120 million records, with a further rise likely for 1942. The 400,000 jukeboxes then operating across the United States accounted for a large portion of the recovery.

The year 1941 had been an unsettled one in the music industry. For months, a complex, acrimonious dispute between the radio networks and the music publishers' organization, ASCAP, had prevented radio stations broadcasting material over which ASCAP had rights—in effect the entire repertoire of current popular music. This dispute had severe effects on the publishers' incomes during most of the year, as ASCAP's material was cut off from its customary outlets. To make matters worse, another organization, BMI, was set up by the radio companies to supply music from new or underexploited sources. So it was that a good deal of music originating outside the professional milieu of Broadway and Hollywood, including regional and country or hillbilly music, benefited from the widest distribution it had so far known.

This was to have an important influence on the future of American popular music. BMI had already produced hit songs such as "Amapola." Like a later success, the Brazilian "Tico-Tico," this represented the Latin strain in their nonstandard output. In 1941, a hidden potential market for country music began to break through with BMI successes like "You Are My Sunshine." A 1941 recording by the country singer Ernest Tubb, "Walking the Floor over You," with an arrangement that either sounded simplistic or refreshingly simple next to the sophisticated song constructions the American public was accustomed to, was on the way to selling 400,000 copies inside a year.

The demographic changes of wartime would enhance the commercial potential of country music even more. But the ASCAP dispute had effects that would carry on through the era of rock and roll. A submerged continent of music, not conforming to styles and standards that had been established through half a century of the musical theater, Broadway, and the movie musical, but informed instead by the energies of folk music and working-class tastes, was ready to surface. Audiences were becoming attracted to directness and simplicity. An idiom later known as "rhythm-and-blues" was about to emerge before a black wartime audience in the same way as the music of Bob Wills and Roy Acuff was addressing audiences of transplanted white Southerners in California and elsewhere.

When the ASCAP ban was lifted in October 1941, one of the first beneficiaries was the Glenn Miller band's recording "Chattanooga Choo-Choo." The tune could now be played on the band's numerous radio broadcasts. The record sold so quickly that by February 1942 it became the first million selling record since 1927 and the first to be awarded a gold disc for the achievement. ASCAP was back on stream, and to that extent it seemed like business as usual. But some new energies were being released, and the arrival of war at the end of 1941 added more complex factors to the picture. In the words of a song recorded by Benny Goodman's orchestra three days after Pearl Harbor and Woody Herman a week later, someone was rocking America's dreamboat.

The war did not affect the recording studios, however, and they were still promoting the products of the songwriting industry. In the last week of 1941, three more versions of the Johnny Mercer and Harold Arlen song "Blues in the Night" were recorded, by Jimmie Lunceford, Benny Goodman, and Harry James (bringing the total to eight since September). James's version of the newly war-resonant "I Don't Want to Walk Without You" was followed by a version by Erskine Hawkins. Direct reference to the war was not widespread, though there had been a burst of compositional activity within days of Pearl Harbor. Fats Waller had a song ready for recording the day after Christmas that supported the government's drive on recycling, "Get More Cash for Your Trash."

Except for the spell of cancellations and blackouts on the West Coast, performances were going ahead untroubled. In Detroit, Louis Armstrong was the main attraction at the Christmas opening of a 2200-seat theater, the Paradise, "an important new show-window for colored bands and shows" (*DB* 12.1.41: 2). The annual Christmas benefit at the Apollo drew a superfluity of participants, with "at least 17 acts, and six orchestras ... unable to go on because of the crush of talent backstage and at 5 a.m. performers were still coming backstage anxious to do their bit for Harlem's most outstanding Christmas charity" (*AN* 12.20.41: 18). Network radio on Christmas Day included two broadcasts by Glenn Miller and his orchestra, including another spot for a broadcast of "Chattanooga Choo-Choo." That night on his long-running show *The Kraft Music Hour*, Bing Crosby sang a new Irving Berlin composition from the score of a film that was not to be premiered until the summer, "White Christmas."

In the first days after the attack on Pearl Harbor, a series of incidents demonstrated the new anxieties of the urban public. There were rumored enemy flights across New York and the eastern seaboard, and California had a number of phantom air raids. The concerns of the music industry followed a similar trajectory, a period of nervous reactions and dire predictions leveling out into engagement with the situation as it was. As a whole, the music industry did not know how wartime conditions would impact upon the economics of playing or administering music. It was easy to imagine music among the commodities of peacetime that would be discarded in the stringencies of wartime. Would people go out or would they stay at home? Would they frequent places of entertainment? Would they save their money or spend it?

Some early indications did not look encouraging. In its first issue of 1942, *Down Beat* placed a front-page article entitled "The Effect War Is Having on Music World," in which immediate reactions were recorded, "When Congress voted war on December 8th, all night clubs, ballrooms and theaters suffered. The public stayed home, with radios on, paralyzed by shock" (*DB* 1.1.42: 1). Some particular losses were also noted, mostly on the West Coast. The Ellington band had been one of the organizations affected by power blackouts in the West in December. Until, as *Down Beat* put it, "the natives get over their blackout jitters," the situation was to remain volatile, with widespread disruption even of booked tour itineraries.

Soon, however, a clearer view of the prospects was possible. In addition to the immediate dynamics within the industry and the public, longer-term social forces were at work. The enormous shifts in population that continued during wartime, drawing workers to war industry locations, had begun in the months leading up to the war, giving some of them a tilt toward an expansive wartime mentality. On the day of Pearl Harbor, the *New York Times* reported the effects on a New England city, "Hartford, Conn., first settled in 1635, is having growing pains. Defense work is the reason. Factories which used to turn out things like typewriters, percolators and toasters are now manufacturing war materials. Defense workers have flooded into the Nutmeg State's sedate old capital on the muddy Connecticut River" (*NYT* 12.7.41: 2). A promising perspective for music and entertainment was emerging from new centers of earning power, such as Jackson, Tennessee: this being a defense boomed area, promoters even until now have had difficulties fitting their dates" (*DB* 1.1.42: 22).

As well as the sheer numbers of people moving to boom areas, there were also cultural and ethnic shifts that this movement brought with it. Writers such as John Dos Passos recorded the wartime mobility of the population in impressionistic surveys of the scene on the roads and railroads and in the depots of the nation, reflecting the randomness and incongruity of the process. Early in 1943, Dos Passos listed the arrivals in Mobile,

Alabama, whose population grew by more than 64 percent between 1940 and 1944, "small farmers and trappers from halfcultivated patches in the piney woods, millhands from industrial towns in the northern part of the state, garage men, filling station attendants, storekeepers, drugclerks from crossroads settlements, longshore fishermen and oyster-men, negroes off plantations who've never seen any town but the county seat on Saturday afternoon" (Dos Passos 1945: 94).

Some people traveled great distances across the United States, taking themselves out of their former cultural settings. Richard Lingeman's (1979: 69) study of the American home front summed up the pattern of this enormous internal migration, among which were the movement of Southern "poor whites" to factories in Michigan and elsewhere, of whites from Kansas and Nebraska to aircraft factories on the West Coast, and of Southern blacks to the East Coast and the shipyards and factories on the West Coast. It was not difficult to foresee difficulties of acculturation that might occur in this massive rush to new centers, as well as the cultural and ethnic encounters that might be brought about. One of Dos Passos's interlocutors, speaking of the strains of life in wartime Washington, D.C., commented on the looming issue of "how people with different colored skins were getting along in this crowded town," and recalled rumors of a "race riot" (Dos Passos 1945: 160). In the manufacturing boom in Mobile, "the shipyards often discriminated against local Negroes and instead imported Southern whites, swelling the population beyond the city's capacity to handle it and fuelling racial tensions" (Lingeman 1979: 165).

In many localities, however, and in the national picture, the war created opportunities for black Americans that had not existed before. Blacks were migrating in numbers unprecedented since the massive move to the northern industrial centers at the time of World War I. Beginning in early 1942, with the Southern Pacific Railroad recruiting a large number of workers, the influx of blacks to southern California over the next three years totaled more than 350,000. Signs of the new economic confidence of the black public and its relevance to music was noted in a report from San Francisco: "the springing up of new defense industries has improved the employment opportunity of the Negro, and he can now afford to enjoy his own traditional music. The sepia crowds rarely attend S. F. downtown theatres, but Duke Ellington's appearance at the Golden Gate Theatre brought them out attired in the best finery, turning the Duke's appearance into both a gala social and musical event" (*DB* 1.15.42: 9).

Even after a few weeks of wartime, it was apparent that early fears of a shrinking market for music and entertainment had been incorrect. In fact, the reverse appeared to be the case. All sectors of the music business were able to envisage expanded rather than diminished cultural and economic roles. Music was going to be an important commodity, a view encouraged by reports such as, "A blitz of show spots is '42's gift to Tank Town. While the wheels of war production spin on 24 hour shifts, Detroit's late goers are jamming the new niteries" (*DB* 1.15.42: 8). An early 1942 ad for the radio station WWJ confirmed the music-business possibilities of Detroit's "13 Billion Dollar Armament Market" (*Var.* 3.25.42: 33).

It was not only the war industries that made certain localities into places of opportunity for musicians. The proximity of army camps and navy and air force bases also encouraged the growth of vibrant night scenes. A contributor to an oral history of the home front mentioned finding casual work as a musician, "I filled in with a band, playing saxophone at a night-club on Franklin Street in Tampa, patronized basically by air force officers. They were living it up—military personnel always pretty well lived it up when it came to night life" (Hoops 1977: 122). Another contributor spoke of the atmosphere of a major city being conditioned by the presence of the military, "Boston was an extremely happy city during the war. We had the Charlestown Navy Yard here, and we had sailors on the streets, going to the movie houses when they had stage shows, and you could hear Vaughn Monroe or Harry James. People—servicemen and nonservicemen—were out for fun" (Hoops 1977: 140).

The military bases themselves, aggregations of men and women with time on their hands, required entertainment, and some camps became extensions to the touring circuit even for big-name bands. The exciting new Lionel Hampton orchestra, for instance, played Fort Meade, Maryland, in early 1942. In March, Tiny Bradshaw's band "'sent' the service men at Fort Miles, Lewis, Del., last Friday in a solid way" (*AN* 3.28.42: 16). The Earl Hines band, dropping in unexpectedly upon the soldiers at Fort Sill, Oklahoma, put on "an impromptu jam session for the delight of all enlisted swing addicts" (*AN* 5.23.42: 12). An orchestra like that of Ada Leonard, with an all-girl personnel, had advantages that produced the *Down Beat* headline

"Ada Leonard Band Clicks in Army Camps" and enabled it to construct a touring schedule made up entirely of such engagements (*DB* 2.15.42: 19).

American popular music was not about to become a casualty of war. A momentary dip in demand was replaced by what *Down Beat* called "an unprecedented upsurge" (1.1.42: 22). The schedules of radio stations and recording studios rolled on. The New York debut of the Stan Kenton band took place at Roseland. Fat's Waller's concert at Carnegie Hall on January 14 went ahead, but was an unhappy experience. Waller seemed at first overwhelmed by the venue and then consumed so much alcohol during the interval that he could not pull the concert together in its second half. One notice offered, "Waller was awed by the hall, its size and acoustics" (*DB* 2.1.42: 3).

The Jay McShann band, trailing glowing reports from out of town, was an immediate success at the Savoy. Live recordings from its broadcasts on the NBC-Blue network give a sense of an excellent band in the Kansas City tradition, with a powerful rhythmic drive. The solos of the alto saxophonist Charlie Parker made an immediate impact among musicians. The trumpeter Howard McGhee related the experience of coming across Parker's playing by chance on the airwaves, "Oh, I heard Bird, it was in '42. I was with Charlie Barnet. We were playing at the Adams theatre in Newark. We came off the show, and I turned on the radio just like I did, and all of a sudden I heard this horn jump through there. Bird, playing 'Cherokee,' with McShann broadcasting—from the Savoy; when I heard this cat play, I said, 'Who in the hell is that? I ain't heard nobody play like *that*'" (Gitler 1985: 71). Through his improvising on the number "Cherokee" (one broadcast solo was allowed to run for forty-five minutes), Parker began to draw a crowd of admirers during the band's stay in New York. The bassist Gene Ramey said, "You couldn't get near the bandstand for musicians who had heard the broadcast. 'Who was that saxophone player?' they all wanted to know" (Dance 1980: 277).

The system that drove the phenomenon of the big bands, that meshed the bands with the business of songwriting, recording, and publication, with radio and live performance, had survived the first few weeks of the war and come out intact. There was no slump in demand—in fact, business was buoyant in the first months of 1942. But the system had some weak links that were vulnerable to the pressures of wartime. Among all sources of income open to musicians and bands, the most profitable was live performance, particularly short-stay or one-night engagements. The main benefit of radio was that it generated demand for this kind of engagement. Bands, therefore, needed to travel.

Early in 1942, there were the first indications that the wartime economy might strike at this basic requirement of transportation. There was a report concerning the Les Hite band, based in California but accustomed to covering the whole of the United States, "their first difficulty arose when the band was unable to find, at any price, a new tire for their bus. Every big band relies on a bus of its own for the long hops between one-night stands, and the Hite boys are still hoping the tire shortage won't leave them busless" (*AN* 2.7.42: 17). This was an early case of essential materials being in short supply. The word *shortage* quickly became so much a feature of wartime vocabulary that Benny Goodman could by March record "There Won't Be a Shortage on Love." As the war continued, the activities of traveling bands were curtailed by regulations and public priorities. As I discuss in chapter 4, these incremental difficulties for the traveling big bands would gradually dismantle the financial platform on which so many bands stood. There was a war on, and ensuring the continued mobility or even the continued existence of groups of itinerant musicians was self-evidently a lower priority than finding the materials to fight the war.

Among the first wartime sacrifices made by the professional music community was one announced by James C. Petrillo, president of the American Federation of Musicians (AFM), within a few days of Pearl Harbor: there would be no strikes by the federation for the duration of the war. As *Down Beat* pointed out, Petrillo "cannily reserved the right to take 'necessary action' should an employer attempt to take advantage of the war situation" (*DB* 1.1.42: 1). However, the agreement seemed to secure an untroubled future for labor relations within the music industry for as long as the war lasted.

In the first wave of reaction to the outbreak of war, some prominent performers had pledged themselves to the war effort, offering help in raising funds or morale or issuing a dedication of their talents to the cause. Al Jolson made such a statement directly after the attack on Pearl Harbor. Fats Waller "immediately threw himself into entertaining the armed forces and to supporting the War Bonds drive and other patriotic activities" (Wright

1992: 258), and other celebrities did likewise. An artist had to possess a relatively high public profile for such pledges to carry value as news or propaganda for the war effort. Especially in the early days of the war and as the first months of 1942 brought news of disastrous losses in the Pacific, however, the propaganda and morale-building efforts drew in performers at all levels.

The music trade press marked out a responsible mission for the music industry. Already observing, in January 1942, that "working people, newly burdened with war pressure at home, and casualty reports from abroad, are seeking the gayer atmosphere of clubs for entertainment and relief." One writer offered weighty predictions of the public mood, "Normal repressions may vanish. A fatalistic spending spree will appear." In this situation, the patriotic duty of the professional musician was clear, "IT WILL BE OUR JOB TO KEEP EMOTIONS NORMAL AND HEALTHY" (original capitals; *DB* 1.1.42: 22).

In the first weeks of wartime people were uncertain that life in the music business would retain its routine character. It became, in time, part of many musicians' normal business to participate in fundraising or other patriotic activities. Such involvement carried both an urgent commitment and a sense of novelty. In December 1941, the *Amsterdam News* carried a report on reactions among black musicians and entertainers, "Harlem's entertainer set are giving generously of their services among this war period. Vivian Harris is knitting sweaters; Pigmeat [Markham] is an air raid warden; Sister [Rosetta] Tharpe has confided that she is seriously thinking of becoming a nurse, and these are but a small share of the performers who are coming to the front with their services" (*AN* 12.20.41: 19).

In January 1942, there was news of a larger voluntary movement by professional musicians. With the permission of the union president, James C. Petrillo, it was announced that more than 200 name bands would be volunteering their services under the auspices of the USO to entertain the troops. During the succeeding three and a half years, performances at all levels of the business were dedicated to war-related causes. In the last days of January 1942, the American Pacific forces, led by General Douglas MacArthur, were under siege at Corregidor in the Philippines. On January 29, Bing Crosby's radio show, the *Kraft Music Hour*, was specially broadcast on short wave to the beleaguered army. Crosby was active in campaigns such as the "Victory Caravan" touring shows and made many benefit appearances with Bob Hope, his partner in the successful "Road" films (*Road to Morocco* began filming in February).

Glenn Miller had identified himself and his orchestra with campaigns for servicemen before the start of the war. In November 1941 he initiated the radio program *Sunset Serenade* in which a feature was a listeners' poll with prizes of radio-phonographs and recordings awarded to military camps. The program was transmitted from Saturday matinee performances at the Hotel Pennsylvania, with the admission money being donated to the USO. It was calculated that these arrangements were costing Miller $1000 a week of his own money.

It is true that such gestures as this earned Miller (described as "no philanthropist at heart"; *DB* 1.1.42: 10) considerable goodwill with the public. There is no reason, however, to doubt the serious concern men such as Miller, a "patriotic American, born and raised in the country's isolationist heartland" (Simon 1974b: 275), felt for the gloomy outlook in view at the turn of 1942. In the first days of the war, Miller went on record with a suggestion that must have caused some disturbance among his fellow professionals—that musicians should volunteer to act as air raid wardens, since most raids were expected at night, when musicians, unlike regular citizens, were awake and at work (*DB* 1.1.42: 10).

One government campaign surpassed others in the voluntary help it received from the entertainment world, the promotion of war bonds. An initiative of the secretary of the treasury, Henry Morgenthau Jr., the war-bonds campaign was conceived "to use *bonds* to sell the *war*, rather than vice versa" (Blum 1976: 17). Movie stars were strongly involved in the war-bond drives (the actress Carol Lombard was killed in a plane crash on January 16, 1942, returning from a bond drive in Indianapolis). Stars of the sports world also participated; for instance, the New York Yankees, visiting Chicago to play the White Sox, "spent part of their time here in the bond-selling business—war bonds." (*NYT* 5.22.42: 27). Given that Morgenthau had organized the campaign via the MGM company and that a star like Dorothy Lamour could sell $350 million dollars' worth of bonds, musicians were junior partners in this massive enterprise, but there are many references to musicians contributing their services. At a performance at the Palace Theater, South Bend, Indiana, in November, Tommy Dorsey was presented by his resident

singer, Frank Sinatra, with a $500 war bond as a birthday gift from the band
(*DB* 12.15.41: 33). In June 1942, the Dorsey band made a recording of the
song "Dig Down Deep," one of the most direct musical appeals for the war-
bond drive, with Sinatra singing, "The land you love the best / Is asking you
to invest / With a personal request from Mr. Morgenthau."

There were many ways in which musicians, as musicians, could contribute to the nation's war effort. An inescapable fact, however, was that many
players in the hundreds of big bands and in the country and blues groups
were young men, whose effort might be better expended in the armed services, as servicemen. George T. Simon, assessing the Glenn Miller band
in 1941, remarked that almost its entire personnel were "obvious draft-
fodder," with ages ranging from nineteen to thirty (Simon 1974b: 262). From
the attack on Pearl Harbor onward, the probability of being called into the
services increased steeply. As Count Basie, then running a nationally successful band, described it, "everything was very close to home, and getting
closer every day. Uncle Sam started building more and more bases and
training camps and manufacturing more and more weapons and ammunition; and, of course, the main thing for us was that those draft numbers
started coming up faster and faster" (Basie and Murray 1987: 319).

The draft had a far-reaching effect upon many bands. Although there
was a large enough pool of available players to ensure that drafted musicians could be replaced, not all replacements were equal to those they
replaced. Ella Fitzgerald's band lost several musicians, including the pianist
Tommy Fulford, who was subsequently killed in the war. The Andy Kirk
band lost several key players in December 1941, "First band casualty of the
war seems to be the Andy Kirk ork which will be gutted by Uncle's beck-
oning to Floyd Smith, ace guitar man, Harold Baker, trumpet, and Henry
Wells, trombone specialist and vocalist" (*AN* 12.20.41: 14). The music press
recorded the accelerating claims made by the draft boards on the nation's
professional musicians, reporting, among many others, the drafting of Joe
Bushkin, pianist in the Tommy Dorsey band, following the draft board's
tracking him down at an engagement at the Hollywood Palladium.

Like other citizens, musicians could avoid the draft by evading it, as
was possible in the roaming lifestyle of a musician, or by being ineligible
through age or fitness classification. At first thirty-five, the upper age limit
was later raised to forty-four. Coleman Hawkins, in Chicago with the band

he had earlier disbanded on hearing of the attack on Pearl Harbor, was older than the limit but sensitive about admitting the fact, "Being over the age fixed for the first recruitment draft was a mixed blessing for Hawkins because he did not want to admit being considerably older than his sidemen. To please his own vanity he pretended that he might be called any day. He even kept up this ploy with friends such as Roy Eldridge and John Kirby. Kirby, increasingly exasperated with Hawk's tactics, said to him one day, 'Damn it, Bean, if you get any younger you'll have to go back into diapers'" (Chilton 1990: 193).

In February 1942, the singer and guitarist Lonnie Johnson made three recordings that dealt with the draft. Just past his forty-third birthday, Johnson was newly eligible for the draft following the raising of the age limit, and the lyrics of "20 to 44" expresses his awareness of the change, "From eighteen to thirty-five, it never crossed my mind / But from twenty to forty-four, looks like everybody's got to go."

For fitness classification, men were ranked from 1-A, the most draft-eligible, to 4-F, those ineligible on health grounds (hence the motif of a song recorded in October 1941 by the Les Brown and Harry James bands, "He's 1-A in the Army and A-1 in My Heart"). One reason for Count Basie's anxiety about the possibility of losing his sidemen was that many of them were classed 1-A. Andy Kirk, having lost key players early in the draft, found the replacements that came to him increasingly difficult to work with, "One night I got disgusted with all the carrying-on and at intermission I said, 'I want everyone in the band room after we're through.' They all came in like school boys. 'What's the matter with you fellows?' I asked them. J. D. King raised his hand, like school kids do. 'You know something's wrong with us,' he said. 'We're all 4Fs'" (Kirk and Lee 1989: 109).

Those excused military service were not necessarily inferior musicians. Benny Goodman had a chronic back problem that required surgery, and Frank Sinatra was exempted because of a perforated eardrum. But the list of musicians called into the service grew rapidly from the end of 1941 onward. Goodman's orchestra lost an influential member in the pianist and arranger Mel Powell. Glenn Miller's orchestra lost a bassist, Trigger Alpert, whose playing was so important to Miller that he arranged a deferment for Alpert and later secured a furlough for him to play in the band over Christmas 1941.

At the start of 1942, *Down Beat* proposed that as many as 37,000 professional musicians might eventually be drafted. Country and blues musicians, as well as those in the purview of the trade press, also were being inducted into service at an increasing rate. The country singer Gene Autry was sworn into service with the Air Force in 1942 live on the radio program *Melody Ranch*. The singer Tennessee Ernie Ford, who had had the task of announcing the Pearl Harbor attack on the Knoxville radio station WROL, joined the Army Air Corps in 1942. The blues singer Memphis Willie B. was an early wartime draftee, in January 1942, and took part in combat in North Africa and Italy. (His 1945 song "Overseas Blues" was a plea to the military not to send him to Japan as well.) The country artist Johnny Barfield, enlisting in 1942, ended the war in a prison camp. Another country performer, Jimmy Bryant, drafted in 1941 and later wounded, had as a fellow soldier the jazz guitarist Tommy Mottola, from whom he learned elements of jazz playing. Artists in all styles of music were reported as having careers "interrupted by the war." In these early months, however, the eventual extent of the process was unforeseeable, and the draft was, for professional musicians as well as for other Americans, an ever-present anxiety.

Just as on the home front women were being drawn into new positions in the work force, so the war began to raise the profile of female musicians. The process was evident even in the early days of the war: all-girl orchestras, previously of interest for novelty value, were reappraised as having employment advantages over males. A band named The International Sweethearts of Rhythm had been formed among students at a women's college in Mississippi. In September 1941 they went as far as the Apollo and the Savoy, two of the prime spots in New York. Reappearing in January 1942, they received the following notice, "Those who heard them . . . were astounded during last week when they heard these same girls from the school in Mississippi playing arrangements that would cause problems for seasoned male musicians as if they were only at practice. The same girls who appeared in slacks last year came on the bandstand attired in long, attractive gowns, adding to the commercial stage presence of the outfit" (*AN* 1.31.42: 16). The Sweethearts and all-female orchestras such as those of Ada Leonard and Phil Spitalny were "100% draft exempt." Some established bands took on female replacements for missing male musicians, but this was a comparatively rare occurrence.

The draft and enlistment were applicable to bandleaders and star players as well as to rank-and-file musicians. The induction into the service of some leaders had considerable news value. By the start of the war, Artie Shaw's orchestra had been for several years one of the most successful in the country. Shaw had achieved a separate fame for successive marriages to Hollywood actresses, among them Lana Turner. The news that Shaw was to join the service was therefore of interest to the general public as well as music fans. One of Shaw's star soloists, the trumpeter Max Kaminsky, described the event, "We were doing a record date at Victor [presumably January 20 or 21, 1942] when Artie's manager handed him his letter of greeting from Uncle Sam. The band was immediately given its notice. 'Well,' I said to Dave Tough as we packed our instruments, 'that's the way it goes. The minute we get a chance to make a little money they have to go and have a war. See you around the Automat, pal'" (Kaminsky and Hughes 1965: 127).

The enlistment of Glenn Miller in the Army later in the year was the most publicized action of this kind, consistent with Miller's success in the two years leading up to his departure. He had had the biggest selling recording of the past fifteen years in "Chattanooga Choo-Choo," and within only a few months Miller was leaving the musical scene, or so it appeared. For many musicians, however, including Miller, Shaw, and Kaminsky, entering the service was anything but a removal from music.

The songwriter Richard Rodgers was turned down for a commission in the Air Force, but he "came to accept that the best thing I could do to help the war effort was to continue doing exactly what I had always been doing," namely working as a composer of popular songs and shows (Rodgers 1976: 210). Rodgers had a show opening on Broadway in early 1942, *By Jupiter*, his last collaboration with lyricist Lorenz Hart. The production experienced a characteristic disruption of wartime, the dimout of street lighting in New York City, "The opening night of . . . 'By Jupiter' saw [theatergoers] completely baffled by the lack of familiar West Side landmarks and feeling their way from Sardi's to the Shubert Theater and back by an elaborate system of navigation based on the Braille system and dead reckoning" (Lingeman 1979: 46). Meanwhile, Oscar Hammerstein saw *Sunny River*, his attempt at a new operetta, fold after thirty-six performances. Hammerstein confided to his agent, "I am trying to write a good song that might do something for the nation's morale." Only a month after the shock of Pearl Harbor, there was already enough new material in circulation for Hammerstein to comment, "I am convinced that all the war songs I have heard so far are on the wrong track" (Fordin 1995: 175). Within a few months, it was not only Hammerstein who was dubious about the quality of the commercial music emerging from these early days of the war.

On December 8, 1941, the composer Aaron Copland, engaged in a cultural mission in Havana, noted in his diary, "The Japanese attacked Pearl Harbor yesterday. It seems strange to be in Cuba with the United States at war" (Copland and Perls 1984: 329). One day later, Copland returned home into an environment where "Americans on the home front were gathering their resources," and where many musicians, both serious and popular, were considering what their role might be in the wartime economy (1984: 341). The songwriter Hoagy Carmichael, enjoying sustained success in the music business, responded to "the dismal shock of Pearl Harbor," by concluding "there was little I could do but give the world something to *hum*" (Carmichael and Longstreet 1966: 285). It was understood that the music for another war would have to be provided.

According to David Ewen (1977: 427), the song "We Did It Before" was "conceived on the day Pearl Harbor was bombed." It was hurriedly inserted into a Broadway musical and performed two days later by Eddie Cantor "as a stirring martial production number that brought down the house." "Remember Pearl Harbor" was also written, according to Ewen, "before the smoke above Pearl Harbor cleared." Other songs directly related to the bombing were written, published, and recorded before the end of December 1941. Ewen commented that "Goodbye Mama (I'm off to Yokohama)," by the established songwriter J. Fred Coots, was written and published within ten days of the bombing. In fact, Coots must have been even quicker off the mark, as the song was recorded by the Teddy Powell band on December 16.

This immediate response in the form of songs about Pearl Harbor itself was a short-lived first phase in the succession of styles of addressing the American public's tastes and emotional states. These approaches quickly led to songs that, while not speaking explicitly of the war, took additional meaning from it. The war temporarily changed the semantics of American popular songs, even transforming some existing songs and giving them a second career. The Irving Kahal and Sammy Fain song "I'll Be

Seeing You," first published in 1938, had a lyric concerning separation and reminiscence that caused it be revived five years later, with the enhanced resonance of the thousands of couples separated by the war.

It took some time for the new context to lead writers to compose love ballads in the same way as before the war. In the early months, there seems to have been the determination to write the definitive war song, as expressed by Oscar Hammerstein. The writing of songs that directly addressed the war soon moved on from the trauma of Pearl Harbor and the raw impact of the war's beginning. But at the end of 1941 and throughout 1942, there were new songs that restated the shock and anger of December 7.[1] The country music entrepreneur Fred Rose, later to partner with Roy Acuff in an important new music-publishing firm, wrote "Cowards over Pearl Harbor," which Acuff featured in stage and radio performances. There were "Martyrs of Pearl Harbor" and two songs with virtually the same title, "Remember Pearl Harbor" and "We'll Always Remember Pearl Harbor," the latter a hit in early 1942 for Sammy Kaye's orchestra, "We'll always remember Pearl Harbor / Brightest jew'l of the blue southern sea / Our lips will be saying 'Pearl Harbor' / On each bead of our rosary."

Closely akin to the spirit of these songs, especially to the bitter tone of Rose's lyric, "out of the sky came hawks of destruction / Piloted by disciples of hate," were the anti-Japanese songs, none of which made much impression commercially. "You're A Sap, Mister Jap" by James Cavanaugh, John Redmond, and Nat Simon was copyrighted before the end of 1941. "We're Gonna Stop Your Yappin', Mister Jap" was copyrighted in 1942 and "Taps for the Japs" in 1943. While references to rising suns (or "sons") and the color yellow were common features, a notable motif in these songs was physical chastisement, "We'll slap the Jap right off the map / We'll hear those yellows yell," and "You're a sap, Mister Jap, to make a Yankee cranky / You're a sap, Mister Jap, Uncle Sam is gonna spanky." The best known of these songs was "We're Gonna Have to Slap the Dirty Little Jap," composed by Bob Miller. The cover of the song copy shows an enormous hand, its cuff labeled "Uncle Sam," striking a minute Japanese soldier in the midriff, while the cover of "You're a Sap" depicts Uncle Sam with a Japanese soldier over his knee, spanking him with a bayoneted rifle.

As Guido van Rijn commented (1997: 154), the attack on Pearl Harbor "seemed to make an impression" on the members of the Lucky Millinder band. In February 1942 they made a recording of "We're Gonna Have to Slap," in a routine swing arrangement, with the title line sung in unison by the whole band, and these lyrics sung by the vocalist, Trevor Bacon, "We'll take the double-crosser to the old woodshed / And start on his bottom and go to his head / When we get through with him he'll wish that he was dead."

At the same session, the Millinder band recorded a new song "Fighting Doug MacArthur," which was also recorded over the following weeks by the bands of Gene Krupa and Tony Pastor. A similar song, "Hats off to MacArthur" was recorded a month later by another orchestra that made a heavy feature of war songs, that of Dick Robertson. The Millinder performance took a brief excursion into hip slang, the band chanting "Dig, dig, dig, Doug, Doug, Doug Macarthur" before Bacon sang the single verse "He's a tough old guy / With a strong reply / He's the guy to slap the Japs / Right down to their size." The verse was followed by a fanfare and drum rolls over which Millinder, in the style of a newsreel announcer, delivered an emotional message of support to MacArthur and his troops, ending "God bless you and all your soldiers, General Douglas MacArthur!"

The song demonstrates how the events of war can undermine the topicality of a lyric, because by the time these recordings were made, it was no longer the case that, "He gave them an awful lickin' / And he kept his soldiers stickin'," for at the beginning of March 1942 the forces under MacArthur's command were compelled to withdraw from the Philippines. It should be borne in mind that activity within the music industry in these early months of 1942 was taking place against the background of a military situation that was steadily deteriorating. This sense of deepening crisis was presumably part of the reason for increasing dissatisfaction with the kinds of popular music that were being produced.

The press at first reported the activities of the songwriters with a mixture of enthusiasm and seriousness, "With one eye on the current situation and the other on his composing pen, tunesmith Walter Bishop has turned out 'They'll Be Blowing Taps for the Japs,' which should be the best this sepia Broadway writer has penned" (*AN* 12.20.41: 19). A month later, *Down Beat* gave precedence to the multi-instrumentalist and bandleader Benny Carter, "Carter is the first colored composer to come through with a war song. Titled 'Harlem on Parade,' it is dedicated to the Negro boys in the U.S. armed services" (*DB* 1.15.42: 1). As performed by the Gene Krupa band as early as January 23, Carter's composition is an effective minor-key swing piece, with a lyric that brings contemporary black style together with a patriotic statement, "Harlem soldiers on the move / See them marching in the groove / Uncle Sam is mighty proud of Harlem on parade. / With those smiles they all perform / In a full-drape uniform / Everybody's here to cheer for Harlem on parade."

In mid-January *Down Beat*'s headline on the progress of the war songs was "Tin Pan Alley Does Its Bit," reporting without unfavorable comment on the spate of new composition, "Shortly after the United States entered the war, Tin Pan Alley was flooded with war songs. The music publishers met the occasion by managing to place a score of songs on the music counters before the end of the first week. Irving Berlin has already written his war tune, 'We'll Wipe You Off the Map, Mr. Jap.' Other new ditties include 'They Asked For It,' 'You're a Sap, Mr. Jap,' 'The Sun Will Be Setting in the Land of the Rising Sun,' and 'We Did It Before and We'll Do It Again.' New comic songs include 'The Japs Haven't Got a Chinaman's Chance' and 'You Can't Push the World Around' " (*DB* 1.15.42: 23). Within a short time, however, the same publication expressed a different view in a review of "We'll Put the Axe to the Axis," by Abe Lyman's orchestra, "This department agrees with the sentiments expressed in the first title, and as wholeheartedly as big-hearted Abe. But music as foul as this is far more likely to *impair* the morale of the nation. Like most of the new so-called 'patriotic' tunes—composed overnight by Broadway writers who figure they can grab a quick bag of loot for their efforts—*Axis* is a feeble piece of music" (*DB* 2.1.42: 14).

By mid-February the editorial opinion of *Down Beat* had hardened into general condemnation of the product being turned out. Under the headline, "Sure We Want Victory But the War Songs Still Smell," an article reported song publishers' dismay that their patriotic compositions are not finding favor either with recording artists or the public, "Songs were coming off the production line like Fords. There must be some other reason they called in their pluggers. What's holding up our songs? Why aren't they selling? What the hell goes? The pluggers gave them the answer. THE SONGS STINK. They aren't so good and the name band leaders won't play them. The NAME BAND LEADERS. The name band leaders won't prostitute their art by playing such cheesy songs. . . . A million half-baked war songs blasted at the public won't build morale. It takes a top-notch tune that can be played well." (*DB* 2.15.42: 11).

Even within the first four months of the war, there were indications that the strategy of the songwriting industry was changing. There were still songs addressed to the war itself, but others showed traces of familiar song genres reasserting themselves. Apart from the Pearl Harbor, anti-Japanese, and MacArthur songs, there were others with a military spirit. The Bob Crosby band made a specialty of applying its big band–Dixieland style to tunes from the nation's military heritage, such as "The Marine's Hymn," "Anchors Aweigh," and "The Caissons Go Rolling Along." Gene Krupa's orchestra made swing versions of several of these at a session in February 1942, and a number of other bands featured military numbers among their repertoire. There were songs about army life, such as Irving Berlin's "This Is the Army, Mr. Jones"; "Six Jerks in a Jeep," sung by the Andrews Sisters; and "Hayfoot, Strawfoot," a song about marching, recorded by Duke Ellington with a rousing vocal by Ivie Anderson.

The earliest wartime song about responsibilities on the home front was Waller's "Cash for Your Trash," later officially adopted by the Waste Paper Conservation Campaign Committee. It was followed by "Saving All I Can for Uncle Sam," recorded by Connee Boswell, and "I Paid My Income Tax Today" recorded by Dick Robertson, and "We Must Be Vigilant," recorded by Phil Spitalny. There were songs about the need for watchfulness and discretion, such as "A Slip of the Lip," recorded by Duke Ellington in July 1942, and songs about patriotic endeavor, such as "For the Good of the Country," recorded by Count Basie in January 1942, and "This Is Worth Fighting For," recorded by Jimmy Dorsey in May.

In the numerous songs published in 1942 dealing with men becoming soldiers, there was sometimes a sense of propagandizing: songs like "He Wears a Pair of Silver Wings," "Wait Till She Sees You in Your Uniform," "You Can't Say No to a Soldier," and other new compositions that dealt with the heightened attractiveness of the male soldier. "He's 1-A in the Army and A-1 in My Heart" celebrated a "guy who's really something / This man of mine he ain't missing nothing," and assured listeners that "He passed the toughest physical, he passed it folks and how." A comparable song, also recorded by Helen Forrest with the Harry James band, was "My Beloved Is Rugged," which described a girl's response to her boyfriend's toning up by army training, "My knees go weak / When I see his new physique." These modulate into a genre of songs dealing with a woman's devotion to a man, such as "He's My Guy," another song associated with Helen Forrest and also recorded by Ella Fitzgerald and Dinah Shore, which had no lyrical reference to the war or the draft but still took some of its meaning from the situation. A subcategory was the generally jocular numbers advocating fidelity, such as "Don't Sit under the Apple Tree (with Anyone Else But Me)." In his composition "Don't Forget to Say No" Hoagy Carmichael wrote, "Don't try to please when I'm overseas / Remember you're not the U.S.O."

Above all, there were songs about separation, some describing a dream or a reverie in which the separation from the loved one is overcome, as in "A Soldier Dreams of You Tonight," recorded by Woody Herman in April 1942, and Irving Berlin's "I'm Getting Tired So I Can Sleep" and Eddie De Lange and John Brooks's "Just As Though You Were Here," recorded in May by Frank Sinatra with Tommy Dorsey's orchestra. The motif of dreams, especially projections into an imagined (postwar) future, connect the love songs with songs of a more global state of feeling: longings, dreams, and prayers about a time or place of exemption from the anxieties of the present, a type perhaps initiated by compositions of the prewar period such as Jerome Kern's "The Last Time I Saw Paris" and Nat Burton and Walter Kent's "The White Cliffs of Dover," with its projection into "Tomorrow, when the world is free." In this vein, the early months of 1942 produced "When the Lights Go on Again," recorded by the bands of Les Brown, Lucky Millinder, and Vaughn Monroe, and "When the Roses Bloom Again," in versions by Jimmy Dorsey, Hal McIntyre, Kay Kyser, and the singer Deanna Durbin.

An idea expressed in songs like "Roses Bloom Again" is renunciation, postponement of the realization of love to a future date when "We'll have time for things like wedding rings / And free hearts will sing." This mood is epitomized by "The Last Call for Love," a song whose melody weaves together fragments of bugle calls and whose message is the need to put aside romantic love in favor of patriotic duty, "With your eyes in the stars of Old Glory / Can I help but be faithful to you? / Till we meet on the day we're dreaming of / It's the last call for love." This song was recorded in February 1942 by the Tommy Dorsey band, with Frank Sinatra as vocalist.

The songs produced in the aftermath of the United States' entry into the war have in many cases not survived their contemporary context. The quality of the new material was variable, to the extent that the industry as a whole attracted condemnation for its approach. The majority of the songs written, published, and recorded, however, were products of the popular music industry following its usual imperatives and procedures. The fact of being at war did not change the idioms of popular music. The level of sentimentality in the song genres remained the same. What changed was the external situation—and this in itself was sometimes enough to enhance or deepen the significance of the songs. The music industry was not required to overhaul its conceptions and representations of romantic love.

It is worth noting how broad a participation there was in the business of exploiting the popular songs of wartime. This is especially important from the point of view of orthodox histories of jazz, which have sought to detach its musicians from implication in the machinery of pop-music production, above all in contexts that involve sentimentality and the genres of romantic song. Among the musicians from the received jazz lineage who in late 1941 and early 1942 made recordings of the songs dealt with in this chapter were Duke Ellington, Count Basie, Benny Goodman, Woody Herman, Lucky Millinder, Louis Armstrong, Fats Waller, Bob Crosby, Charlie Barnet, Gene Krupa, Claude Thornhill, and Muggsy Spanier; and, from the fringes of jazz legitimacy, Jimmy Dorsey, Tommy Dorsey, Harry James, Artie Shaw, and Les Brown. Jazz musicians made numerous recordings of this type of material. Such musicians did not seem to be detached from the popular-song process in any way that distinguished them from musicians of other kinds.

By February 1942 Aaron Copland had completed first sketches for a newly commissioned wartime work, *Lincoln Portrait*. Copland had accepted the commission to compose "a musical portrait of a great American" despite his skepticism about "expressing patriotism in music," which he considered "difficult to achieve without becoming maudlin or bombastic, or both" (Copland and Perls 1984: 341). Not all of the music published in the early days of the war avoided these problematic qualities. But within a short time, the business of musical composition, publication, and recording had become normalized. Producers of popular songs, along with people in other phases of the industry, had recognized that the rules of the game were much the same as before, that the industry's practices would carry over into wartime with only minor adjustments. In discovering the viability in a time of war of the emotions of regret, nostalgia, loneliness, and the imagery of dreams, hearts, and roses, songwriters found themselves dealing in a familiar currency and one that still deeply conditioned the musical tastes of the American public.

A popular song from the early months of 1942, "Johnny Doughboy Found a Rose in Ireland," provides an example. Written by Kay Twomey and John Goodhart, the song was recorded by the orchestras of Freddy Martin, Kay Kyser, and Guy Lombardo and by the singer Kenny Baker. The song could have come out of the publishing industry at any time since the 1890s, and in some respects it returns to the idiom of George M. Cohan at the time of World War I, "Johnny Doughboy found a rose in Ireland, / Sure the fairest rose that Erin ever grew. / Though the blarney in her talk took him back to old New York, / Where his mother spoke the sweetest blarney, too." The song uses long-established images of Irish ethnicity and even older elements of the sentimental popular song, including a mother, a rose (a sweet Irish rose, at that), and "smilin' eyes of blue." In the version by Freddy Martin's band, "Johnny Doughboy" reached number 8 in the national music chart in June 1942. Its story of an American falling for an Irish colleen could have been the subject for a song at any time, and its minimal reference to wartime is the fact that he is a "doughboy," itself a dated, nostalgic term. Though more recent histories barely acknowledge the continued prominence of such song genres, songs like "Johnny Doughboy" were close to what remained the main line of popular musical taste even as late as 1942.

Chapter 3

The Alley

American taste in general was indiscriminate.

—BARRY KERNFELD, *The New Grove Dictionary of Jazz*

Popular music composed or performed before rock and roll has usually been reckoned with only as it impinges on the narrative of jazz or some other codified canon. Other idioms also have their own narratives, which guarantee acceptance for the diverse musical forms that fall within their terms of reference. *Country music,* with a generally agreed historical narrative holding it together (Carr 1980; Malone 1987), is a term that lends a validity, a basis of respect to the works of performers such as Jimmie Rodgers, Hank Williams, Merle Haggard, and Bob Wills. "Jazz" gives a conceptual focus to the discussion of performers as disparate as Billie Holiday, Albert Ayler, Lennie Tristano, Fats Waller, and Jimmy Yancey (though Yancey's visibility is also derived from the tradition labeled "blues").

In giving an account of the musical world that many Americans inhabited in the early 1940s, therefore, some areas are organized and legitimized under one of these received headings. In 1941–1942 there was a style of music called "jazz," even if its identity was not easily extricable from an idiom known as "swing." There was a field of musical activity today called "blues," though it also became mixed with other things under the more

42

problematic heading of "race" music. There was also an upsurge of country music, even though it also was not the same music as is now so called; in some publications country came mixed in with black idioms under the title of *folk music*. The definition of these terms is problematic now and was even more so in the early 1940s.

What is also clear is that a large area of American popular music is completely missed by all of these narratives. There is a gap in the history of American popular music, and it extends across musical activity that has not found itself the validating narrative that has established the visibility of these other forms. The result of this hiatus is that a large proportion of the music that Americans chose to perform, record, and be entertained by in the decades before rock and roll is subject to disregard. This affects the valuation of such music. If singers such as Dinah Shore or Allen Jones do not qualify for attention as "jazz" singers (and neither of them do), they remain marginalized by music historians. The same applies to material: some songs written in the 1920s and 1930s have achieved the status of standards for jazz musicians, and this is interpreted as a guarantee of artistic merit—although only on the grounds that jazz redeems these songs from their original condition. In general, however, popular song recorded before 1955 has not been considered worthy of attention in its own right, *as* popular song rather than as raw material for jazz or another so-called authentic idiom.[1]

The model is one of separating wheat from chaff, with the wheat being what belongs to jazz, country, blues, and other valorized forms, and the chaff being everything else. The narrative of jazz has for a long time informed us that up to the mid-1950s American popular music, with the possible exception of some other accredited traditions, was virtually devoid of value. The performers and creators of this critically stigmatized or critically invisible music were, to name only a few, Helen Morgan, Ruth Etting, Norah Bayes, Bing Crosby, Al Jolson, Jo Stafford, Johnny Mercer, Jimmy Durante, Eddie Cantor, Alice Faye, The Ink Spots, Vaughn Monroe, Gene Austin, Connee Boswell, Lena Horne, and presumably also Harry Warren, Richard Rodgers, Jerome Kern, Hoagy Carmichael, and Harold Arlen. The status of songwriters such as these last four, together with Cole Porter, George Gershwin, and a few others has been elevated by a construct known as "The Great American Songbook" and a wave of critically accepted performers of such music. But the popular music of the pre-1950s, in its original form, remains under a historical cloud.

Consequently, some readers may have a sense of categories being confused or distinctions of quality not being made. However, this book is concerned with filling some of the gaps in the historical record resulting from the selectivity of jazz and other narratives. Unless it is possible to confront the reality of what Americans were singing, playing, and listening to in those murky pre-Elvis days and to treat such music with historical imagination, we are left with the proposition that, apart from jazz in its various forms and some other acceptable musical canons, the American public spent decades wasting its time and money on inferior forms of music.

To get a sense of the commonalties of musical experience, taste, and awareness—of what music *meant* to an American public—requires research outside the confines of the existing narratives, taking account of performers and styles that currently have no place in them. To take a lead from film studies, a critical appraisal of popular song in the early 1940s might follow an approach such as this, "Film history is concerned both with the analysis of films as texts and with placing them in context. Contextual analysis involves exploring the production histories of films (who made them and how were they made?), the historical reception of films (who saw them and how did the viewers respond?), and how the films were informed by and responded to the societies and cultures in which they were made" (Chapman 2002: ix). Applying this to a piece of music, we may ask the following questions. Who performed the piece? How did its performance come about? In what style was it performed? Who were the audience for the performance and how did they respond to it? How did this piece of music relate to the society and culture in which it was produced and performed? A historical study of any cultural product ought to be able to answer such questions.

In the selective process that critics have used to deal with American popular music, what is lost is the background musical experience. We cannot know fully what "Johnny Doughboy" meant to a listener in 1942 because the musical-social matrix in which the song was heard has gone, and few writers on the subject seem to want to recreate it for the purpose of understanding it better. Consequently, today's listeners can only respond to such music ironically, through an after-the-fact sensation called "nostalgia" (now a regular category for the racks in record stores), or, most commonly, by rejecting it outright.

The common background experience of music in the early 1940s was very different from that of today. To look at the types of music available in a single community in 1941–1942 gives a strong sense of the changes that have taken place. A 1941 musical directory for Buffalo, New York, and its county lists a large number of singing societies, often distinguished by ethnic identity: the Buffalo Choral Society, the Buffalo Jewish Choral Society, the Frederick Chopin Singing Society, the United German-American Singing Societies, and The Welsh Singers of Buffalo. There were pipe bands and drum corps. The directory comments that "Buffalo in the nineteenth century was famous for its singing societies," and it is clear that the tradition lived on at least up to the 1940s (*Directory of Music* 1941: 14). The radio stations WBNY, WBEN, and WBBW each maintained a musical director and up to fifteen staff musicians. A popular item in radio programming was organ recitals, with ten a week broadcast on WBNY. Buffalo was also a center for polka music, which had a touring circuit of several northeastern states and, even in competition with name swing bands, was doing well up to the start of the war. All of this, varying with the ethnicity of the individual subject, provided a background of musical experience that differs markedly from what is common today.

Some popular song traditions persisted as active idioms without the associations of the past they have since acquired. Charles Hamm (1983: 350) commented upon the "continuity of musical style" that was "one of the most striking features of the Tin Pan Alley era" from the 1880s onward. The years of World War II were late within that era, but songs from that stylistic continuity were still popular. A tradition of lyric singing, associated with Italian *bel canto* and the Irish tenor style, was still current in 1942, even as Stan Kenton was playing at Roseland and Charlie Parker was sitting in at Monroe's. An evening of network radio offered, in addition to Glenn Miller and Dinah Shore, the following: Lanny Ross, tenor, on WABC; Frank Parker, tenor, on WABC; Morton Downey ("The Irish Nightingale") on WHN; and the Dubuque A Cappella Choir on WJZ (*NYT* 3.11.42: 28).

A newly composed song such as "When the Roses Bloom Again," even with its reference to the world after Pearl Harbor, had echoes of a piece from the very beginning of this continuity, "When the Robins Nest

Again," described by Hamm (1983: 285) as "a sentimental verse-chorus bal-lad" from 1883. During 1941 and 1942, theaters on Broadway put on seasons of Gilbert and Sullivan and reruns and revamps of operettas. The 1909 *The Chocolate Soldier* had a run at Carnegie Hall, and a version of *Die Fledermaus* entitled *Rosalinda* opened in October 1942 and ran for 521 per-formances. What Oscar Hammerstein had written in disgust at the failure of his *Sunny River* was evidently not yet true, "Operetta is a dead pigeon and if it ever is revived it won't be by me" (Fordin 1995: 175).

In its reception of songs in 1941 and 1942, an American audience was bringing to them a different set of responses from those of later times, when these traditions and idioms were obsolete or had taken on unfavor-able connotations. The audience represented an interpretative community with a different set of norms and criteria from those of the period since then. A 1942 audience had no knowledge of Elvis Presley, Chuck Berry, The Beatles, or Kurt Cobain. They had not experienced rock and roll, soul music, punk, grunge, or hip-hop. Our judgments of the music of 1942 are conditioned by what has come after; their judgments were conditioned by what went before. However, it is possible to extrapolate a set of values that is assumed or generated by the music of this early wartime period by asking several questions. What assertion was it making? What issues was it interested in? How did it treat the human person, the male, the female, the natural world, the family, life and death, society, morality?

As I discussed in chapter 2, the song repertoire of 1941–1942 had a focus on the subject of romantic love that was little changed by wartime. It is common to contrast the treatment of this subject in popular song with its treatment in folk forms like the blues, as in this passage from Samuel Charters, "The 'love' that fills the blues has little of the sentimen-tality of the 'love' that dominates American popular song. The love that is expressed in popular song is an adolescent emotion, and the words are filled with the vague yearning and misunderstandings of adolescent affairs. 'Are you true?', 'Can you be true?', 'Will you keep yourself true to me?'" (1963: 37). By contrast, the treatment of love in the blues is general-ized by Charters as direct and "real." It is true that the physicality of sex is not represented in the love song of the 1940s, not even in the allusive way to which the blues, too, was confined, "arms" and "kisses" represent the only stated consummation of love. However, it is clear that these songs were operating within a set of conventions, both in lyrical content and in musical structure, and that meanings were given and received within those parameters.

There is a central construction of love that is related to an image of *home*. The notion of a love affair that reaches its culmination in peaceful domesticity goes back to songs like Rodgers and Hart's "Blue Room" of 1926, "We'll build a blue room, / A new room, for two room. / Where every day's a holiday / Just because you're married to me." Another example is Walter Donaldson's "My Blue Heaven," which in a 1927 version by Gene Austin remained the best-selling recording of all time until surpassed by "Chattanooga Choo-Choo" early in 1942.

Romantic love in this convention is *paradisal* and is located in places that can contribute a particular quality to this paradise. Sometimes love is enhanced by exoticism, as in the many songs concerned with tropical islands or foreign locations identified as romantic, "Blue Tahitian Moon," "Sing Me a Song of the Islands," "Sleepy Lagoon," and "Remember Hawaii." Sometimes the idyll is discovered in American places, where an added emotion is one of return, familiarity, and reassurance, as in "Chattanooga Choo-Choo," where the speaker finds the feminine image of "satin and lace" and a homecoming from which he will "never roam." This image of love in the American homeland is epitomized by another song, recorded by the Mills Bothers in January 1942, "Dreamsville, Ohio."

In the formal language of the 1940s love song, the ideal is not urban but quasi-pastoral. Unlike the Western film genre, and other American texts in literature and art, it shows no hankering for the wilderness or escape from civilization. Instead, it expresses a desire for a private retreat, a space where the speaker is surrounded by love and beauty. The notion of beauty is represented by recurrent symbols, such as the frequent use of the state of dreaming as referred to in chapter 2. There are many references in the lyrics to roses or to other flowers that have a similar function in the convention, "One Dozen Roses" (recorded by Connee Boswell), "When the Roses Bloom Again" (Boswell, Deanna Durbin, Arthur Tracy), "When the White Azaleas Start Blooming" (Bing Crosby), "Blue Shadows and White Gardenias" (Crosby, Lanny Ross), and "Yesterday's Gardenias" (Tony Martin). The natural world or its symbols is present in references to seasons and times of the year and sometimes to birds.

A large proportion of an older repertoire of Tin Pan Alley songs that supplied nostalgia remained current up to the early 1940s. In early 1942 Buddy Clark recorded "That Old Gang of Mine," "My Buddy," and "Keep the Home Fires Burning"; Bing Crosby recorded "Wait Till the Sun Shines, Nellie"; and Dick Todd recorded "Dear Old Pal of Mine." A song like "The Lamplighter's Serenade," written by Hoagy Carmichael and first recorded in January 1942, confirms what is apparent in these other songs: that notions of romantic love include the ideas of home and family and an image of intergenerational harmony that is frequent in the love ballads of the period, but which disappears soon afterward.

"The Lamplighter's Serenade" was one that Frank Sinatra recorded in his first session as a solo artist, on January 19, 1942, and another version was recorded a few days later by Bing Crosby. As Will Friedwald remarked (1995: 109), the song was "one Sinatra never remade and no one else ever bothered with after 1942." The story of an ageing lamplighter who takes benign pleasure in lighting the lamps for young lovers in a park, it seems a surprising choice for such an important session in Sinatra's career. Friedwald commented that the song suited Crosby's "well-established paternal identity" better than it sat with Sinatra. (Chapter 7, however, will examine the idea that Sinatra was an artist less of our own time than we might think.) As with anyone involved in music in the early 1940s, Sinatra's perspective on this "sentimental" material was not the same as ours. "The Lamplighter's Serenade" was accessible to Sinatra and his audience in January 1942 in ways in which it is not accessible to us today. The sympathetic treatment given to a song like this indicates a whole ethos of song that was about to disappear, together with the combinations of emotions it was intended to evoke, "And if a lady or a beau should answer no, / He sprinkles their hearts with his magic; / Then he steals away / To sing another day / The lamplighter's serenade."

At the start of World War II, there were other now-disregarded strands in the fabric of American popular song. The polka produced upbeat songs such as "The Beer Barrel Polka." The light classics and sacred songs, still being recorded by artists like Crosby, Deanna Durbin, and Grace Moore, included "Danny Boy" and "Adeste Fideles." The growing prominence of the cowboy song produced Tin Pan Alley evocations of the West (the January 1942 *Down Beat* reported that "Fred Wise and Mart Fryberg, writers of 'Purple Hills of Idaho,' have never been farther west than Newark, N.J.") and two massive hits of 1942, "(I've Got Spurs That) Jingle Jangle Jingle" by Frank Loesser and a hillbilly ballad that stayed at number 1 on the sales charts for five weeks, "Deep in the Heart of Texas."

Musically, too, many of the songs produced during this period followed conventions that were ingrained in song-production over the entire Tin Pan Alley period. Song structures remained within the pattern of the thirty-two-bar chorus, though variations on this were not uncommon. Stylistically, a change had occurred that enabled listeners to detect an older style in a new song, "Somebody Else Is Taking My Place," for instance, a song that did well commercially in versions by Benny Goodman and others, was reviewed as "a brand new song, but it's constructed like an oldie" (*DB* 1.15.42: 13).

By 1942, however, popular song had become increasingly sophisticated melodically and harmonically. The chains of secondary dominant chords that typified many earlier songs had been replaced by a greater use of chromaticism and "a willingness to alter almost any note in a chord for richer harmonic color" (Hamm 1983: 366). This use of a variety of chord forms and chord movements went together with melodic lines also characterized by chromaticism. This increasing chromatic freedom is exemplified in a feature that Alec Wilder pointed out: a downward movement to a note that is not in the key of the piece. This movement appeared in the third bar of the 1929 "Can't We Be Friends?" (recorded in 1942 in a big-band version by Muggsy Spanier); having previously used notes in the F-major scale, the phrase in the third bar drops to D-flat, which lies between the fifth and sixth degrees of the F scale. A song with the same feature is Jimmy van Heusen's "Darn That Dream," written in 1939. Of this song, Wilder (1972: 444) said, it "has a very interesting and difficult melody in that its chromatic character makes the notes hard to find." The chromaticism begins almost immediately: the first two notes, D and G, are the tonic and fifth in G-major; but the next note, under the word *dream*, is D-sharp—again the raised fifth of the scale. In each of these melodies, the three-note phrase ending on the aberrant note also has a similar rhythmic pattern. The release, or third eight-bar section, of this song was described by Wilder as "very far out."

A very similar phrase is found in "Serenade in Blue," written by Harry Warren for the 1942 Glenn Miller movie *Orchestra Wives* and recorded by the Miller, Benny Goodman, and Jimmy Dorsey bands. In this melody (in the key of E-flat) the most striking chromatic shift occurs in the second half of the fourth bar: it is very similar to the two other examples, with a downward three-note phrase that lands on D-flat (the same notes as in "Can't We Be Friends?"). The melody of "Serenade of Blue," however, is chromatic at several other points. Wilder's comment on "Darn That Dream" can be applied to this piece, too, "It's a melody, I'm certain, built around the chromatic harmony."

Charles Hamm summed up this development in popular songwriting as follows, "The harmonic language of Tin Pan Alley had been so expanded that almost every chord could have added tones, nonharmonic tones, and chromatically altered notes, alone or in combination" (1983: 367). Harmony in American popular song was moving in the direction that Aaron Copland had outlined for modern classical music in his *Our New Music*, "All chords are now judged alike, according to their appositeness to the situation in which they are placed" (1941: vii). In popular song of the late 1930s and the early 1940s, every possible chromatic addition to the diatonic scale had been used: the lowered ninth, the raised fourth, and the raised fifth having been used by writers such as Harry Warren and Hoagy Carmichael, there was now a spread of all twelve tones of the chromatic scale to be found in the harmonic and melodic structures of popular music. By 1942, any professional musician who played a wide enough selection from the current repertoire would come across these chromatic alterations.

This included jazz musicians. At a point of intense activity in the winter of 1941–1942, jazz players such as Charlie Parker and Dizzy Gillespie were in the process of developing a style later to be known as "bebop." The three chromatic alterations mentioned above are also the notes that have been taken to typify the harmonic aspect of bebop. The raised fifth is referred to by theorists as the distinctive element in the bebop scale (Levine 1995: 175). The raised fourth (or "flatted fifth," as it was called at the time) was for a long time considered a defining feature of the new style; and the lowered ninth note over a dominant chord made frequent appearances in the improvised lines of Charlie Parker, among other bebop players.

This kind of chromaticism may have been derived by jazz players from their experiences of playing the popular song repertoire. The stimulus for using, say, a lowered ninth, in a bebop theme or improvisation could come from hearing it in a song from the contemporary repertoire. The development of harmony in jazz of the period exactly parallels the development of harmony in popular songwriting. It is not generally argued, however, that jazz was influenced in this way. Jazz has been seen as producing its innovations in an internal way, discovering various intervals and tones by a process of pure research (DeVeaux 1991: 541). Writers on jazz have preferred to keep it separate from popular music; in actuality, however, jazz players spent a lot of time playing nothing but the popular song repertoire. The internal approach of jazz historians holds that the development of harmony in jazz in the early 1940s did not come from outside of jazz music itself—and definitely not from the efforts of popular songwriters like Harold Arlen or Harry Warren.

This approach is counter-intuitive. It implies that when jazz players played popular songs they were in mode of operation completely divorced from the one they were in when playing jazz, and that no influence of one upon the other was possible. However, being around popular music, continually playing its melodies, and dealing with its harmonies would likely have an influence on the harmonic vocabulary of jazz players. Moreover, the harmonic changes that popular music had been through were precisely the same ones as appeared in bebop a few years later. Hamm (1983: 352) made a similar point with reference to George Gershwin's influence on jazz harmony in the 1930s. William Howland Kenney (1993: 46) suggested that in 1920s Chicago, the experience of jazz musicians exposed to the new popular songs extended the harmonic variety of jazz. Even more specifically, Lewis Porter discussed the possibility that John Coltrane derived the harmonic progression of his celebrated "Giant Steps" from the 1937 Rodgers and Hart song "Have You Met Miss Jones?" (Porter 1998: 146). Each of these instances entails moving away from the narrative of a music called jazz that does everything for itself, has a history that no other music impinges upon, and that has never benefited from its more or less essentially constant contact with popular music. Jazz was more than in contact with popular music—it was implicated in popular music, it could hardly be distinguished from it, although, as we shall see in chapter 5, efforts were already being made to articulate its separation.

The absence of a suitable model for their work has stood in the way of recognition for the popular songwriter in American culture. This difficulty was overcome for many songwriters of the 1960s and after: for writers like Bob Dylan it is appropriate to use the model of the lyric poet, owing to the content of his songs and his relative freedom from the constraints of the music industry. This model does not work for professional songwriters of an earlier era, however, such as Johnny Mercer or Harry Warren. When evaluating their work, we must consider that songwriters of 1941–1942 were working within a cultural context that was particular to their time and situation.

The distinction between these two types of writers is akin to the difference between the relatively free artists of filmmaking, such as Federico Fellini or Ingmar Bergman, and filmmakers who worked within the American studio system, such as Howard Hawks or John Ford. This distinction, discussed in film studies under the auteur theory, is equally applicable to the songwriting business. Writers like Warren were not directly expressing their ideas and emotions: they were often working to order, within song genres, in situations where creative autonomy was secondary. Just as film theorists argue that studio directors like Hawks were nonetheless auteurs who produced distinctive bodies of work, so it should be possible to approach the work of songwriters like Warren and Mercer.

Harry Warren, born Salvatore Guaragna to an Italian immigrant family, received no formal education in music but taught himself to play six instruments and to read music. Warren's career as writer of some of the best-known songs of the 1930s and 1940s was strongly associated with movies; in fact, it can be largely summed up in a listing of the films he worked on. Although Warren worked for a number of the major film studios, from 1940 was under contract at Twentieth Century Fox. There he wrote songs for ten films by the end of 1942.

Warren's songs for the wartime Fox musicals were performed by a stock company of actors and singers, including Betty Grable, Alice Faye, John Payne, and Carmen Miranda, and were inserted into some lightweight, generic scenarios. On two occasions Warren wrote music for the Glenn Miller orchestra, first in the 1941 *Sun Valley Serenade*, a musical set in an Idaho ski resort. Warren's writing for this film, with the lyricist Mack Gordon, produced the million-selling "Chattanooga Choo-Choo," performed in a dynamic sequence featuring the black dance team the Nicholas Brothers. In early 1942, Warren and Gordon worked on a film starring

Miller about the lives of big-band musicians, *Orchestra Wives*. The score contained the abovementioned "Serenade in Blue," written by Warren in the confidence that the Miller band would handle its chromatic complexities, and another place-name song, "I've Got a Gal in Kalamazoo."

Also issued in 1942 were two other Fox films with scores by Warren. First was *Iceland*, for which Warren wrote several war-topical songs and one that has become a standard, "There Will Never Be Another You." Alec Wilder wrote of this song, "There's not a poorly chosen note in the melody. It's sinuous, graceful, gracious, sentimental, totally lacking in cliché" (1972: 401). Warren and Gordon's final assignment for 1942 was *Springtime in the Rockies*, featuring the Fox ensemble together with the big band of Harry James, who made a hit of Warren's ballad "I Had the Craziest Dream."

There was a permanent link between the popular song and the film industry—something impossible to ignore in Warren's case but also, as I discuss in chapter 6, an essential factor for popular music as a whole. This determined the variety of the creative demands made of the songwriter. Even in the limited time span of 1941–1942, Warren wrote music for romantic ballads, humorous songs, and what were classified as "rhythm numbers," for example, "Kalamazoo," which Warren claimed he wrote initially as "a kind of rhythmic exercise." For *Orchestra Wives* he wrote the highly chromatic "Serenade in Blue," and a few months later, for the 1943 *Hello, Frisco, Hello*, the eloquently straightforward "You'll Never Know."

Warren's work is paradigmatic of the position of a successful songwriter at this time in the history of American music. He was deeply enmeshed in the workings of the film industry, having to take account of plot, character, the genres of film and song itself; the identity of the performer(s) for whom the song was designed; and of wider commercial implications, such as the potential for sales of records and sheet music. The songwriter was also, as Warren frequently stated, subject to the power exerted by others in the filmmaking process. In his words, the songwriter was considered "the lowest form of animal life" (Wilk 1974: 121).

At the time it was difficult to develop and express an identity in one's music within the film industry, and in a sense this was not required. As with studio-bound directors, the essential character of a songwriter's work had to be inferred from a view of their whole output, which could be astonishingly diverse, as in the case of Warren or Irving Berlin. As a result, it is not easy to locate a specifically "Harry Warren" tendency in Warren's work, while for a songwriter in a later cultural-industrial context, such as Dylan, the essential character of their work is written all over it. This same point might be made about all of the major songwriters of the early 1940s.

Warren's musical background enabled him to bring many styles to the table, "I can run the gamut of all music because I love music so much. I used to know all the overtures by heart. 'Light Cavalry,' 'Poet and Peasant,' 'Morning, Noon, and Night,' any one you could think of, I knew them all. I knew all the church music, all the Catholic mass music. I knew all the Debussy, I knew all the Ravel. I love them . . . and of course, Puccini" (Wilk 1974: 133). Warren was of a generation in which white ethnicity, including Italianness, tended to be effaced, as the surname change from Guaragna to Warren indicates. This cultural background determined Warren's exposure to the musical influences he listed.[2] This suggests a further dimension of the background to music of the early 1940s: the tradition of lyric opera still formed an element of the musical language, even in a composer who worked in Hollywood and wrote songs that ultimately became part of the jazz repertoire.

In terms of background, antecedents, and musical culture, Warren was a long way apart from Johnny Mercer, a middle-class Southerner from Savannah, Georgia, with, as he put it, "a thing about jazz and blues" (Wilk 1974: 133). The style of Johnny Mercer, both as a singer and as a lyricist, was close to the jazz idiom, and this inevitably involved him in boundary disputes among jazz critics. Mercer became a songwriter through a career as a big-band singer. The status of singers in jazz or outside of it has been a troubling question for jazz writers. There is perhaps more argument about what a "jazz singer" is than over any other kind of musical performance in this field. Many singers who seemed to have some claim to be classed as jazz singers were explicitly denied this status. For example, in Leonard Feather's *Encyclopedia of Jazz*, Helen Ward, singer in the Benny Goodman band, was summed up this way, "Like many pop singers, she earned a quasi-jazz reputation through her chance association with a band that played jazz" (Feather 1960: 452). Presumably "chance association" did not mean that Ward was in the Goodman band by accident (especially given Ward's story that Goodman once made her a proposal of marriage to keep her with the band). Ward at least had an entry in the *Encyclopedia*, while Helen Forrest, an even more popular band singer, did not, though her bandleader, Harry James, did appear. Similarly, praise for Frank Sinatra's musicality was preceded with a negative, "Though he is not basically a jazz performer" (1960: 421). Mercer came off slightly better, "A good rhythm singer in a semi-jazz vein, he made his major contribution as a songwriter"(1960: 331).

In Feather's remarks, as in other jazz criticism, there is an effort to detach an essence called "jazz" from other substances with which it has gotten itself mixed up. Singers pose this difficulty for the ideology of jazz because they are inevitably involved with popular songs, and the relationship of the popular song to jazz is itself a troubling issue. Here I am concerned with Mercer as a songwriter, but it is worth noting the "semi-" status he has been granted in the discourse of jazz. The *Encyclopedia* went on to say that Mercer's contribution to jazz was as a songwriter, since he wrote "lyrics and sometimes music for many that became jazz standards."

As a lyricist Mercer collaborated with the best-known song composers of his day, and in the early 1940s he was at the height of his success. Among the successful songs he published in 1942 were "That Old Black Magic," "I'm Old Fashioned," and "Tangerine." A later part of this chapter will deal with songs Mercer produced in 1942 with Jerome Kern, Harold Arlen, and Hoagy Carmichael. Like Warren, with whom he wrote on occasion, Mercer worked primarily and most successfully for films. His work is therefore also conditioned by the requirements of film styles and narratives and kinds of song that were usable in specific contexts. He also worked primarily as a collaborator, writing lyrics for music composed by his partners. These conditions work against viewing Mercer as an auteur with his own artistic vision. Nevertheless, critics have identified certain qualities, a particular stance or attitude that give Mercer's work an identity of its own. Gene Lees wrote of Mercer's "emotional warmth," his "powerful vivid use of Anglo-Saxon imagery" (Lees 1987: 48) and, a quality he related to Mercer's roots in Southern culture, a diction that is "free and flashing and open" (1987: 52). Alec Wilder (1972: 272) described qualities that he claimed Mercer shared with his collaborator, Arlen, "their love of the lonely and sentimental, the witty and the warm and the bittersweet."

Like the question of jazz status, the critical discourses available for writing about lyricists shows the same propensity for the popular song culture of early to mid-century America to slip under the radar. Mercer is one of the few writers of standard songs to attract the label "poet" (Lees 1987: 11). While this is a compliment, implying creative achievement, it reinstates the model that was referred to above, which is more applicable to a writer with the creative autonomy of Bob Dylan. The work of Mercer and Warren needs to be understood in its historical context, recognizing ways in which a writer or composer's output was conditioned by the structures of a profession and an industry. This is not to imply that these conditions were solely constraints, that, given unconditioned creative freedom, artists like Mercer or Warren would have been able to express themselves more "authentically." Mercer may have functioned to better effect within the music business than in any hypothetical freedom from its constraints. He was an active participant in all the entertainment structures of the time: he appeared in films, wrote songs for them, appeared on network radio, and from 1943 presented his own high-profile radio program. In addition, from the summer of 1942 onward he was cofounder and co-owner of a major new independent record company, Capitol, the first for many years to threaten the hegemony of the existing majors Decca, Victor, and Columbia.

Not being accorded the status of a jazz performer and a "poet" only of a kind that the traditional model would not recognize, Mercer, like others of this period, falls into conceptual gaps in the history of American music. This brings the discussion back to the difficulties of discussing the popular music of this phase of history. A narrative that would give it its positive justification is missing. The popular songs of 1942, or of any year prior to Presley, are usually seen as important to the extent that they contribute toward the development of jazz. A band like Benny Goodman's is seen as having some components, such as a popular female singer, that can be discarded, along with anything else that does not further the received narrative of jazz, without doing any historical injustices.

The work of the writers of popular song such as Warren and Mercer is predominantly remembered as a secondary contribution to a field they never claimed to belong to. Warren, in particular, was the product of a completely different cultural and musical context, and the question of how his work related to "jazz" would have seemed irrelevant to him. The work of the creators and the performers of early 1940s popular music should be seen separately from the narrative compulsions of other idioms of music.

Their music should be viewed within the contexts in which it was produced and in which it had its real meaning.

Songs and songwriting were accommodated within a network of media that supported them, commented on them, or even brought them into being. The principal means through which songs were made available to the American public in the early 1940s were films and phonograph records and radio. Many songs that have become standards were once movie songs, "I Don't Want to Walk Without You" was "a tune from the pic *Sweater Girl* which is coming up, but fast" (*DB* 2.1.42: 15). Mercer's "That Old Black Magic" was written for the film "Star Spangled Rhythm" and "I'm Old Fashioned" and "Dearly Beloved" for *You Were Never Lovelier,* a movie vehicle for Rita Hayworth and Fred Astaire.

The format in which songs were issued on record was the double-sided 78 rpm shellac disc with a running time of about three minutes per side. The technology that would make the long-playing record possible was still six years away. At this time, all of an artist's output was issued in what were, in effect, singles. Issues would usually come out a couple of months apart, so that a typical recording session of six sides would produce a three- to six-months' supply of releases for that artist. For example, the Gene Krupa band's recording of "Skylark," with a vocal by Anita O'Day, was recorded at a session on November 25, 1941, and released together with a version of "Harlem on Parade," recorded two months later. All four tracks recorded on November 25 came out coupled with recordings from other sessions. Lucky Millinder's "That's All," recorded in November 1941, with vocal by Sister Rosetta Tharpe, was released together with the wartime ballad "When the Lights Go on Again," recorded eight months later.

Artists were subject to decisions taken by the record company on when and in what sequence and combination recordings were put on the market. Once issued, the music was open for promotion and publicity. The trade papers carried reviews of recordings, as well as listings of the most popular records and sheet-music issues. *Down Beat* featured a listing of the most played records in jukeboxes (selected by "One of the score of charming operators employed by the Chicago Automatic Hostess Co."), a matter of great weight in the market for phonograph records at that time.

Reviews were generally brief and could give strong judgments even on established artists. The Glenn Miller issue of "American Patrol" and

"Soldier Let Me Read Your Letter" was given this verdict, "A very classy job on the old Texas march. Rhythm section sounds much less sodden than usual" (*DB* 11.1.42: 8). A Woody Herman release featuring "Amen" and "Deliver Me to Tennessee" prompted this opening, "Brother, this one really comes on, but like something. A terrific Lunceford bounce beat, and Woody singing one of his terrific blues" (*DB* 11.1.42: 8). A review of a Duke Ellington release, coupling "Hayfoot, Strawfoot" and "Sherman Shuffle" was couched in the same kind of language, "It's sheer powerhouse—and anybody that thinks Duke has lost his musical innards, should rub his nose in this" (*DB* 11.1.42: 8).

New material, consisting for the most part of new popular songs, was appearing continuously, introduced via films or as individually published songs. Once a newly written song was available, there was a response by the recording companies, whether to pick up the song or leave it alone. A significant number of songs in 1941 and 1942 were issued in competing versions by different artists and different companies, in a process similar to the later practice of cover versions. The life cycle of a song can be traced though the versions that were marketed, this cycle measured in a few weeks or a few months, dating from the release of the movie the song appeared in or from the release of the first recording.

References in the music press gave indications of songs that were attracting interest through competing versions. On "Somebody Else Is Taking My Place," *Down Beat* gave this report, "Benny Goodman grabbed it first . . . his Okeh platter is getting a heavy play in the [juke]boxes" (*DB* 1.15.42: 13). A song the Goodman band recorded just after Pearl Harbor, "Someone's Rocking My Dreamboat," was by February the focus of much recording activity, "there are several versions which are going well in the machines. The Ink Spots' Decca, Benny Goodman's Okeh, Woody Herman's Decca and Erskine Hawkins's Bluebird are all excellent treatments" (*DB* 2.1.42: 15). Competition to exploit "I Don't Want to Walk Without You" seems to have had a clear winner, "Harry James's Columbia is the only disc worth spotting. . . . Helen Forrest's vocal helps. Only other competition for James is Casa Loma's Decca" (*DB* 2.1.42: 15).

Competition to exploit new songs occurred not only between artists but between recording companies. Recording activity in late 1941 and early 1942 following the arrival on the market of new songs by Johnny Mercer illustrates the process. One was "Skylark," which remains a jazz standard and was recorded in later decades by artists including Art Blakey and Stan Getz and singers such as Carmen McRae and Bette Midler. "Skylark" is not a straightforward song, in particular, its third eight-bar section, described by Alec Wilder (1972: 383) as "one of the most extraordinary releases I've ever heard."

Around the time of Pearl Harbor, nine versions of "Skylark" were recorded, five of them in January 1942 alone. The sequence began with a version by Gene Krupa's orchestra, featuring the singer Anita O'Day, recorded November 25. On January 8 the tune was recorded by Glenn Miller, and there were three new versions recorded between January 24 and 29 by Bing Crosby, Woody Herman, and Harry James. The band of the trumpeter Bunny Berigan also recorded the tune in January. In February "Skylark" was done by the singer Dinah Shore, and on March 19 there were two final recordings in the cycle, by the band of Earl Hines and the operatic singer Gertrude Niesen. The recordings of "Skylark" by Crosby, Herman, and Niesen were on the Decca label, the James version was on Columbia and Krupa's on its subsidiary label Okeh, while the Miller band's recording was on the Victor label and those by Shore and Hines on its subsidiary Bluebird.

The strategies of the record companies in taking up this promising new property are clear. Companies that had two labels, one at a budget price, as was the case with Columbia and Okeh, put out versions on each label. The Columbia "Skylark" by Harry James and the Okeh "Skylark" by Krupa have similarities, though the James version shows off a string section and a characteristic trumpet-based orchestral sound. The three Decca versions are by contrasting performers: Crosby, a solo male singer; Niesen, a solo female singer; and Herman's big band. The three RCA versions are by a successful swing band (Miller) and, on the partner label, one by a popular singer with a networked radio show (Dinah Shore) and another by Earl Hines's orchestra, a black band that did not rank among the top thirty nationally—an issue aimed at a "race" market, as was sometimes the case on labels such as Bluebird. Some versions were coupled with other tracks that made the disc a more attractive proposition. The James-Forrest "Skylark" was backed with a swing instrumental, "The Clipper," and was the most successful release, reaching the top 10 listings by the beginning of

June. The cycle of recordings of "Skylark" ran from November 1941 through March 1942, by when it had run its course as a potential hit item.

Its cycle overlapped with that of another Johnny Mercer song, written in collaboration with Harold Arlen, that was to make a much bigger impression during its span of popular exposure, "Blues in the Night." Like many other examples, *Blues in the Night* shows the interdependence of the film and music industries and the methods of exploiting a potentially profitable creative property. But, unusually and more importantly, its history also demonstrates how a popular song can enter into the lives of its listeners and be used by them, how a popular song can penetrate the culture as a whole.

Mercer and Arlen were engaged to write for an RKO movie called *Hot Nocturne*. The scenario had a scene in which a group of white jazz players are thrown into jail in St. Louis. While in their cell, they hear some black prisoners sing a song, supposedly an authentic blues number. The song, "Blues in the Night," was in fact written by Mercer and Arlen for the movie. So strong was its impact that the title of the film was changed to that of the song. Faced with the task of writing a blues song, Arlen had decided to undertake research on blues songs already published. It is surprising in a songwriter whose work is frequently placed close to jazz that he seemingly had no knowledge of how a blues song was constructed. The song Arlen produced consists of a twelve-bar verse, followed by another twelve-bar verse with different harmonies, followed by an eighteen-bar strain in a minor tonality. Arlen's model for "the blues" was probably a song like W. C. Handy's "St. Louis Blues," which also has a minor strain contrasting with twelve-bar choruses. This is borne out by Arlen's standard for authenticity, "I've got to write one that sounds authentic, that sounds as if it were born in New Orleans or St Louis" (Wilk 1974: 147). This is not a definition of a blues that many later writers would accept as authentic.[3]

The decisive stroke during the song's composition was Arlen's suggestion that Mercer move the line "My momma done tol' me" from the middle of the lyric to become the opening line. As Alec Wilder remembered, "All I ever heard the public sing was the 'My momma done tol' me' phrase. That seemed all they needed in order to like and accept it" (1972: 272). The song was informally premiered by its writers at a party at the Hollywood home of the songwriter Richard Whiting, among a gathering of singers and movie stars. It produced a sensational response, "Around nine thirty or ten Harold and Johnny came by, they'd just finished the song, and they went to our piano and did 'Blues' for the first time. Well, I want to tell you, it was like a Paramount Pictures finish—socko, boffo, *wham*! At one end of the room, Martha Raye almost passed out; for once, she didn't have a funny line. [Mel] Tormé was so knocked out by the musicianship, he just sat there. Mickey Rooney kept saying, 'My God, this is unbelievable!' And Judy [Garland] and I raced over to the piano to see which of us could learn the song first! You knew right away the song was so *important*" (Sackett 1995: 46).

All of the leading bands, those of Miller, Shaw, James, Goodman, and Tommy Dorsey, recorded the song during the cycle that ran from September 1941 to March 1942, with thirteen versions recorded in all. The movie *Blues in the Night* was on release throughout the autumn of 1941 into 1942; in mid-November 1941 it was showing at the Strand on 47th Street and Broadway, as part of a stage show that also featured Hattie McDaniel and the Count Basie orchestra.

The song was at its hottest in the last two weeks of December, when four recordings were made. Artie Shaw's band made the first recording in September, with vocal and improvisation by the trumpeter Hot Lips Page, one of the elite black musicians then breaking the color line in white bands. There quickly followed recordings by the Cab Calloway, Charlie Barnet, and Woody Herman orchestras. Glenn Miller recorded "Blues" on December 18, just three days after *Down Beat* registered the song as a sleeper, "Blues in the Night. Woody Herman has the strongest record, Decca, with Art Shaw's Victor and Cab Calloway's Okeh runners-up" (*DB*, 12.15.41: 15). The Jimmie Lunceford orchestra, which had been featured in a scene in the movie itself, made a recording on December 22, and on Christmas Eve a seven-piece band out of the Goodman orchestra included "Blues in the Night" in a session based around the singer Peggy Lee. The Goodman version has a strong Dixieland feeling, indicative of the older styles implicit in the song's blues construction. The Dixieland trait is also heard in Harry James's recording, made on December 30. The James orchestra, despite the presence of a string section, sounded at times like the Bob Crosby band, which had long made a specialty of its reference to older jazz styles.

By January 1, the Woody Herman recording had reached number 5 in the charts. In January the song was recorded by the band of Guy Lombardo and by three singers, Bing Crosby, Dinah Shore, and the Kansas City blues shouter Joe Turner. Shore's recording, introduced by a "growl" trumpet and with a more pronounced backbeat than other versions, did well commercially. However, by the beginning of February, in a review of the Lunceford recording, *Down Beat* already was warning that it was "too late to mean anything as a money-grabber" (2.1.42: 14). Woody Herman was then at number 2 in the charts and due to hit number 1 at the beginning of March.

Any first-run commercial potential in "Blues in the Night" was exhausted, with the country's first-rank recording musicians having pushed it through its cycle, but reverberations of the song continued outside of the commercial arena. The public had taken up the song in the way that Alec Wilder noted, but it seemed to seep into its consciousness by other routes as well. It exemplified the capacity of an effective popular song to permeate the culture.

The Harlem pianist Willie "The Lion" Smith, relating the musicians' habit of improvising dirty lyrics to some of the best-known popular tunes, told of how applying the habit to "Blues in the Night" rebounded on Fats Waller during a road tour at this time, "They had been using up the time on the bus improvising new barroom verses to 'Blues in the Night' and Fats was having a ball. They opened at the Paradise Theater in Detroit after an all-night run on the highway. During the first show, Fats started singing some of the smelliest phrases from the night before into the microphone. The management banged down the curtain and called the cops" (Smith and Hoefer 1964: 232).

In a very different sector of society, "Blues in the Night" found a use in another way. In May, the *Amsterdam News*, under the headline "Uses Popular Ditty as Mother's Day Text," related that "A phrase from the popular song 'Blues in the Night' was selected by the Rev. Baxter Carroll Duke, pastor of Avalon Christian Church for his sermon subject" (*AN* 5.16.42: 1), the phrase presumably being the inevitable "My momma done tol' me."

On July 29, 1942, the folklorist Alan Lomax conducted an interview with a young field hand and musician, McKinley Morganfield, at his home near Clarksdale, Mississippi. Morganfield, who was later to change his name to Muddy Waters, was the most outstanding musician encountered by Lomax and his fellow researchers from the Library of Congress in field research into black musical folklore in the Deep South. Among other notations, Lomax made a list of the songs that the young singer had in his current repertoire. The list contained blues songs by himself, Sonny Boy Williamson, and Walter Davis as well as some surprising selections: a Bill Monroe bluegrass number "Be Honest with Me"; popular standards like "I Ain't Got Nobody" and "Dinah"; and current hit songs like "Deep in the Heart of Texas," "Chattanooga Choo-Choo," and "Blues in the Night." Lomax ran into "Blues in the Night" once more on the same trip, a group of Mississippi girls wanted to perform the song rather than the contemporary spiritual that they eventually sang into his recording machine.

The history of "Blues in the Night" and its popular reception in 1941–1942 suggests some further reconsiderations of the narrative of jazz. In the competition for a best-selling recording of a new popular song, we see jazz artists taking part in a popular-music process. The twelve versions of "Blues in the Night" that were recorded over six months do not show great stylistic variations, regardless of whether the artist concerned was a "jazz" musician or not. Herman, Lunceford, Goodman, and Turner would be so categorized. James, Shaw, Calloway, Barnet, and possibly Miller figure in most accounts as jazz musicians of a lower order; Shore, Lombardo, and Crosby would almost certainly not qualify. However, all twelve recordings produced during the song's cycle approached it in a similar way. It cannot be said that the Lunceford recording is definitively jazz, while the Dinah Shore recording is definitively not—in fact, Dinah Shore's "Blues in the Night" is one of the funkier versions. All the artists trying to make something of the Mercer-Arlen hit song seem to have playing the same game.

The products of the popular music industry had a broad constituency. "Blues in the Night" turned up in the repertoire of a blues player in Mississippi only a year after the song's inception. Surely, Muddy Waters saw the movie or heard some of the thirteen versions over the radio. The thirty-four songs the young musician was playing were much more varied than the blues narratives would lead one to expect. Fourteen are not blues numbers, but selections from various kinds of American music—from country ("You Are My Sunshine," "Boots and My Saddles") through spirituals ("Down by the Riverside") to pop songs ("Dark Town Strutters' Ball" and "Red Sails in the Sunset").

Similarly, all jazz bands played a high proportion of popular songs and did them in a way that it is difficult to identify as categorically jazz treatments. In the early 1940s, all major bands, black and white, recorded versions of the entire gamut of popular songs. As we saw, bands such as those Gene Krupa, Bob Crosby, and Lucky Millinder had a special line in military numbers. Benny Goodman's band made recordings between December 1941 and July 1942 of virtually nothing but contemporary pop songs, with only six tracks from that period lacking a vocal by Peggy Lee or Art Lund. The Count Basie band, whose 1941–1942 output did contain some blues material, made versions of songs like "Blue Shadows and White Gardenias," with a straight vocal by Earle Warren. The Duke Ellington orchestra, the most definitively jazz of all, had in its repertoire the Helen Forrest hit "I Don't Want to Walk Without You" and the Mercer-Arlen song "Dearly Beloved" from the film "You Were Never Lovelier." Jazz players were making pop records. Blues players were singing pop tunes.

The normative traditions of jazz and blues, as discussed in chapter 5, were first being constructed at around this time. Writers in these traditions have devised arguments to explain how and why jazz and blues players sometimes behaved in these noncanonical ways. If a jazz player performed a popular song, he was either parodying and subverting it (although it does not *sound* as if this is what Basie was doing to "White Shadows") or giving in to some form of coercion (Townsend 2000: 170–172). A record company, an agency, a song-plugger, or other interested party had compelled the jazz player to make a recording of this kind of material. According to these theorists, jazz players just play jazz and blues singers just sing blues, unless they are forced to make concessions.

A similar problem of categorization was faced a generation later by Chuck Berry, "Last night you heard me do 'Mountain Dew,' a hillbilly song. I do that and I look out and the people are stompin' their feet and goin' 'Heehaw!' Tonight you heard me do [Nat King Cole's] 'Ramblin' Rose.' Does that mean I'm doing ballads now? No, I followed it with 'Johnny B. Goode'" (Flanagan 1987: 80). Berry nevertheless saw his performance, indeed his personal style, as having coherence and wholeness. It is not as if he was ceasing to be a rock-and-roll artist (if, in fact, that is what he is) as he moved from one song to another, becoming now a hillbilly, now a ballad singer, and so on. The material that he used was intended, as he put it, "to break things up."

Likewise, the repertoire of a band like Goodman's was not made up of disparate elements some of which were "jazz" and some of which were "not jazz." The vocals, the ballads, the swing numbers, and so on were components of a band style that did not necessarily conform to an ahistorical definition of an entity called "jazz." What Goodman, Ellington, or Basie did was part of a continuum with what Dinah Shore, Johnny Mercer, and Bing Crosby did. Musicians whom later histories regard as jazz musicians were close to the popular music industry; indeed, it is often impossible to distinguish their practices from those of "popular" performers. Another way of putting this is to say that jazz was part of popular music. In dealing with the products of Tin Pan Alley, the performers later categorized as jazz artists demonstrate the absence of any fundamental separation between them and the rest of American popular musicians.

Bandleaders, their managers, and their accountants had several sources of income to consider. A well-placed band or artist could pull in a substantial income from personal appearances, with movies an occasional possibility, and dates in theaters and ballrooms the staple element. There could be session fees and royalties from recordings and other avenues that were open to some musicians, such as fees for compositions and arrangements and endorsements of products. A few, such as Benny Goodman's guitarist Allen Reuss, made money through teaching. Most artists had a variety of ways of earning a living, the component parts reinforcing one another. For instance, personal appearances created interest in songs and records, records generated interest in personal appearances, radio influenced sales of records and created interest in movies and gigs, and so on, in what could be a self-reinforcing circle.

In the late 1930s and early 1940s, a major development affected the balance between the different forces: the rise of the jukebox. The need to consider outcomes in terms of jukebox exposure determined some decisions taken by musicians at this level of the market. According to *Down Beat*, "America's more than 400,000 coin machines (jukes) are the goal of every recording artist nowadays, and every master made in the studio is accompanied by a prayer that it will be 'the one' which will 'hit the boxes'" (*DB* 12.15.41: 35). This is borne out, for example, by the switch by Benny Goodman from the Columbia label to its partner Okeh. This was intended "to push Goodman into more coin machines" (*DB* 12.1.41: 14). At thirty-five cents a copy, Okeh discs were cheaper than Columbia's, creating the probability that more operators would put Goodman's records on their machines. The greater volume of sales would, it was hoped, more than make up for the lesser royalty on the cheaper disc. If a jukebox was stocked with discs at thirty-five instead of, say, fifty cents, the operator made a 30 percent savings. With high-quality artists, such as Goodman, available at that price, the operators should still get the same revenue.

Record reviews were conscious of jukebox sales in their assessment of the commercial potential of new releases. "Someone's Rocking My Dreamboat" in its various versions was "going well in the machines," and, in a comment that shows how the contents of the jukebox could be targeted to specific locations, "[it] can hardly miss no matter where the machine is" (*DB* 2.1.42: 15). This was a way of saying the song would do as well in a colored location as in a white one. Conversely, the Jay McShann band's follow-up to its recent successes, "New Confessin' the Blues" was estimated as "excellent for colored and swing locations" (*DB* 2.15.42: 15).

Jukeboxes were placed in a wide variety of venues, and the social scene around the machines was the subject of commentary. In July 1942, the Glenn Miller orchestra, a major beneficiary of coin-machine business, recorded "Juke Box Saturday Night." The song left a permanent marker of the machine's centrality among the recreations of American youth of the 1940s. The fact that RCA Victor almost blocked the release because of the possibility of giving offence to jukebox operators is further evidence of the financial clout of the market. The Miller track cuts the swing vocal choruses, sung by the Modernaires, with accurate imitations of two contemporary coin-machine favorites, Harry James and the Ink Spots. The lyric sets a scene of a crowd of teenagers "Mopping up soda-pop rickies to our heart's delight," and enjoying the free entertainment as "somebody else plays the record machine." A columnist in the *Amsterdam News* gave a view of a jukebox in another setting, "A bunch of the cats were in the candy store around the corner on the mid-watch, getting groovey off Pepsi-Cola and the throb of the piccolo [jukebox]. Somebody lamped the Waller label and promptly shot a buffalo [nickel] into the slot, expecting to be 'sent' the usual way. The others had their chicks all ready, set for some of the Harlem style rug-cutting in close quarters" (*AN* 5.30.42: 16).

It was largely due to the stimulus of the jukebox market that sales of phonograph records pulled out of the dive they took after 1929. The combination of economic depression and radio supplying the appetite for music meant that sales declined from the late-1920s to bottom out ten years later. The large numbers of jukeboxes installed in the late 1930s, however, resulted in an expansion of record sales to supply the machines, and by 1941 this had translated into a stimulus to sales of records for home consumption. This was all good news for operators, record companies, and retailers and for the musicians making records and earning royalties. But it was viewed by many of the rank and file of professional musicians and their representatives as another channel through which work was disappearing from real, live musicians.

As recorded music was taking up more program time, the need for radio stations to maintain in-house orchestras was diminishing. Bars and restaurants that installed jukeboxes did not need to hire musicians. Though there was still a lot of music broadcast on radio from the remote linkups with ballrooms and clubs, the total amount of music coming to Americans in recorded form was increasing. Although this had financial advantages, these did not necessarily benefit the musicians. The issue of jukeboxes and musicians' employment became another cause within the attritional war between the AFM and the radio and recording companies. The AFM, through its abrasive leader James C. Petrillo, had agreed to a ban on strikes "for the duration" of the war. However, the cluster of grievances against the practices of the media companies was difficult to ignore.

Radio had long raised anxieties about long-term prospects for professional musicians. The financial benefits from radio, however, were at least more evenly spread than those from recording. There were radio stations across the country, according to an April 1942 survey, each putting out on average twenty-nine hours of live music each week (in addition to forty-eight hours of recorded music; Sanjek 1988: 267). Of this, a large proportion were remote broadcasts from venues in the vicinity of the station or on the networks from New York, Chicago, and other major cities, often featuring name artists. Many stations provided employment to in-house musicians, from country artists like Hank Williams, who began his career on a small Alabama station, to formal orchestras like the ones attached to the Buffalo stations. In all, the total number of musicians heard on radio even in a single week of 1942 was still high. As a character in Garrison Keillor's *Radio Romance* put it, this was the last time there were shows "that let people sing on the radio who were not famous" (1991: 318).

A characteristic of the way in which music was presented and experienced on radio was sheer variety—or, to put it more accurately, an absence of generic programming. As Gene Lees noted, "It was a glorious and indiscriminate mélange in which jazz and classical and country music were mixed on the same station or network, so that it was impossible not to know what the full range of America's music was" (1987: 87). This is demonstrable from radio listings during this period. For example, the music broadcast on the night of December 7 included the swing bands of Bunny Berigan and Claude Thornhill, the Latin band of Xavier Cugat, the country singer Gene Autry, Judy Garland, and Dinah Shore. Radio listings in March 1942 gave slots for the three tenors Lanny Ross, Frank Parker, and Morton Downey but a listener might also take in the U.S. Navy Band and Glenn Miller's show on WABC. Steering among the soap operas on the dial in Providence, Rhode Island, on an afternoon in 1942, a listener could pick up Bing Crosby, Kate Smith, *Masterworks of Music,* and *Italian Melodies.* The weighting of music increased as the evening went on: Fred Waring, Harry James, The Metropolitan Opera, Bing Crosby again, Teddy Powell, Rudy Vallee, and later Stan Kenton, Johnny Long, Joe Marsala, and Duke Ellington (the last on WPRO at 12:30 a.m.).

For fans of swing music, prime time came toward the end of programming into the small hours, with the networks picking up remote broadcasts from ballrooms and clubs across the country. Another enriching factor was the different time zones, which prolonged the entertainment even further. The trumpeter Ruby Braff, who grew up in Boston around this time, described the selection of music that was available to him on late-night radio, "I could hear the broadcasts from 11 o'clock onward 15 minutes apiece. They came in from all over the country, it would be: And now from Chicago, Stuff Smith, how the hell could I go to bed? Then: Now we go to New York for Art Tatum. It just never ended until two or three o'clock in the morning" (*JJI* 8.2002: 10).

Early evening scheduling generally did not have this air of wild discovery, with the main stations featuring established singing stars or name bands sponsored by major companies. Tobacco companies had the largest stake in sponsoring programs, one of the most prominent being Glenn Miller's *Moonlight Serenade,* sponsored by Chesterfield cigarettes. By mid-1942 the Miller band was doing the Chesterfield show three nights a week, in a fifteen-minute early evening slot. A few months into the war, the program had a strong orientation to its audiences in the military training camps and their families. Each week a military base was awarded a deluxe radio-phonograph as a prize for winning a listeners' poll. The sponsor's presence was difficult to miss, as in this introduction to the June 29 edition, which combined the advertising message with patriotism:

ANNOUNCER: Chesterfield, the favorite cigarette of Uncle Sam's fighting forces and you folks at home, brings you Glenn Miller's "Moonlight Serenade." Now here's Glenn himself.
MILLER: Thank you, Gil, and Chesterfield greetings, everybody. Here's the first of this week's Serenades, with a special salute for Fort Benning, Georgia. And while you folks are lighting up the cigarette that satisfies, our Serenade starts with the band playing "Give Me Something to Remember You By."

Another networked program that pulled in a large share of the audience was *The Kraft Music Hour*, featuring Bing Crosby. The show went out on Thursday evenings. Despite its title, the show had many guest stars who were not musicians, including the actors Humphrey Bogart and Ronald Reagan and the boxer Gene Tunney. Musicians featured alongside Crosby included Paul Robeson, Johnny Mercer, Harry James, and the Ink Spots. Crosby's salary as star and host was $5000 per show for the 1942–1943 season. But opportunities for contracts with shows at the level of the *Kraft Music Hour*, the *Camel Caravan*, and the *Fitch Bandwagon* were few. Most of the sustaining broadcasts fed into radio stations from ballrooms and other locations paid nothing, neither to the artists nor the venue. For both of the latter parties the radio broadcast was a means to an end: for the club or ballroom, a means to attract patrons, for the artists, to gain exposure that would lead to moneymaking opportunities elsewhere.

For musicians, the primary goal among such opportunities was live engagements. Even for the best-paid artists and bands, live gigs were financially significant. For the lower-ranked organizations, they were vital to survival. Someone like Glenn Miller made a large income by different means: royalties on records, especially with "Chattanooga Choo-Choo" hitting sales of 1.2 million copies; film appearances; and two long-running, salary-paying radio shows. Miller could also command large sums for live ballroom and theater performances. Most other bands had this last element alone.

Musicians needed to think of radio and records purely as channels for securing the live engagements that were their only significant source of income. Therefore, musicians' lives revolved around travel. Live performances were not always offered within range of a band's home base, and so bands and musicians had to travel to reach as many gigs as they could manage to secure. For many American musicians, no other location—not the radio or the studios—meant as much as the domain of the road.

Chapter 4

The Road

But you're a road man, Willy, and we do a road business.

—ARTHUR MILLER, *Death of a Salesman*

The Duke Ellington band began 1942 at the Mainstreet Theatre in Kansas City, Missouri, where they were booked to play a week. Before the end of February, the band played dates in Junction City, Omaha, Madison, Waukegan, Elkhart, Chicago, Detroit, Canton, Pittsburgh, Uniontown, Boston, Lawrence, Portland, Worcester, Toronto, Buffalo, and Washington, D.C. The dates in Chicago, Detroit, and Boston were for one week, and all the others were one-night stands. Between Elkhart, Indiana, and Chicago, the band spent a day at the Victor studios in Chicago, and another recording session required a day at the studios in New York, between the Buffalo and Washington engagements.[1]

For the Saturday performance at Waukegan, Illinois, there was a buildup in the local press over the previous week. The *Waukegan News-Sun* gave lavish praise to the players in the band (including Jimmy Blanton, who was hospitalized in California) and suggested that, "This attraction should be one of the high spots of the current dance season." Thursday's edition had an artist's caricature of Ellington, with the caption reading, "Ellington's band is as far ahead of the usual bands now as it was ten years ago, and it was tops then." Friday's *News-Sun* quoted *Metronome* and *Swing* magazine, and Saturday's edition published figures for a *Down Beat* poll in which Ellington rated high in all categories (*WNS* 1.14–17.42). The advertisement on the day of the gig called Ellington "one of the greatest musicians alive," and gave a line to the singers Ivie Anderson, billed as the "California Song Star," and Herb Jeffries, the "Bronze Buckaroo." An ad for the date at the State Theatre in Uniontown, Pennsylvania, made mention of the show "Jump for Joy," which Ellington had premiered the previous summer. The feature film that Uniontown patrons would get on the bill with the Ellington band, a newsreel, and a Donald Duck cartoon, was *No Hands on the Clock*, starring Chester Morris and Jean Parker.

For these first months of 1942, Ellington's band traveled north to Chicago, east via Detroit and Pittsburgh to New England, and to Toronto and Buffalo before a longer trip to Washington, D.C., via New York. The later months of 1941 had been spent in comparative stasis on the West Coast, with a run of engagements taking advantage of interest generated by "Jump for Joy" and radio coverage. The first week of November was spent at the Golden Gate Theatre in San Francisco. While in residence at the Golden Gate, Ellington and several members of the band went out to eat at a restaurant, and what occurred there was not an isolated incident, "Duke Ellington's recent visit to the Bay region to play a week at the Golden Gate Theatre found the usual number of so-called 'Good Americans' who run restaurants and hotels doing their best to make the Duke and his party feel out of place. Just about the silliest deal of all happened at one of the downtown eateries across the bay. The arrival of Duke and his party caused some confusion among the waiters, etc., who finally allowed the Duke to sit out in the open but seated the other members of his party at another table and placed a screen in front of them" (*DB* 12.15.41: 24).

The Midwestern and eastern dates paid as little as $300, for the night at Omaha. Junction City paid $400, and Waukegan $450, while Madison and Elkhart brought in $687 and $767. For four nights at the Palace Theatre, in Canton, Ohio, the band received $2750, a week at the RKO Boston Theatre was worth $5500, and the week at the Howard in Washington, D.C., $4688. Some differences in the payments may be due to the itinerary. Assuming that full-week and other longer engagements determined the framework of the trip, then dates like Omaha may have been fillers designed to fit into the schedule and at the same time bring in extra revenue. The billing of the Waukegan engagement as "A Scoop!" suggests that it, too, was a filler engagement, the management of the Rink Ballroom having been offered the chance to catch the band on its way to Chicago.

The mode of transportation for the Ellington band at this time was primarily the railroad. This was unusual for traveling bands and an indication of the band's relatively good financial status. Another reason may have been the need for security for a black band. When in the South, Cab Calloway's band, another black band with a busy road schedule, carried its crew in a Pullman railroad car and otherwise preferred to used railroads, as Danny Barker related, "We left New York City on first class trains: the New York Central, the Twentieth Century Limited, the Broadway Limited. Hugh Wright, our road manager, was a wonderful and understanding human being; he always made it a practice to get the band the best train transportation if it was possible" (Barker and Shipton 1986: 163).

The Ellington band's accounts list payments to the Kansas City Missouri Lines, Rock Island Railroad, Milwaukee Railroad, North Shore Electric Railroad, New York Central, Pennsylvania Railroad, and New York and New Hampshire. Some accounts specify Pullman cars, for example, for the journeys between Canton, Pittsburgh, and Philadelphia in February. As wartime conditions began to bite, however, the band could not always rely on superior train accommodations. The band manager, Jack Boyd, referred late in 1942 to times when "they always had their own two Pullmans and baggage cars, living in them for weeks at a time" as "the good old days." [2] Boyd recalled an occasion when the band played successive nights in Sioux Falls, South Dakota, and 875 miles away in Indianapolis, with a journey of nineteen hours. By 1942, the AFM had imposed a limit of 400 miles travel between one-nighters, but some of the Ellington band's shifts strained this limit, such as the move between Boston on February 23 and Toronto the next night.

Ellington's band's accounts for 1942 show how marginal its financial position was. In the week of gigs at Madison, Waukegan, and Elkhart, once band members and staff (including Ellington himself) received salaries and expenses were paid, only $25 was left. A better week came at the end of February, with gigs in Buffalo, Toronto, and New England, including $1000 for performing at Symphony Hall in Boston; the account cleared a profit of

$1038. The incidental expenses give a picture of the logistical complications of running of a band. There were payments to Grey Line buses for a move in Boston; to transfer companies in Portland, Worcester, Buffalo, Toronto, and New York; to customs officers for the trip into Canada; expense claims by individuals including Ellington himself; a sum for tips to bus drivers; and items including "cleaning and pressing," wires and phone calls, and, an unexplained entry that indicates a world of mundane concerns, "Chicago Shoes, $14.44." According to Robert Boyer's *New Yorker* essay on Ellington, the Ellington organization grossed $210,000 in 1942 but came out with a margin of $4000. This was an advance on 1941, when the band showed a loss of $1500 on an income of $135,000 (Boyer reprinted in Tucker 1993a: 245).

It seems the weekly accounts were kept by Boyd as the band traveled the country—most were typed on stationery borrowed from hotels. The largest outgoing was payroll, with salary paid to twenty-one individuals. Ellington took $250, and other performers, including some famous names, received salaries that varied interestingly. The trumpeter Rex Stewart's $125 was equaled by the clarinetist Barney Bigard, singer Ivie Anderson, and saxophonist Johnny Hodges. Tenor saxophonist Ben Webster made $90, while the newcomers, trumpeter Ray Nance and bassist Junior Raglin, were paid $77.10 and $64.20.

The company that traveled with the band, performed in stage shows, and was paid out of the organization's income frequently included singers, comedians, and dancers. For the week at the Paradise in Detroit, the payroll included the singer and dancer Marie Bryant; the comedian Al Guster; and the dance act Pot, Pan, and Skillet. The last received $250 for the week—an amount equal to Ellington's. When the band had a longer residency—as they did in the summer of 1942 in Los Angeles and Chicago—personnel were sometimes limited to band members and staff, but it was normal on the many theater dates to hook up with these other performers. In August the Ellington payroll supported the dancer Baby Lawrence, Jig Saw Jackson, Pops and Louie, and Dusty Fletcher. This troupe undertook a Midwestern tour with the band, and they came back on board in November for dates around the theater circuit in Chicago and the East.

To anyone familiar with the writings of jazz historians, it may be surprising to find such an institution as the Duke Ellington band sharing its traveling and working space with these other performers. They were, however, part of the context in which musicians like Ellington and his band worked. The interpretation placed upon this is of some significance historically. Historians of jazz, including some expressing this opinion at the time, felt that the coexistence of Duke Ellington with dancers and singers and his playing in ballrooms and cinemas was an unfortunate necessity, brought about by the poorly evolved infrastructure of the music business (see Leonard Feather's 1943 comment on Ellington's not needing to "tickle the toes of a mob of jitterbugs"; Tucker 1993a: 175). However, musicians, writers, instrumentalists, composers, dancers, singers, and comedians appeared on the same bills, took part in the same performances, and were part of what customers got for their entrance money.

The Ellington band, in this respect, was behaving no differently from others. Some leaders enthusiastically embraced the presence of dancers and other acts. The black performer Cholly Atkins, who had a long career in dance, related how in the early 1940s he developed an act with Cab Calloway's band in which Calloway himself danced. Atkins's troupe frequently toured with bands, "We started doing a lot of 'round the world' dates with other big bands, like Andy Kirk and Lucky Millinder. This included black theatres in Baltimore, Washington, New York, and Philadelphia" (Atkins and Malone 2001: 47). Atkins was working with Louis Armstrong's band at the time of Pearl Harbor; Armstrong, like Count Basie, "had a special fondness for dance acts. He'd even strut a little bit on stage, himself" (2001: 52). As a dancer, Atkins saw nothing unusual about working with a band. "Many big bands," he wrote, "carried a boy-and-girl team, a comedy dancing act, and usually a couple of vocalists" (2001: 52). This is exactly what the Ellington band did throughout 1942.

Another band that traveled with singers, dancers, and other acts was that of Fats Waller, whose tour in early 1942 was taken with comedy performers such as Apus and Estrellita. Waller himself could be considered a singer and dancer. From another point of view, however, Waller was a jazz musician, and some critics have taken a stern view of what they see as the frivolous incidentals in Waller's performance. Leonard Feather's comment in his *Encyclopedia of Jazz* is representative, "Fats left a legacy of great records recalling a gay, insouciant personality that contrasted oddly with his serious stature as a major jazz creator" (1960: 452). This implies what became an axiom of jazz criticism: that jazz is a serious music that has no truck with "entertainment." Subsequent histories of jazz overlook the fact that for years jazz players performed with and among dancers, singers, comedians—turns of all kinds. This was the case in venues such as the Apollo in Harlem: Lucky Millinder's band appeared with the dancer Honi Coles; Count Basie with the same Pot, Pan, and Skillet who toured with Ellington; Earl Hines with the singer and dancer "Rubberlegs" Williams (who later recorded with Charlie Parker); and Fletcher Henderson with the comedian Jackie "Moms" Mabley. The show at the Apollo the week of March 7 offered both Fats Waller and Clifford Fisher's Football Dogs, an act described as "a new high in canine artistry" (*AN* 2.28.42: 17).

Another ingredient in the entertainment package in which jazz came wrapped was movies. When a band like Ellington's was performing a theater date, as in its 1942 circuit, a film would generally be provided. The film *Blues in the Night* could be watched between performances by Count Basie at the Strand on 47th Street in New York or by Glenn Miller at the Palace in Cleveland. The next film on the bill with Miller was Preston Sturges's *Sullivan's Travels* at the Michigan Theater in Detroit. A Red Allen date at the Apollo in March featured John Ford's *The Young Mr. Lincoln,* starring Henry Fonda. In May at the Paramount in Times Square, a stage show of the Woody Herman band and the Ink Spots accompanied the movie *This Gun for Hire.*

The film could be a factor in a band's success or failure in a venue. *Variety* reported that Ellington's appearance at the Oriental in Chicago did good business "despite a weak Jinx Falkenburg film" (2.18.42: 31). Was the sense of a film affected by seeing it in a show featuring a band, and did it make a difference which band it was? Was *Blues in the Night* given different nuances by being seen with Miller rather than Basie? Ellington himself, as I discuss in chapter 7, claimed that on at least one occasion the film with which his band's performance was coupled had a direct influence upon his compositions.

Presentation in a theater determined the nature of the set a band played. Many stage shows were timed to achieve the desired number of performances of the bill within the allotted time, with six shows a day being customary. For instance, when Benny Goodman's band played the Paramount in May 1942, the schedule began at 9:15 a.m., with exact timings of trailers, the film *Take a Letter, Darling,* the band performance, intermission, a film short, and a trailer promoting war bonds; the final show ended at 2:52 a.m. Goodman's band knew that its sets would begin at 10:56, 1:33, 4:10, 6:57, 9:42, and 12:27, each lasting for fifty-two minutes (Latzgo 1995: 34).

A band had a different role in ballroom dates, where an important function was to play for dancers. This determined the balance between the different elements the band could provide. An important engagement for the Ellington band was the huge Trianon Ballroom in Los Angeles, which provided a six-week booking in April and May 1942. The format at the Trianon included a floorshow in which the band accompanied its singers and three dance acts. For the remainder of the time, the band played music for customers to dance to, using a wide selection from its repertoire.

Above all others, Ellington's band was known for basing its repertoire upon its leader's compositions. But, like other bands, Ellington's was operating in a popular-music environment. A recording was made of a one-night performance by the Ellington band at a ballroom in Fargo, North Dakota, in November 1940. On that occasion, a large proportion of the selections were compositions by Ellington, but the band also played popular numbers, such as "Whispering Grass," "Star Dust," and "All This and Heaven Too." In one of only two brief recordings that exist of the 1942 Trianon engagement, the band played Frank Loesser's "I Don't Want to Walk Without You," the popular hit of the early months of the year.

For bands with the stature of Ellington's, there was normally advance publicity drawn up by the agency that managed the band and arranged bookings. By 1942 Ellington was managed by the William Morris agency. Agencies employed local agents to supply information to media about upcoming performances and artists. The material about Ellington in the *Waukegan News-Sun* was an example of a local newspaper making use of information supplied by the agencies. Ellington's previous agency was Mills Artists, which stressed to its agents the need to have Ellington's recordings and sheet music on display in music stores and indicated that Ellington and his band would be available for "autograph stunts" and publicity events. The Mills write-up recommended using Ellington himself for radio and newspaper interviews, as "He is as genial as he is intelligent, always creates a good impression upon newspaper people . . . and invariably supplies them with good copy."[3]

The William Morris publicity, like the Mills material, is significant in the way it positioned Ellington. Mills referred to authorities in classical music, Percy Grainger and Constant Lambert, who "accepted Ellington's genius quite seriously and have hailed him as one of the most influential factors in the current trend of popular music." The Morris approach continued to promote the idea of Ellington as a serious artist with claims to attention in the legitimate field. Among the "punch lines" mailed out to agents were "America's Foremost Modern Composer" and "America's Genius of Modern Music." This characterization of Ellington on the model of the serious composer was to be taken up in a more ambitious initiative before the year was over.

Because of the reputation and the publicity angle that went before it, the Ellington band was booked in venues that had something of the concert hall about them. In this early 1942 itinerary, one date that stands out among places of normal commercial entertainment was an appearance at the Memorial Auditorium in Buffalo, New York, on February 25. The "Aud," as it became known locally, was a reminder of recent troubled economic times. Buffalo, like other industrial cities, had suffered greatly from the economic depression of the 1930s, and under the Roosevelt administration money was allocated through the Public Works Administration for building projects in the city. The Memorial Auditorium was a convention hall, inaugurated in 1940 and capable of seating 15,000 people. A performance by a band like Ellington's evidently used only part of the available space, since the press reported "a swell gate of 1500 admissions at $1" (*Var.* 3.4.42: 42). The ad for the performance at the auditorium shared the page with an assortment of movies, a concert by the Buffalo Philharmonic, and the Palace Burlesque, featuring "Peaches, Sheba of Shimmy."

In these first months of wartime, Buffalo was a center of intense industrial and economic activity. Two airplane plants, Bell and Curtiss-Wright, had been in operation for some time. Curtiss-Wright expanded during the early war years from a workforce of 5300 to 43,000. General Motors employed 87,000 workers in Buffalo and the surrounding areas. There were two giant steel mills, Bethlehem Steel and Republic Steel. In the view of one historian, "The war was good for Buffalo. It was the best thing, in fact, that ever happened to the city" (Goldman 1983: 233). With about half the workforce employed in war-related industries and a weekly earning power of $10 million, "prosperity was unprecedented" (1983: 234).

Of direct relevance to black musicians coming into the city, such as Ellington and his players, was the Colored Musicians' Union, which was founded in 1927 when black musicians were denied entry to the white local. Duke Ellington and his musicians, as well as such performers as Ella Fitzgerald, Lionel Hampton, and Billie Holiday, used the union hall as a place to relax after performing in the city. Another place of resort, a nightclub and social center, was the Little Harlem Hotel, whose clients over its long lifetime included Louis Armstrong, Count Basie, Sugar Ray Robinson, and Bing Crosby. At the time of the 1942 visit by the Ellington band, Buffalo's south-central area had clubs and showplaces such as the Moonglow, Paradise Ballroom, and Vendome Hotel, where Count Basie and the jazz violinist Stuff Smith performed. There was a complex of theaters, movie houses, clubs, bars, and ballrooms catering for a city doing booming wartime business. The Glen Casino, presenting a variety bill of a tenor, a soft-shoe dancer, and music by Bono and his orchestra, was later in the year advertising new opening hours, "WAR WORKERS ATTENTION: We have arranged our show time so that you will be able to see the COMPLETE FLOOR SHOW starting at 1.45 a.m."

Ellington and his musicians were on the train into New York the day after their Buffalo show for a recording session at the Victor studios and then on to Washington, D.C., for a week at the Howard Theatre. The week in Washington was followed by week-long dates on the eastern circuit at the Royal in Baltimore, the Earl in Philadelphia, and the Stanley in Pittsburgh. The band then played three nights in Camden, New Jersey, and, setting off on the Rock Island Railroad on the long trail to the West Coast, two nights in Steubenville, Ohio, and one at Moline, Illinois.

The arc of the year carried the band to the West Coast, back to Chicago for an extended stay, and then to more one-nighters in the East. The process was continuous. In his autobiography, Ellington claimed that his was "the only band in the world that works fifty-two weeks a year. It is probably the only organization of any kind doing anything fifty-two weeks a year, with no holidays and no weekends off" (1974: 41). This was a tough schedule, offset by the relative comfort in which the band traveled at this time. Their total mileage on the road in 1942 was around 30,000 miles. Andy Kirk, whose band could never afford the kinds of transportation that Ellington's had, reckoned to cover 50,000 miles every year from 1937 until the late 1940s (Kirk and Lee 1989: 88).

It could be a grueling experience to travel with a band that had not reached the income of Ellington, or Calloway, or the popular white bands. The saxophonist Dexter Gordon joined Lionel Hampton's band at the end of 1940, before its big successes, "Gladys [Mrs. Lionel Hampton] was economizing. It was a line called All-American—All-American Bus Line—and the whole band could fit in there, but it was tight, and it was strictly a California [unheated] bus, and it's December, and so our first stop was Fort Worth, Texas, which I think is about fifteen hundred miles. It took about three days to get there. And after we got out of Arizona, we got into New Mexico, it started getting cold, and so then we got to El Paso, there was a mutiny.... And this cat Jack Lee was the road manager with the band. And the cats said 'No, no, man, shuck this bus. We got to get a real bus'" (Gitler 1985: 14).

Even highly ranked and efficiently run bands, such as Jimmie Lunceford's, could impose a burden of traveling verging on exploitation. It was in response to this that in 1941 the AFM brought in its restriction on distances. The greatest traveling privations were probably felt by musicians in the lesser-known bands whose sphere of operation was restricted to a region or locality, what were sometimes called "territory bands." Memoirs of players are full of bus breakdowns, overcrowding, extremes of heat and cold, lack of sleep, lack of food, unreliable incomes, and humiliations, which could be many times worse for black musicians. All the bands traveled, even those of white leaders such as Glenn Miller, Artie Shaw, and Harry James. But the white bands and successful black bands such as those of Ellington, Lunceford, and Calloway, were to some degree insulated from some of the problems of the road.

The U.S. circuit the Ellington band made in 1942 covered New England, Maryland, New Jersey, Pennsylvania, New York (though they played only recording sessions in New York City), Ohio, Illinois, Indiana, Wisconsin, Minnesota, Nebraska, Kansas, Missouri, Iowa, Michigan, Utah, Colorado, California, Oregon, and Washington and in Canada Ontario and British Columbia. Of major cities, the band worked in Boston, Washington, Detroit, Philadelphia, Baltimore, Seattle, San Francisco, and St. Louis twice; Los Angeles three times; and Chicago five times. St. Louis was as far as the Ellington band went into the South throughout 1942. It was also where, later in wartime, an incident occurred that is described in Richard Boyer's *New Yorker* piece (reprinted in Tucker 1993a: 232). Arriving at the Union Station in St. Louis, second only to Chicago as a railroad center, the black musicians of Ellington's band were unable to get taxis. The next day, even using a white man as an intermediary and despite the enthusiastic response they received to their performance on stage, they were unable to buy food (Tucker 1993a: 232).

The much-traveled Andy Kirk remembered the Jim Crow screens from wartime travels between army camps, "In those days there were curtains in diners to use when the southbound trains crossed the Mason-Dixon line. They were always pulled across the dining-car to separate the Blacks from the Whites." Kirk recalled an occasion between Little Rock, Arkansas, and Jackson, Mississippi, when a black steward refused to pull a curtain in front of the Kirk musicians seated in the diner, "The conductor yanked it across again and said, 'I want you to know'—and he was shaking his finger at Mr. Smith—'I'm in charge of this train from the engine to the last car.' The waiter in charge said, 'And I want you to know,' pointing his finger right back at the conductor, 'I'm in charge of this car from the kitchen to the other end! And if you don't want this car on your train, put it on the side track.' And he opened the curtain with a yank." Andy Kirk regarded the waiter's action less as a protest than a determination to provide good service in his dining car. "But," Kirk went on to say, "this kind of confrontation would never have happened before the war" (Kirk and Lee 1989: 106).

There were signs of change, but it is worth remembering that this was still a time of Jim Crow cars, those on a train to be used by colored passengers only. Like much of the infrastructure of certain parts of the country, the Jim Crow cars were separate but not equal—they were generally placed immediately behind the engine, where they caught sparks and ash that flew in its wake. Many travelers spoke of having to wash dirt and soot from their skin and clothing after riding in a Jim Crow car.

Beyond the Jim Crow cars stood a violent and troubled system of segregation. This was the time of segregationist "white demagogues," in John Gunther's phrase: Martin Dies, Father Coughlin, Senator Bilbo of Mississippi, and Governor Talmadge of Georgia. During 1941 and 1942

Langston Hughes produced poetry like "Merry-go-Round," subtitled "Colored child at carnival" ("Where is the Jim Crow section / On this merry-go-round, / Mister, cause I want to ride?") and "The Bitter River," dedicated to two fourteen-year-old boys lynched under a bridge on the Chicasawhay River in October 1942 (Rampersad 1995: 240, 242). In January, the singer Helen Humes was performing "Governor Talmadge Blues" at the Café Society Downtown in New York.

The *Amsterdam News* carried frequent stories of outrages against black Americans, including front-page photographs of lynchings and other violent acts. In January it reported six black soldiers killed in Alexandria, Louisiana (*AN* 1.17.42: 1), and in February it published a story about a battle in Virginia between police and 200 black servicemen denied entry to a local hotel (*AN* 2.7.42: 1). A front-page leader in February decried a wave of "terrorism against colored soldiers" (*AN* 2.12.42). The July 18 edition carried a front-page photograph of a lynching in Texarkana, Texas, and a report of a white mob in Hamilton, Georgia, that had attempted the lynching of a black draftee.

The increased output of wartime industries, coupled with the absence of part of the workforce on military duty, created employment opportunities for black Americans, but this opportunity had been difficult to win and was difficult to sustain. The opening up of the new jobs was achieved only after a threatened march on Washington, D.C., proposed in June 1941 by A. Philips Randolph, president of the Brotherhood of Pullman Porters, which led the Roosevelt administration to enforce equality of employment in the defense industries. Subsequently, even with Executive Order 8802, which forbade discrimination in such employment, and the Fair Employment Practices Committee, which existed to monitor its application, employers and organizations in some areas dragged their feet on the matter or resisted it outright.

The interracial context in which the music business and traveling bands found themselves showed signs of progress alongside signs of resistance. The hiring of black musicians by top-ranked white bandleaders was a movement in the music industry that had attracted publicity. This was initiated by Benny Goodman employing Lionel Hampton and Teddy Wilson. Later, Billie Holiday performed and traveled for a brief, troubled time with Artie Shaw's orchestra, and Lena Horne sang with Charlie Barnet's band.

Shaw also hired the trumpeter Hot Lips Page. In each of these cases, breaking down barriers was only part of the motivation. Most leaders insisted that they hired these star black soloists on the grounds of musical quality, though this also implicitly supported a principle of equality. Goodman had a musical perfectionism that, over and above racial politics, made him seek out players like Hampton and Wilson. Most of the players concerned spoke well of the men who employed them; Lena Horne, for instance, often spoke appreciatively of the support she received from Barnet and his musicians.

Roy Eldridge, a trumpeter with a brilliant, extroverted style as well as a capable singer, joined the Gene Krupa band in April 1941. Krupa was a white Chicagoan who became a star through his drumming performances with Benny Goodman's band. Soon after Eldridge joined Krupa, he had a share in a hit recording, "Let Me off Uptown" in which he sang, exchanged patter with the white singer Anita O'Day, and played a resounding trumpet solo. Two reports shortly after Pearl Harbor confirmed Krupa's commitment. The *Amsterdam News* ran the self-explanatory headline "Crackers Don't Want Roy Eldridge—So Krupa Nixes Southern Tour" (*AN* 12.13.41: 20). Two days later in *Down Beat*, a report from York, Pennsylvania, appeared under the headline "Krupa Fined after Fight over Eldridge," "Gene Krupa used his fists two weeks ago to subdue the operator of a restaurant here who refused to allow Roy Eldridge admittance. Gene and his band were playing a one-nighter at the Valencia Ballroom. . . . It was reported that the restaurant man made 'unfair' and ungentlemanly remarks regarding Eldridge, and then asked that Roy leave the place" (*DB* 12.15.41: 1).

Eldridge's account of his time with Krupa's band locates the beginning of his problems during this series of one-nighters. The tour was destined to finish in California, where, Eldridge related, it was acceptable for him to meet Hollywood stars but dangerous to mix with the rest of the clientele. Being turned away from hotels and suffering other indignities, Eldridge succumbed to a nervous breakdown while performing at the Palladium Theatre. He ended the story, "When I went back a few nights later I heard that people were asking for their money back because they couldn't hear 'Let Me off Uptown.' This time they let me sit at the bar" (Hentoff and Shapiro 1962: 320).

As in some labor issues that were surfacing in 1942, the spectacle of racial mixing seemed to provoke more objection than black people working in an exclusive environment, whether in the music business or in industry. Whatever difficulties it faced, a black traveling band was implicitly less of a challenge to the status quo than a band in which blacks and whites were working together, in what could be seen as a model of an integrated society. In hostile contexts, amicable interracial contact between musicians, even off the bandstand, could lead to trouble. Andy Kirk described such an occasion, "We were playing a white dance in a big warehouse in Montgomery, Alabama, and who should come in but Joe Bushkin. He was stationed there with the air force, along with some other New York musicians we knew. At intermission we were really fraternizing—shaking hands, hugging each other, like old buddies. Finally, this cracker who'd been watching got closer and closer so he could hear what we were saying. You could tell by the look on his face he couldn't understand how Bushkin and I could be so friendly on a social basis" (Kirk and Lee 1989: 107). Kirk saw this incident, on the whole, as a sign of positive change, in that the cracker's interest in the sight of black-white friendship indicated puzzlement rather than outright hostility.

In the context of performance, there were few instances of black and white musicians playing together in the early 1940s. In recording studios, however, this was possible owing to the literal invisibility of the event. The culture of the jam session, with its somewhat covert sphere of operation, also provided conditions in which black and white musicians could meet and interact. The popular white bands, with their featured black players, were another area of exception. But it was a different matter at the grass-roots level of working musicians and potentially in all parts of the country, as in a 1941 instance in Minneapolis reported by *Down Beat*, "The initial attempt by a Minneapolis musician, drummer Bob Benham, to successfully integrate the best in colored and white musicians by using the first mixed band in a downtown spot, ended in dismal failure last month when manager Art Murray was forced to give notice to three of the northwest's top men, Popeye Booker, and Oscar and Ira Pettiford." The clientele were "taken aback by the sight of these men playing together, and complained vociferously." One of the three musicians, the bassist Oscar Pettiford, went on to join the Charlie Barnet band a year later, becoming another of the featured black players in a white orchestra. Later he played with other white bands, including Boyd Raeburn and Woody Herman's, as well as becoming for a time a member of Duke Ellington's orchestra. The report concluded that at this time, "Minneapolis still takes its music by sight, and not sound" (*DB* 1.15.42: 22).

The presence of a white musician in a black group could be equally newsworthy. In February 1942, *Down Beat* reported that a "mixed Boston band," led by Sabby Lewis, was featured at Kelly's Stable in New York City, "playing hot tenor, and making most of the arrangements, is an ofay. He is Jerry Heffron" (*DB* 2.1.42: 3). The use of the slightly barbed black slang term *ofay* for a white man suggests an ironic perspective on the part of the writer. The preferred terms for blacks in the same publications were, at the time, *colored* or *sepia*. The black newspaper *Amsterdam News*, in a report on another exclusion, referred to the singer Lena Horne, who had recently left the Charlie Barnet band, as "The 'New Type' Sepia Movie Star." Miss Horne had been in Hollywood working in the all-black film *Cabin in the Sky* and was exhilarated with the upturn in her career. However, the problem of getting served in an eatery recurred, "Only one little incident marred her otherwise perfect stay in Movietown, and that happened at the MGM commissary when she and several sepia players were refused admission by the doorman" (*AN* 6.20.42: 16).

Incidents reflecting the same situation litter contemporary press reports and the reminiscences of black musicians. The *Amsterdam News* nevertheless expressed surprise at an incident in which the Earl Hines band, performing at a rally in aid of defense at the Mosque Theatre in Newark, were refused an order of food in the same building. The headline ran "It Happened in Newark—and in 1942!" (*AN* 2.7.42: 16). The memoirs of Andy Kirk contain a catalogue of such incidents. During the early 1940s, Kirk was compiling information for a guidebook intended to help black travelers avoid what Kirk called "embarrassing situations." Its slogan was "Vacation, recreation, without humiliation." Not that Kirk had a comfortable time off the road—in the spring of 1942 his attempt to buy a house in a residential district of Long Island was blocked by white residents invoking a covenant that would mean "colored people would be barred from the neighborhood until 1975" (*AN* 5.9.42: 1). Many road situations that Kirk described took place in wartime, the conditions hardly mitigated by the fact that Kirk and his men were traveling and performing for the benefit of the army camps, "On the way from California to play a camp in Yuma,

Arizona, we had to cross the Colorado River at Yuma. There was a toll-bridge, and if you were on government detail the toll-booth man always passed you through without charging the toll. This guy in the toll-booth saw we were a black band and made us pay. We explained our mission but his answer was, 'If you don't like this country, why don't you move out?'"(Kirk and Lee 1989: 105).

The road was tough for anybody, even the best-supported white bands. As noted earlier, financially there could be a slim margin even for the strongest of the black bands such as Ellington's or Basie's. Lower down the scale, the experience was tougher still: higher exposure to racism, greater physical discomfort, fewer opportunities to branch out through radio and recording, and, most importantly, less chance of breaking even financially. In the end, whether a band could keep going was less a question of being able to endure the hardships than of remaining financially viable. Conditions were changing as the United States moved through the first months of the war, and getting no easier, especially for bands that had been closer to the red line in normal times.

The saxophonist Coleman Hawkins, whose band's departure on the road was delayed by Pearl Harbor, was an early voice arguing that black bandleaders needed to scale down. Early in 1942 he was saying that they would be well advised to abandon the big-band format, "The number of places where big Negro bands can go on location is becoming limited, but there are any number of spots open to jumping small bands—such as the Café Society and Famous Door in New York, for instance. And few colored bands of today are getting rich, anyway" (DB 1.15.42: 4). A few months later, Ella Fitzgerald, a singer with a strong popular appeal, announced that she was giving up her big band, which she had taken over in 1939 upon the death of its former leader, Chick Webb. She cited "the strain of constant traveling and hardships of one-night stands" (AN 5.23.42: 16). As conditions worsened, there was an increasing likelihood that others, especially black musicians, would decide the rewards of running a traveling big band were not equal to the pains.

On March 4, the fifth annual "Red, White, and Blue Ball" was held at the Savoy Ballroom, with a patriotic theme and featuring the song "We Are Americans, Too." At the same time, members of the Les Hite band were singing a parody of a current hit song, "It ain't no place for our fine race / Deep in the heart of Texas, / You are a cinch for them to lynch, / Deep in the heart of Texas" (*AN* 4.4.42: 16)

The choices facing black musicians regarding the road were more urgent than for most white players, and there was less room to maneuver in. The choice of transportation was a more difficult one. In early 1942, decades before the age of mass air travel, there were three ways of getting around the country: bus, private car, and train. Buses were uncomfortable, exhausting, and did not isolate the traveler from Jim Crow, as exemplified by Danny Barker's description of traveling musicians not being allowed to use public restrooms (Barker and Shipton 1986: 166). The private car had the advantage that "those who have automobiles are relieved of much Jim Crow nuisance," though "some filling stations may refuse to serve them" (Gunther 1997: 682). Traveling bands had used cars from the earliest days, but they were not always adequate to the job of carrying a large team of players and their equipment. Trains were generally the least stressful way of traveling, though segregation might be encountered in its most formalized aspect. Train travel was also relatively expensive, as detailed in a pessimistic statement in the summer of 1942 by Joe Glaser, manager of several successful black bands, including Louis Armstrong's, "It cost almost $1800 last week to move Louis Armstrong and his band by train for seven one-nighters. A trip which can be made for $75 by bus may cost anything from $250 to $350 by train. . . . Outside of that, there are some jumps that simply can't be made by train. It looks as though the only solution is to charge at least $150 extra for any band sold on a one-nighter, to cover the extra costs" (*AN* 8.1.42: 15). But bands that imposed Glaser's suggested extra charge would become less competitive. The costs of traveling by train, if his figures were accurate, could increase by 200 to 300 percent over the cost of bus travel.

The conditions of wartime continued to squeeze the basic commodities of the band business, principal among these being travel. Private travel by car or bus, if for purposes that had nothing to do with the war effort, was not considered a high priority by government agencies. In the first weeks of the war, cars became problematic and buses soon afterward. The option of traveling by train remained, but, along with other disadvantages, there was now a problem of severe overcrowding. Troops, individual service personnel, and people whose jobs were important to the war effort traveled by train. The claims of traveling swing bands to move around the country in wartime seated in comfort on busy railroad trains were not strong. Joe Glaser's final line was "eventually half the bands will have to get off the road" (*AN* 8.1.42: 15). Everyone concerned with the issue knew that all bands now had problems, that black bands had severe problems, and that traveling was at the center of them. A few months on, in the summer and fall of 1942, the issue of the position of black bands was taken all the way to Washington, D.C.

A distinction can be made between means of travel and systems of travel, the latter embracing the total rationale for a performer's mode of traveling. One example of a system of travel, practiced by country musicians in the 1930s, was what Richard Petersen (1997: 118) called "radio station barnstorming." The term *barnstorming* was used in other occupations, from theater to stunt flying; its principal use at this time was in baseball—one of many analogies between baseball and popular music. Radio station barnstorming referred to performers, individuals, or small groups securing an outlet with a radio station and profiting from local exposure by playing live dates around the area within reach of the radio signal. When local interest was used up, the performer would move on to a radio station somewhere else and begin the process again. This system tended to be continued for long periods, as the sojourn with each new station might last for months. This was the main way for country performers to make a living in the 1920s and 1930s.

Something like this system was operated occasionally by touring big bands. In the last few weeks of 1941, for instance, the Ellington band did a cleanup tour of the West Coast, taking advantage of radio exposure to put together a string of dates while interest was still active. The imperative was to fit in as many engagements as possible within the available time frame. The bluegrass musician Bill Monroe spent some time playing two different radio stations per day, one in Greenville, South Carolina, the other a hundred miles away in Charlotte, North Carolina, and fitting in live engagements in the evenings. The barnstorming method, the main means of survival for professional country players, became particularly difficult to sustain in the increasing stringencies of wartime travel.

For a relatively successful stratum of country musicians, another system of traveling was in the barn-dance aggregations. Country radio shows like the *Grand Ole Opry*, broadcast from Nashville on WSM, and the *National*

Barn Dance, from Chicago on WLS, generated opportunities for the featured performers. Tours of live engagements were put together for troupes of performers to travel as live versions of the radio programs. According to Petersen, for these performers these tours were, "by far the most common means of profiting from the name recognition and legitimacy that came from performing on the radio" (1997: 118). They also offered, as distinct from the individual enterprise of barnstorming, a structured pattern of working and the financial backup of the sponsors. By 1942 the organization and the impact of these shows were both on a grand scale. Bill Malone (1987: 183) noted that the Camel Caravan, a company of twenty Grand Ole Opry performers, traveled 50,000 miles and put on 175 shows in the sixteenth months up to the end of 1942. WLS-sponsored shows had made more than 6000 appearances between 1932 and 1942.

The barn-dance tours required a considerable logistical effort, comparable to a circus troupe, an analogy that several swing bandleaders also drew with the experience of big-band touring. There was a hierarchy of touring units and networks, ranging from the big, highly organized units following national itineraries to the smaller independent units such as the barnstorming groups, with an informal localized touring circuit, to performers and units at the line between professional and amateur, who either did not travel at all or did so in the manner of the itinerant blues players. In the 1930s the travels of the last were hard to distinguish from the movement of other black Southerners to the northern cities or, in the swirl of the Depression years, from the general displacement of people in the harsh economic climate.

In the 1930s and the first years of wartime, there was an enormous number and diversity of people traveling in the profession of music. Much of this has not been fully documented, in part because of the dominance of the accepted historical narratives, and partly because some regions and styles of music have received little research. To give a picture of the aggregate of musicians and bands traveling in the United States in 1942, it would be necessary to note, among other instances, the polka-band circuit of the Northeast, whose orbit overlapped with the itineraries of the big swing bands. Walt Grabek, a Polish-American polka musician, returning to civilian life at the end of 1942, set up a band that toured its territory until after the end of the war, "Their best territory was Pennsylvania, Ohio and West

Virginia: Union Town, Paw Paw, West Virginia, out in Fairmount. All the name bands used to play out there, a crummy place. A lot of miners out there, and they came. Jimmy Dorsey played there, and we outdrew him" (Blau 1992: 42). The way in which a tour by a band like Grabek's was set up was essentially the same as for Ellington or Lunceford, "An advance man would set up jobs, make deals with halls and parishes, put up posters so that the band would work steadily and efficiently, making the most of each swing through the Midwest and back through upstate New York" (1992: 43).

This account of a polka band in the Northeast uses the word *territory*, which has an almost mythical significance in the history of music and traveling bands in the United States. According to Ross Russell, in the music industry the term *territorial band* was, "applied to those orchestras that are based in outlying districts, tend to monopolize bookings in their home area, and enjoy local prestige but no national reputation" (1971: 54). This seems to be the way the term was used in the trade press at the time. The account given in Gunther Schuller's *The Swing Era* differs, in that Schuller added, "Territory bands by definition were black," on the grounds that white bands in the territories did exist but were better able to secure permanent location jobs, "and therefore were not required to travel as much as the black bands" (1989: 770 fn.) This description makes extensive, rather than occasional, traveling essential to the definition of a territory band. Therefore, a band like that of Alphonso Trent, based in the Adolphus Hotel in Dallas and represented on few recordings but not noted for extensive traveling, would not be defined as a territory band. Some other commentators, however, would cite Trent as a prime example of a territory band.

The status is unclear of bands like those that had little or no national reputation and were clearly territorial or local, those of Buddy Arnold, Jimmy Parette, Bob Hutsell, Bill Sawyer, Emil Flindt, Buddy Johnston, Glenn Williams, Billy Hughes, Charlie Baker, Johnny McGee, Frank Lombardo, and the rest. They were elements in the overall picture of contemporary music and the roster of bands on the road, but their reputations are not preserved under the heading of *territory bands*. The term has tended to be applied to those organizations that have some accepted connection with the history of jazz music. As elsewhere in this book, we see the abstraction of an essence "jazz" from a broader context in which it subsisted.

Schuller's *The Swing Era* provided a map of the main centers and the territory bands associated with them (1989: 774). For a historical view, other sources include Ross Russell's *Jazz Style in Kansas City and the Southwest* (1971) and Albert McCarthy's *Big Band Jazz* (1983). Russell divided the territory bands into three main groups: Texas bands, those associated with the urban center of Kansas City, and those linked with other cities. The picture that we get from these sources tends to identify a territory with one particular part of the United States. Ira Gitler (1985: 13) noted that the contemporary usage of *the territory* "included Kansas, Missouri, Texas, Oklahoma, Wisconsin, Minnesota, Iowa and the Dakotas. Bands also made forays into Montana and Wyoming, but these states weren't included when someone referred to 'the territory.'" Schuller's map of the territory bands extends to include Georgia, Louisiana, North Carolina, Indiana, Alabama, Ohio, Colorado, and Los Angeles. The definition of the territory seems to depend on where the writers concerned believed that there were jazz or proto-jazz bands worthy of historical consideration.

By Schuller's count, there were forty-one such organizations operating from the mid-1920s onward; by some other definitions, there were many, perhaps hundreds, more. McCarthy (1983: 88–182) added others to Schuller's list, originating in such towns as Nashville, Tennessee, and Amarillo, Texas. He included eastern and New England orchestras, such as the Boston-based Sabby Lewis band (in the news for an "ofay" among its ranks). Between them, jazz writers on the subject arrived at a final figure of around fifty territory bands worth noting. Because this portion of the much larger number that must have been in the road is comparatively well documented, it provides an indicator of the progress of traveling bands and of the ways in which their situation changed through the first year of the war.

About one-quarter of the Midwestern bands listed by Schuller never made recordings, and in other regions the proportion was probably the same. Few secured radio outlets, so that the radio-barnstorming option was not open to them. For most of these black bands, with no access to radio or recording, traveling was in itself the only means of creating a reputation. This meant that the travel schedules were intense and the rewards rather low. Many of these bands, consequently, existed close to the line of solvency and were vulnerable to any changes in the economic situation. The Depression of the early 1930s had already finished off a number of them, and the conditions of wartime were about to increase the pressure on the survivors.

The principal Texas bands, apart from the aforementioned Trent orchestra, were Troy Floyd's and Don Albert's, both from San Antonio.

To designate a territory band as, for example, a San Antonio band, can say little about the band's actual sphere of operation; bands could cover the whole expanse from Canada to the Mexican border. The Don Albert band is one of few whose itineraries have been researched in some detail. Chris Wilkinson's *Jazz on the Road* (2001) traced Albert's excellent band through its extended forays from its home base across the eastern half of the nation. One tour, beginning in the spring of 1935 and ending almost a year later, tracked around the Gulf of Mexico, through Florida and the Carolinas, to Buffalo and Detroit, across to Pittsburgh and New York, and eventually south to New Orleans and then home to Texas (Wilkinson 2001: 120).

San Antonio also produced a band named Boots and His Buddies; Amarillo, in West Texas, was the home of Gene Coy's Happy Aces, whose bass player at one time was Junior Raglin, the successor in Duke Ellington's band to the ailing Jimmy Blanton. Dallas produced Alphonso Trent and the band of T. Holder, which later became known under the name of its new leader, Andy Kirk. Houston was the base of a powerful band led by Milt Larkins, which featured several saxophonists in the Texan style, most notably Illinois Jacquet, who became the new star in the Lionel Hampton band in 1942. Another member of Larkins's band was T-Bone Walker, whose electric guitar playing was to have an enormous effect upon postwar popular music.

In the 1930s, Kansas City was a center of musical activity—perhaps surpassing even New York—and its territory bands traveled far. The Count Basie band left for New York and success in 1936, and other Kansas City bands lined up to make the same jump. Another band that had a strong regional reputation and made a few recordings, but never expanded beyond its territory, was Harlan Leonard and His Rockets. In its saxophone section in the late 1930s—the main reason for historical interest in Leonard's band—was Charlie Parker, still a teenager and about to move to the more promising environs of Jay McShann's orchestra. Other southern cities had bands that are remembered as serving their territories: Atlanta, Charlotte, Little Rock, New Orleans, Tulsa, and Birmingham had orchestras noted by historians of jazz. The saxophonist Dexter Gordon's brief description of meeting a Birmingham-based band carries a flavor of the territory band's way of life, "I remember we ran into the Carolina Cotton Pickers somewhere. Had a raggedy old bus, and the cats were wearing overalls. They really looked like the . . . territory band, you know. There were a lot of them at the time. A lot of bands" (Gitler 1985: 22). Although Schuller, on the basis of the Cotton Pickers' single recording session, rated them a "functional provincial band at best" (1989: 778), they featured around 1941 a saxophonist, Porter Kilbert, whom Charlie Parker regarded as a peer after meeting him at a jam session (Gitler 1985: 61).

Other Midwestern cities that had renowned territory bands were St. Louis, which produced a succession of bands in the 1920s, Cincinnati (Zack Whyte), Indianapolis (Speed Webb), and Omaha. The early band scene in Omaha has the benefit of a fuller written record than others. Red Perkins's band survived from the 1920s to the early 1940s and made a few recordings in the middle of that span. Two Omaha bands, regarded by Schuller as "rather outstanding" (1989: 787), were still operating in the first year of the war: Lloyd Hunter's Serenaders and the band of Nat Towles.

The Nat Towles orchestra is sometimes considered the best of all the territory bands, in Schuller's view, "one of the most remarkable but least celebrated orchestras of the Swing Era" (1989: 790). A recording like "You Don't Mean Me No Good" suggests a band with a rhythmic drive comparable to that of the Count Basie or Jimmie Lunceford bands. The Towles band traveled in a more expansive style than most other territory bands. According to the saxophonist Buddy Tate, who spent several years with Towles before moving on to Basie, the band was bankrolled by a gangster in Dallas and could afford higher salaries and a superior means of transportation, "We had a sleeper bus, like a Pullman car. There was a cab up front and then seats you could let down like a bunk. There was plenty of room and next to the cab a huge closet where we put all our uniforms and instruments. There was a john on it, too, and altogether it cost Towles a lot of money" (Dance 1980: 121).

The saxophonist Preston Love, who joined Towles in 1942 and whose *A Thousand Honey Creeks Later* is a good account of territory band life, had a different opinion of the same vehicle, which he described as "somewhat overcrowded and at time odorous inside" (Love 1997: 58). Love had graduated from the rival band of Lloyd Hunter, whose 1933 school bus he described as "miserable-looking" and "very inadequate for sixteen or seventeen adults" (1997: 53). Moving to the Towles band, as Love did in June 1942, was also a step up musically. Buddy Tate mentioned players like T-Bone

Walker, "who used to go out on the floor and make all the money for us," and the singer Duke Groner, whom he called a "show-stopper," "He used to sing *Trees* and *I'm in the Mood for Love*, and women would just fall out" (Dance 1980: 121).

Several points emerge from players' descriptions of territory orchestras. First, despite their being drawn into the retrospective narrative of jazz, they were evidently delivering something other than what later critics would consider "pure jazz." Buddy Tate, a player with excellent credentials within the jazz field, spoke with enthusiasm about the qualities and skills that made the Towles band superior, "Towles had a big book and I learned to read a lot in that band. It was harder music than Basie's, because it was an entertaining band and we did everything, all with a lot of class. We did ballads, and we had good singing groups like Lunceford" (Dance 1980: 122). Tate's phrase "we did everything" is a more accurate description of what most jazz players were doing than that they were "playing jazz," in the sense that phrase has come to have. The musical repertoire was varied, to the point of being uncategorizable in a present-day perspective, they "did ballads," the band's singer performed "Trees," there were singing groups, and there was the element contributed by T-Bone Walker. None of this makes the Towles band, whatever its quality, sound like a *jazz band* according to later understandings of the term.

Second, it appears that some bands were of equal ability to others that achieved nationwide prominence. Tate expressed certainty that Towles's band could outplay the Basie orchestra, at least at a certain stage. Evidently, there were also outstanding individual players. Some went on to work in more famous bands, but it seems there were many whose abilities never became known to the wider world. The case of Nat Towles shows how fortuitous the process of fame, and hence of history, can be. According to several accounts, the Towles band might have shared the trajectory of the Basie band had they not been out of town on the day the promoter John Hammond stopped over in Kansas City to contact Basie (Schuller 1989: 788).

A third observation on the histories of the territory bands is that, by the time of Pearl Harbor, there were few surviving. Those surviving bands included the Omaha bands of Hunter and Towles, the Jeter-Pilars and George Hudson orchestras from St. Louis, the Carolina Cotton Pickers (who folded in 1943), Gene Coy's band from Amarillo, Milt Larkins's from

Houston, Ernie Fields's from Tulsa, and a few bands from Kansas City, including Harlan Leonard and the bands of Tommy Douglas, Clarence Love and Paul Banks, and Jay McShann. Before the end of the war more would be winnowed out. According to Schuller, Banks and Hunter quit before the end of 1942 and Douglas, Leonard, Larkins, and McShann followed before the war's end (though the last two organized new bands later).

In another baseball analogy, Preston Love described the Nebraska bands as "minor league" (1997: 80). The hope of leaders and players in the territories was to follow the trail blazed by Count Basie from the minors to the majors. At the time of the attack on Pearl Harbor and in the first year of the war, this was happening to only one territory band, that of Jay McShann. The historical significance granted the McShann band derives mostly from the fact that it brought Charlie Parker to notice—and to New York. It is also significant as the last of the territory bands to achieve a measure of national prominence at a time when Kansas City had gone about as far as it could go.

The McShann band had been on the road for a couple of years and had made recordings. At the end of 1941 there was a buildup of press recognition for the recordings and for successes on the road. A single, "Confessin' the Blues," was reported in early December as reaching 100,000 sales and was to hit half a million. In the first few months of wartime, *Down Beat* carried seven mentions of the McShann band: reviews of recordings, rumors about management moves and upcoming bookings, and reports of attendance records being broken at territory venues as far apart as Houston, Texas, and Davenport, Iowa. The correspondent in Iowa wrote, "This McShann band really has something on the ball" (*DB* 1.15.42: 8). A report early in 1942, days before the band's debut at the Savoy Ballroom, described them as "the most sensational to come out of the Middle West since Count Basie" (*DB* 2.1.42: 2). It is significant that the acclaim was for the band as a whole: Charlie Parker's soloing was mentioned only as one of its assets. A review of "Dexter Blues" said, "there's a mess of nice growl trumpet, Charlie Parker alto and McShann ivory to set it off" (*DB* 12.1.41: 14).

The Savoy Ballroom, for a black band the prime location in the country, was also a tough environment in which to debut in the majors. The dancers and the public in the Harlem venue were accustomed to the highest levels of dance musicianship, and bands that played regular engagements there were often fiercely defensive of their turf. According to McShann's bassist, Gene Ramey, the competitive message reached them early, "Before we went to New York to play at the Savoy Ballroom, we got a postcard from Lucky Millinder which said 'We're going to send you hicks back to the sticks.'" This was a statement of the perceived difference between a New York band and one from the territories (Dance 1980: 276).

The band experienced transportation problems that caused them to arrive late at the Harlem ballroom. Gene Ramey took responsibility, "McShann had one of those big old long Buicks, and I was driving, with about five or six guys in it. I took what I thought was the shortest route to New York, up and over the mountains, instead of taking the Pennsylvania Turnpike. We struggled and struggled, but we finally got to New York, raggedy and tired" (Dance 1980: 276). The drummer Gus Johnson, however, blamed the manager's wartime economizing on tires, "Everybody was mad with us when we came into New York, because we were late. The cars had broken down. Johnny Tumino had retreads on one car and they all blew off, so we had to buy new tires. We were supposed to be at the Savoy at five that evening, but it was almost nine when we got there. [In another account, Johnson says that it was eleven o'clock.] We didn't have time to change clothes, so we just got up and played in what we were wearing" (1980: 292).

Accounts of how the McShann band recovered the composure to defeat the Millinder band that night differ slightly. Early in 1942, the Lucky Millinder band was establishing popularity locally and nationally for its earthy swing and its star vocalist Sister Rosetta Tharpe. Setting up on the opposite bandstand, the McShann musicians were aware of their disadvantage in visual appeal, "the people were looking at us like we were nothing" said Ramey. "Everything we had was shabby-looking, including our cardboard stands, and we only had one uniform—a blue coat and brown pants" (Dance 1980: 276). McShann and Johnson both recalled Millinder referring to them as "Western dogs" (1980: 248, 292).

The McShann musicians described their own band as triumphant in this encounter. Gus Johnson's summary was, "we got there and stayed on one tempo—one of those jump tempos—and blew Lucky Millinder off the stage" (Gitler 1985: 65). Gene Ramey's version was that "from the time we hit the first note until the time we got off the bandstand, we didn't let up," and that Millinder was driven to climb onto his piano and to direct his band from there, in an effort to match the drive being generated by these Midwestern usurpers (Dance 1980: 276). McShann emphasized his tight control over his players, describing how he instructed them "we'd hold off for another set. . . . But after Lucky's guys had really carried on, mine began to get restless. Now we had a tremendous number named *Roll 'Em* that we used to play for about twenty-five minutes, and if we got it going, moving right, we would extend it to thirty minutes or more. This particular night my cats—mostly young and wild—were so eager that we just turned them loose and played that number ten minutes into Lucky's time. That broke the house up! Lucky came back on the stand and fired seven of his guys right there." Despite this angry gesture and the near-broken leg that he sustained in jumping off his piano, Millinder was reportedly prepared to concede. "He took me out to some night spots," said McShann, "and we hung around for a while and had a little taste. 'Man,' he kept saying, 'you cats came and blew me out tonight'" (Dance 1980: 248).

It should be noted that in accounts referring to the Savoy confrontation no mention is made of soloists, not even of Charlie Parker, as an element in the appeal of the band to the audience. The musicians stress rhythm, "one of them jump tempos," and the power and cohesion of the whole ensemble "moving right." To a 1942 audience, what was important was an ensemble, an *orchestra*, presenting many phases of musicianship, among which the improvised solos no doubt had a significant position, but which were contained within the effect of the whole presentation. Even among the soloists, contemporary valuations were not necessarily in line with later canonical judgments, "McShann, of course," said a July 1942 review, "is the outstanding instrumentalist," going on to note that a certain Charlie Parker "offers inspired alto solos, using a minimum of notes in a fluid style, with a somewhat thin tone but a wealth of pleasing ideas" (*DB* 7.1.42: 4). McShann and others pointed out that it was the tenor saxophone solos of Jimmy Forrest that invariably won the greatest applause in theaters and ballrooms.

These contemporary opinions may be seen as perverse or simply wrong. Decades of jazz criticism have established an order of precedence that places Charlie Parker in a higher category than men like McShann and Forrest. There has been little or no effort to understand their respective performances in a context of their times, or to give due attention to the way that audiences listened to music and what they were listening for. Similarly, the McShann band itself, which presented such an exciting experience for the Savoy audience, is seen primarily as a means of transporting Parker to New York (Collier 1978: 365–367; Gioia 1997: 206–208), a host body through which bebop was enabled to enter the historical bloodstream of jazz. This attitude has also conditioned listening: the recordings of the McShann band are offered as items of "historical interest" deriving not from the band's performances but from a negation of them. Jazz historians suggest that it was from this environment that Charlie Parker achieved liberation into the next historical phase of jazz. We can detect the embryonic stages of bebop, but only in the brief solos played by Parker himself.

In New York in 1942, the Jay McShann orchestra was an ensemble and was enjoying growing success as such. It worked superbly for the clientele of the Savoy on its debut, as it continued to do elsewhere. From the Savoy the band went to the Apollo, had a return engagement at the Savoy, and continued to win rave notices in the black press and the music papers. The *Amsterdam News* reported in April that, "McShann and his band created a sensation in Detroit last week, playing to capacity audiences during the normally dull pre-Easter season" (*AN* 4.18.42: 17), and the following week carried a story headlined "Jay McShann Scoring Big Hit in Eastern Appearances." A full-length review in *Variety* (4.22.42: 49) of one of the band's Apollo performances did not mention Parker.

The beginning of 1942 was not an auspicious time for a band to be experiencing a breakthrough. Even after its successful arrival in New York, the band did not record for five months, and the month in which they did record, July 1942, was the least propitious moment in the history of popular music for a recording career. An article in *Down Beat*, written by Bob Locke, begged recording companies to "Put Full McShann Ork on Wax" (7.1.42: 4). Locke's point was that the band had a wider repertoire than was reflected in their previous recordings, but it also assumed that it was the band's complete resources that would be of interest to the public. More recent writers on jazz, by contrast, have encouraged a retrospective cherry-picking of the McShann recordings, directing listeners to the few precious moments of Parker's improvisations in among the performance of the whole band. We listen for confirmation of the historical inevitability of

the rise of bebop, and the decline of such historically dispensable phenomena as the Jay McShann orchestra and the big bands in general. But
the decline, or rather the discontinuation, of the careers of McShann's
and comparable organizations was not a historical inevitability and certainly not driven by the internal logic of jazz. It is only the later teleological
assumption that bebop was an evolutionarily necessary higher development of jazz, what David Ake (2002: 56) has called the bop-centrism of
much jazz writing, that has led to this view. In fact, Harold Baker, one of
Parker's friends, remarked, "Charlie loved big bands" (Reisner 1965: 29).

A McShann personnel listing in the *Amsterdam News* in April omitted Parker's name; he was back in the list for a July 2 recording session, so
the April omission perhaps refers to a phase when Parker was temporarily
AWOL (*AN* 4.25.42: 16). The band continued to tour the South and Midwest
and was still operating successfully at the end of 1942, when Parker, whose
behavior was increasingly erratic, was hired to play in the Earl Hines band.
The McShann band folded in 1943, when its leader was inducted into the
U.S. Navy. By then, wartime conditions had dramatically closed off possibilities for the touring big bands.

Many territory bands had to give in to tightening restrictions, the
draft, and economic pressures. Ross Russell's study of the Texas territory
bands cites Boots and His Buddies as "another wartime casualty" (1971: 58).
For the Harlan Leonard band of Kansas City, "wartime pressures became
acute" (1971: 178). The pressures were increasingly felt at a higher level of
the market as well. In July 1942 Ella Fitzgerald gave up the orchestra she had
taken over upon the death of her friend and mentor, Chick Webb. A report
in the *Amsterdam News* made clear her reason, "the strain of constant
travel and hardships of one-night stands" (5.23.42: 16). The men working
in Fitzgerald's band had on occasion refused to travel in their substandard
transportation, and a combination of transportation costs, salary demands,
and uncertain incomes had made the responsibilities intolerable. It was still
early in the war. Even in the remaining months of 1942, the situation would
grow more difficult still for the bands that tried to stay on the road.

By the early summer of 1942 there was no sign that the war might end
soon and few indications that it was progressing other than disastrously.
MacArthur's retreat from Corregidor was not the last of the losses sustained in the Pacific. In March a *New York Times* piece, accompanied by

very graphic maps of the possibilities, announced "the Japanese have a selection of future offensives, but Australia and India seem to be marked for attack next" (*NYT* 3.12.42: 3). Only the stunning victory at Midway Island, in the last days of June, gave any promise of an end to the prolonged retreat and the possibility of a turning point in the conflict.

The fact that there was a war on had a gradual but dramatic effect upon a range of commodities, not only those that directly concerned musicians. Government agencies such as the Office of Price Administration and the Office of Defense Transportation exercised increasing control over staple items of American home and working life. The Office of Price Administration had begun to ration tires as early as January 1942, with effects on orchestras' touring schedules. Rubber was in extremely short supply, with the inflow of material from abroad reduced by 97 percent. Many initiatives tried to recoup this massive loss, including recycling schemes and development of alternative materials. Among individual efforts, those of a New Jersey inventor named Claude Habberstadt, who reached a speed of 75 mph on an experimental set of wooden tires, received mention in the national press (*NYT* 3.13.42: 38).

Food products were becoming scarce: sugar was rationed from April and coffee, meat, and alcoholic drinks in the following months. Gasoline shortages and the rationing that was gradually introduced from May onward had the most drastic immediate effects of all these restrictions. Production of private automobiles had stopped within five weeks of the attack on Pearl Harbor, and directives concerning automobile transport began to impose strains on the entire transportation system. By the end of 1942, government measures had imposed gasoline rationing across the nation, banned "pleasure driving," and introduced a national speed limit of 35 mph. Priorities in the allocation of whatever means of transport remained were controlled by the Office of Defense Transportation. The federal government had powers to requisition trucks and buses for defense purposes, and in May there were hints that there might be some requisitioning of private automobiles. Consequently, much of the traffic that normally traveled on the roads was displaced to the railroads, with the further result that by the early summer there was already a recognition of a "rising tide of passenger traffic" on train systems across the country (*NYT* 5.22.42: 21).

Many writers on the tenor and quality of life in the United States during this period associate it with long, slow journeys on severely overcrowded passenger trains. John Dos Passos, in his accounts of the journeys he undertook in the early months of 1943 for the writing of *The State of the Nation*, described the exhausted human traffic on the nation's railroads, the waiting crowds slumped in Washington's Union Station, "The floor, the benches, the entrances are dark with shifting masses of people. About half of them are young men in uniform. Negro families are spread around the benches. Cues fan out in shifting tentacles from every ticket window, from the information booths, from the newsstands, from the telegraph offices. In the telephone room, men sitting on upended suitcases wait glumly for a chance at the booths" (Dos Passos 1945: 215). He also described a more vital and expectant crowd on a California-bound transcontinental train, "There were sailors and soldiers and a great many young women out of textile mills and department stores and Negro families all dressed up in new duds, and middle-aged mechanics and old day-laborers and cocky young kids out of high school in leather jackets. They were all going through to the Coast. The civilians were headed for war industries. The soldiers and sailors were headed for the Pacific" (1945: 263).

To sum up the magnitude of wartime migration, according to U.S. Census Bureau figures, more than 15 million Americans relocated during World War II. Added to the enormous civilian traffic was the massive and essential mobility of the military; according to Verlyn Klinkenborg, "Soldiers came from anywhere, trained anywhere, and were deployed anywhere in a seemingly endless shuffling of the country's young men" (1991: 168). Among the priorities of a federal agency like the Office of Defense Transportation, it can be imagined where the claims of traveling band musicians ranked.

As mentioned earlier, the bus had an intimate importance for the musician on the road. Experienced players came to regard the band bus as a temporary home, and some were commended for their ability to adapt to bus conditions. The young Frank Sinatra, traveling with the Tommy Dorsey band, was noted for his fastidiousness and care for his appearance, and a *Down Beat* write-up for a singer in the Charlie Barnet band, Hazel Bruce, praised her thus, "She's from San Antonio, 22, and can dress in a bus in 6 seconds" (1.15.42: 13). The importance of bus travel in keeping transport costs low is seen by an ad featuring the Midwestern bandleader Dick Jurgens that appeared the week after Pearl Harbor, "There's more money in har-mony when you travel by Greyhound" (*DB* 12.15.41: 8). For bands, buses were economically the most attractive proposition of all the alternatives, with trains a luxury option, at least under normal circumstances. All forms of transportation had their advantages and disadvantages, but on balance the bus was and would have remained the normal preference. The removal of bus travel happened in stages, but it began to affect the operations of traveling musicians almost immediately after Pearl Harbor, with restrictions and bans on the availability of buses.

This was the beginning of a rapid change in the earning prospects for musicians, with the combined effect of limited gasoline and tire supplies, blackouts of entertainment districts, and embargos on manufacture of such non-war-essential items as musical instruments and, equally important, jukeboxes. Another critical commodity suddenly almost unobtainable was shellac, the basic ingredient for the manufacture of phonograph records. Shellac was produced by a secretion from insects that were only found in India. The record manufacturers had to deal with this problem as a matter of urgency, and it would take longer to affect musicians. An increasingly critical outlook for the bands must have been clear by April, when James C. Petrillo, the AFM president who had promised in December that musicians would take no industrial action "for the duration," made a special appeal to the U.S. authorities.

The main issue was tires, for which Petrillo wanted his union members to be granted priority. But there was a convergence of problems and a pessimistic assessment of the long-term results, "While the dance industry is worried over the eventual effects of rubber shortages and eastern gasoline rationing, so far there has been no clear indication of how much damage will be done" (*Var.* 4.8.42). At the end of May, *Variety* carried the headline "More Grief Promised Bands" above the report of the extension to the restriction on buses to companies that had so far been allowed to operate normally. "If their work is stopped," the report said, "the band business will be faced with a problem much more serious than it is now" (5.27.42: 39). The extended ban, due to take effect on June 15, provoked urgent discussion in the press and the music industry. The ban was postponed, but only by one week, and bandleaders were understandably cautious about traveling commitments even a short time ahead, "Lack of transportation and the fear of having buses pulled from under them during a tour has made many bands shy away from the road the last couple weeks" (*Var.* 6.17.42: 40). No leader or musician wanted to suffer being stranded far away from home base by any sudden yanking of the band bus. Many were switching to the next best transportation option. *Variety* reported that even though "buses are available until the 22nd, various leaders heading out of New York and other keys are almost all moving their men by private car" (6.17.42: 40).

The situation had some parallel benefits for hometown bands that could substitute for the immobilized big names, as was reported from Boston in June (*Var.* 6.17.42: 41). Bands like those of Duke Ellington and Cab Calloway, continuing to do most of their traveling by train, were still managing to get around relatively unimpeded. In the week of the bus ban, the *Amsterdam News* reported on another band in a position of advantage, the all-girl orchestra The International Sweethearts of Rhythm, described as the "most war-proof" orchestra in the world. The paper referred to a general panic in the band industry, "Many leaders who depend on constant road-work for their income are at a complete loss." The Sweethearts, however, in addition to being "100 percent draft-proof," enjoyed the biggest advantage of all at this particular time, "Just as important, though, is the fact that, unlike the majority of orchestras, they have their own bus instead of a rented one, and a very remarkable bus it is too. Costing them a cool $15,000, it's a Pullman affair with perfect sleeping accommodation for 22 people, and has everything from running hot and cold water to air-conditioning" (*AN* 6.20.42: 16). Such a facility would have been exceptional at any time, but as war conditions started to bite, the Sweethearts' investment in a means of transport put them among the bands most likely to survive this crisis.

It was not difficult to predict that the situation would have the most drastic impact on black bands. The racial implications of the worsening transport problem were the subject of statements issued by the very influential Joe Glaser and Moe Gale, both of whom managed several prominent black bands. Glaser and Gale, who individually controlled venues such as the Savoy in New York and the Grand Terrace in Chicago, were considering combining their resources to counteract the effects of the impending ban. When it came into force, they suggested, "it will be almost impossible for Negro orchestras to move" (*Var.* 6.17.42: 41). On June 22, when the buses were yanked, the situation of the black bands, particularly those that traveled in the southern states, became critical.

In the expression used in a *Variety* headline in the week the ban came into force, the black bands were in effect "Jim Crowed." There had been an effort by representatives of the black music community to gain a special dispensation from the Office of Defense Transportation for black bands traveling in the South, but this was not granted. The bands would be forced onto other forms of transportation, but would do so at a further disadvantage, "Train riding isn't easy for colored bands . . . particularly in the South, the best territory for them. Jim Crow rules on southern lines make routing a difficult task" (*Var.* 6.24.42: 41). Finding feasible train routes between one-night locations was a complex undertaking for all bands, but the rules that came with racial segregation made this much worse. Furthermore, trains were expensive and now overcrowded with wartime travelers.

The dispute over buses rolled on into summer. By the end of June, the NAACP was taking an active interest in the plight of black orchestras. The organization communicated with the federal departments responsible for the decision, "Because restrictions on bus accommodation have hit Negro musicians hard, the NAACP wired Joseph Eastman, head of the Office of Defense Transportation . . . asking him to withhold application of the restrictive order to buses used by Negro orchestras"; this intervention placed the issue of tour buses in a perspective of the wider racial situation, "discrimination against Negroes in the South and other parts of the country makes it impossible for Negro bands to get Pullman, eating, housing or other accommodations" (*AN* 7.4.42: 16).

In June a delegation visited Washington to lobby the Office of Defense Transportation: its members included the labor leader Wilbur White and the singer-bandleader Cab Calloway. Calloway's consistent commercial success, together with his performance style, has not stood him in good stead with some jazz historians, but it paid dividends for his band members. Calloway was, in Danny Barker's estimation, "first-class all the way . . . he was a great performer and he knew what he wanted . . . and he is a helluva singer. He could sing a ballad, sing a swing song"; and the Calloway band, at the time of Barker's tenure, was "a hell of a band" (Barker and Shipton 1986: 168). Calloway was an accomplished dancer, a singer who could sustain the role of Sportin' Life in Gershwin's *Porgy and Bess*, and later an actor in movies. In 1942 during the transportation crisis, Calloway was a leading spokesman in the campaign to secure rights for black musicians. In July, a proposal was submitted to the Office of Defense Transportation to make special provisions for black orchestras. Calloway spelled out the larger picture of prejudice and disadvantage, he "explained that Negro orchestras cannot get 'location spots' because of the greater number of white orchestras and because, in spite of the musical superiority of some Negro orchestras, management of 'location spots' will not hire Negro outfits. He estimated that the average Negro band spends eight to ten months a year playing one-night stands" (*AN* 7.11.42: 15). The same report predicted that, unless there was some relaxation to the bus ban, there would be an "elimination" of bands in the lower ranks of the business, and even the more successful bands would be seriously affected. The Negro Actors Guild issued an official statement of praise for Calloway's efforts in taking the bus issue to Washington, D.C.

The *Chicago Defender* saw the accumulating difficulties besetting black bands as foreshadowing an end to the entire musical economy, "What with colored bands not being able to secure buses for transportation, Petriollo's [sic] edict banning the making of commercial records after July 30 and the biggest name orks losing men fed up with long road jumps, local musical observers are glancing in their crystal balls to determine the future of sepia aggregations" (*CD* 7.25.42: 12). Moe Gale and Joe Glaser's press releases were posing the same questions. On July 29, drawing the attention of U.S. musicians to this major change in their circumstances, *Variety* ran a full-page ad spelling out to bands that "YOU CAN'T MAKE MONEY ON LOCATION" and that "ONE-NIGHTERS ARE UNCERTAIN AND HAPHAZARD because of transportation problems, gas rationing, etc." The magazine directed readers to a forthcoming edition containing a guide to "other profitable fields" (7.29.42: 39). Most bands, however, had for many years depended on one-night and short engagements. It was difficult to conceive that other "profitable fields" could fill the hole left by the removal of the road tours. This loss, moreover, was not the only one that bands and musicians had sustained or were about to sustain.

During the week of August 12, *Variety* and the *Amsterdam News* reported the death of Marcellus Green, a member of the Erskine Hawkins band, in a car crash near Chattanooga in which the pianist Avery Parrish was also seriously injured. Automobile accidents involving musicians were by no means rare, but the occasion of Green's death was conspicuous. Both publications reporting the accident spelled out its significance in the context of the transportation crisis. In *Variety* (8.12.42: 46), the headline described Green as the "Latest Victim of Dance Jump Made by Automobile," while the *Amsterdam News* pinned the blame indirectly on the Office of Defense Transportation, "the accident happened in one of the private cars in which the band is forced to travel because the Office of Defense Transportation has not acted upon the problem of buses for Negro bands" (8.15.42: 1). Green's death had highlighted the twin problems of wartime and Jim Crow and indicated once more the possibly terminal crisis the bands were facing, "the risk incurred in traveling in private cars through the South threatens to force them out of business."

The importance of this crisis for the viability of the large traveling bands can hardly be overstated. Any profession would find it difficult to survive the loss of an activity that produced by far the largest portion of its income. The parties lobbying the Office of Defense Transportation in Washington, including Cab Calloway, carried on their campaign into the fall but with limited expectations that anything could change the direction of developments. The prewar economy that had enabled many bands to flourish and many more to make a living was changed "for the duration" at least, and it was not possible to foresee whether prewar conditions could be re-created after the war was over. Within eight months of the attack on Pearl Harbor, the economic basis on which the musical culture of the large popular band had depended was radically revised.

The changes that flowed from this would have decisive effects upon the character of American popular music. Not only the swing orchestras had this essential prop pulled from under them; according to Bill Malone, "hillbilly entertainers" also found that "gas and tire shortages curtailed their abilities to tour" (1987: 181). For country as well as big-band musicians, the live engagement tours had an interdependent relationship with all their other sources of revenue: recordings advertised their live shows, live shows advertised the recordings, and radio made up the third leg of the relationship. Radio appearances were diminishing in the face of recorded music; the war restrictions were strangling live engagements; and finally, recording was about to be declared off limits. In view of these multiple threats to all their significant means of making a living, all converging in the summer of 1942, the question of why the big bands were entering into decline hardly seems to need any other explanation.

The system that drove the bands on the road was a competitive laissez-faire economy in which conditions of working and living were for the most part unregulated. Organizations such as the AFM had succeeded in mitigating some stress factors, for example, by limiting the maximum distance traveled between one-night gigs, although to a still-generous 400 miles. The interiors of buses, in which musicians spent many hours a day for weeks or months at a time, were not always salubrious. As Preston Love noted, buses could be "odorous." Traveling musicians were subject to the personal habits of their colleagues in an environment in which, except for heroes of personal grooming such as Frank Sinatra and Buddy Rich, standards might be lower than in normal living. Most buses lacked air conditioning and could be sweltering in summer and freezing in winter.

The death of Marcellus Green was notable for its timing, in the midst of a national dispute about the very traveling conditions involved in Green's death. But as a statistic, the death of a professional musician in a highway accident was unremarkable. A survey published in 1941 by the magazine *Music and Rhythm* disclosed that 200 musicians had died in automobile accidents in the preceding two years. The death of the singer Bessie Smith in an accident near Clarksdale, Mississippi, in 1937 was on its way to mythic status by the early 1940s. Musicians traveling the road in the winter of 1941–1942 might also have been aware of the death of Chu Berry, saxophone soloist with Cab Calloway's band, killed in an automobile crash in Ohio in October 1941.

To judge by press reports, there was every sign that the road remained as hazardous as ever. The blues singer Peetie Wheatstraw was killed a few days before Christmas 1941 in a collision between his automobile and a train near St. Louis (*DB* 1.15.42: 1 noted that Wheatstraw had recently made a recording entitled "Hearseman Blues"). The winter brought a cluster of reports of other accidents, some resulting in loss of life. The issue of *Down Beat* that related Wheatstraw's death also reported two other road accidents involving prominent musicians. Skinnay Ennis was a singer and bandleader whose former employer, Hal Kemp, had been killed in an accident in California in December 1940. One year on from Kemp's fatal accident, Ennis and his band almost suffered the same fate in what *Down Beat* described as a "bus smashup" (1.15.42: 1). On December 31, 1941, the bus of Al Donahue's band was involved in a serious accident on a notorious "dead man's curve," between Providence and Worcester (1.15.42: 21). Eleven days later, near Pittsburgh, California, the West Coast bandleader Jo Atria was killed in a car accident (2.1.42: 11).

In March 1942, the bandleader Tiny Bradshaw, later a major force in rhythm-and-blues, was reported seriously injured on the road between Cincinnati and Detroit (*DB* 3.1.42: 5). Bradshaw was later commissioned into the U.S. Army, so this accident seems not to have been as serious as reported. In April, the band bus of the singer Eddy Howard was wrecked in an accident near Rockford, Illinois (*DB* 5.15.42: 2). Teddy Powell, another prominent bandleader, was involved in a road accident that *Variety* reported largely for its curiosity value. Powell "crawled out of the wreckage of his overturned car" on the West Side Highway in New York after a collision with a car driven by fans who were trying to locate the gig in Armonk, New York, from which Powell was returning when the cars collided (*Var.* 5.13.42: 41).

One cannot accurately extrapolate from known incidents how many were occurring among musicians of all ranks traveling the roads in wartime. The cases mentioned here involved well-known bands worth reporting on. It is a reasonable assumption, however, that the hazards of traveling increased in correlation with the standard of transportation provided: hence, a greater number of accidents can be assumed to have happened among grass-roots territory bands. One instance, preserved because of the later career of one of those involved, was the accident in 1936 in the Ozarks in which Charlie Parker was injured and the bass player George Wilkerson was killed. The continued occurrence of injurious or fatal automobile accidents before and after the period of this study, from one that partially paralyzed the bandleader and arranger Fletcher Henderson in the 1920s to another that killed the trumpeter Clifford Brown in the 1950s, suggests that the toll was more or less constant over many decades.

Fires were not as frequent events in the lives of traveling musicians as were road accidents, but the press and musicians' memoirs for the period indicate that fires were not an uncommon occurrence. Both the venues, especially nightclubs and ballrooms, and means of transport, especially buses, could be the sites of serious fires. The burning down in 1939 of the Palomar Ballroom in Los Angeles had destroyed the property belonging to the Charlie Barnet orchestra, including instruments and its stock of music. The most notorious and, up to that time, most destructive incident occurred in a nightclub in Natchez, Mississippi, in April 1940. The Natchez venue had provided perfect conditions for the spread of fire and maximum loss of life: flammable hanging decorations, a crowded floor, and doors and windows locked to keep patrons in and gatecrashers out. Ten members of the Walter Barnes band and 200 other people died in the fire.

The end of 1942 was marked by an even more destructive fire occurring under similar conditions, the infamous Cocoanut Grove blaze. But the early months of the year provided indications of this continuing hazard in the lives of traveling musicians. In Pittsburgh in January, the New Penn Ballroom burned down, consuming the "horns and paper" of a territory band led by Henry Blauth (*DB* 1.15.42: 22). Two weeks later, *Down Beat* reported that a venue in Roanoke, Virginia, in which the Eddie Wiggins band were rehearsing went up in flames, prompting a headline about the Wiggins band "blowing hot" (2.1.42: 22). The first issue of *Down Beat* for March reported a fire in a restaurant in Macon, Georgia, in which the Glenn Williams orchestra lost its entire library of sheet music (3.1.42: 19), and the burning of the Billy Hughes band's bus at a ballroom in Worthington, Iowa (3.1.42: 11). In April, the band bus of the extremely popular Kay Kyser orchestra was destroyed in a fire in a New York garage (4.15.42: 11). A month later another nightclub, in Paducah, Kentucky, was the scene of a fire while the band of Ray Franklin was playing there (5.15.42: 20).

On the night of Saturday, November 28, the Cocoanut Grove in Boston became the site of one of the worst disasters that ever struck an American place of entertainment. The description in *Variety* a few days after the fire that engulfed the nightclub referred to a "holocaust" in which "panic-stricken patrons at the Cocoanut Grove nitery trampled and clawed each other to death as smoke and flame choked and seared them" (12.2.42: 1). The total of fatalities was 449.

Among those who died in the Cocoanut Grove fire were entertainers and musicians. "Two musician friends of mine died in that fire," Max Kaminsky wrote, "Bernie Faisioli, the violinist band leader, and Ecky Watson, a trumpet player, who was one of my best friends" (Kaminsky and

Hughes 1965: 75). There were the inevitable stories about people who had just missed being caught in the disaster, in this case a visiting company of Irving Berlin's Army show, who had enjoyed a complimentary dinner and left the club shortly before the fire broke out. Among other fatalities was a country singer, Buck Jones, "a long-time fave of cowboy fans" (*Var.* 12.2.42: 1). The entertainers Maxine Coleman and Guy Howard also died. A singer and pianist named Grace Vaughn had been working at the Grove for some time. In the notice of her death, she was described as "a singer of Irish songs, playing her own piano accompaniment." Those who lost their lives in the Cocoanut Grove fire did so from various causes. Grace Vaughn "died as a result of suffocation, and was found slumped near the piano without any fire having touched her" (*Var.* 12.2.42: 24).

Within days, authorities in a number of cities imposed emergency controls on nightclubs in their jurisdictions. Beginning on December 1, all 1161 entertainment venues in the Boston area were closed until further notice. In New York, a "special fireman" rule requiring fire personnel in theaters was introduced. "That the tragedy will profoundly affect the local night spots," commented *Variety*, "and even those in other cities, was without question tonight." It seemed as though the disaster in one location in Boston had opened up a problem that existed everywhere and involved potentially many thousands of venues. "Many of them are considered firetraps," the report went on, "and all of them, certainly, will come in for a terrific inspection, with construction changes ordered—or else" (12.2.42: 24).

Beyond the terrible losses of life, losses of equipment and sheet music could be difficult to recoup. A band's repertoire, embodied in its written music, took time to build up and was difficult to reconstruct. Charlie Barnet was loaned material by other leaders to keep his band working following the Palomar fire. Financial losses could be substantial: damages to the relatively obscure Hughes band in Iowa were estimated at several thousand dollars. An item in *Variety* (7.29.42: 41) recounted a delayed effect of an earlier fire affecting Teddy Powell. Following a fire in 1941, Powell had been obliged to take a loan from the bandleader Tommy Dorsey that Dorsey was now intent on collecting, "Powell borrowed the cash from Dorsey after the Rustic Cabin, Englewood Cliffs, N.J., burned down last winter and Powell's band lost all its instruments and library." The light tone of fire and accident reports is partly an effect of the house style of publications like *Down Beat* and *Variety*, but there is also a sense that, except where deaths occurred, such incidents were a regular part of the chances in the industry.

Musicians traveled and worked in environments that, even when not dangerous, did not promote physical and mental health. The world of popular musicians shared some of the conditions associated with poverty: overcrowding, bad air, poor nutrition, sleep deprivation, alcoholism, and reduced life expectancy. The disease that most notoriously prevailed in these conditions was tuberculosis, an ever-present fact of life even in the United States until streptomycin was produced in 1944. The primary cause of tuberculosis, inhalation of airborne tuberculosis germs, is more likely to occur in overcrowded and poorly ventilated places—hence the spread of the disease in such housing as in the Lower East Side of Manhattan. As one investigator told a congressional committee, with reference to the slums of Little Italy, "If we had invented machines to create tuberculosis, we could not have succeeded better in increasing it" (Mangione and Morreale 1993: 143).

At its worst, the lifestyle of the traveling musician could be another effective machine for delivering the same result. Tuberculosis had long been known as an occupational hazard, in addition to the fact that many musicians were drawn from working-class populations, black and white, which were exposed to the infection to begin with. Blues and country music had long spoken of the disease. The song "T.B. Blues" of the hugely popular white Mississippi singer Jimmie Rodgers drew upon his own fatal condition, "Been fightin' like a lion, looks like I'm gonna lose. / Ain't nobody ever whipped those T.B. blues."

Tuberculosis was not an uncommon condition in the environment of the big bands, though it found its best encouragement in the smaller, more irregular locations of nightclubs. The medical historian of jazz, Frederick Spencer, wrote, "As jazz spread throughout America, the 'white plague' tagged along, thriving in poorly ventilated, late-night venues, with drink and drugs to hand" (Spencer 2002: 226). Some musicians contracted tuberculosis and survived, among them the singer Lee Wiley, the pianist Joe Sullivan, and the arranger with the Benny Goodman band, Eddie Sauter. Some well-known musicians died of the disease, however: in the early 1930s, one of Duke Ellington's most valued soloists, the trumpeter Bubber Miley, and the trombonist Charlie "Big" Green.

The rate of the disease among musicians remained a constant into the 1940s, but there was an apparent spike around the winter of 1941–1942. The first *Down Beat* after Pearl Harbor carried reports on three high-profile cases. Dick Wilson, tenor saxophonist with the Andy Kirk orchestra, died in New York on November 24 after five weeks in the hospital. *Down Beat's* first two pages also reported the condition of two better-known musicians, Charlie Christian and Jimmy Blanton, the bassist with the Ellington band. Christian was said to be "making rapid progress" in a sanitarium in Staten Island, where he had been confined since July. Blanton, on the other hand, was described as "a mighty sick boy" (*DB* 12.15.42: 2).

Charlie Christian, one of the most influential of jazz guitarists, was diagnosed with tuberculosis as early as the spring of 1940, but the treatment prescribed, "fresh air, rest and regular healthy meals," reads like an ironic negation of the habits of the jazz player—and of Christian more than most. As well as being featured in the heavy performance schedule of the Goodman band, Christian was a habitual late-night jam session participant, as indicated by his regular presence at the celebrated sessions at Minton's in New York. A year after his initial diagnosis, Christian collapsed again. The trumpeter Jimmy Maxwell related that visitors supplied Christian with "an ounce of pot and some bottles and some professional girls from uptown," with, in his opinion, the result that "thinking they were giving him a good time . . . they were only speeding him along on the way out" (Spencer 2002: 229). Such occasions may not have accelerated Christian's death on March 2, 1942, but they did indicate habits and environments that represented the problem more than the solution.

Awareness of tuberculosis as a professional hazard and its incidence around that time were reflected in a *Down Beat* interview with Count Basie in January. The article referred to tuberculosis as "the greatest scourge to the musician," and quoted Basie's account of half of his band members becoming ill a year earlier. All his musicians were then given a full medical examination twice a year (with the ironic result that most of them were now 1-A for the draft). Basie commented that he had "seen some very fine musicians forced to give up their horns or even their lives to T.B." Musicians on the road were in Basie's view "easily susceptible" to tuberculosis, "because of the bad conditions which prevail" (*DB* 2.1.42: 10).

In his autobiography, Ellington commented that in 1940 and 1941 the phenomenal young bass player Jimmy Blanton "had given us something new, a new beat, and new sounds ... altogether it was a great period. Then he got T.B." (1974: 164). The bassist Milt Hinton implied that the lifestyle of jam sessions and long road trips led to Blanton's condition (Gitler 1985: 44). He fell ill during the band's stay in California in 1941 during the run of Ellington's musical "Jump for Joy." Blanton reportedly moved out of a hotel room he was sharing with the arranger Billy Strayhorn in order not to expose Strayhorn to the illness, "One day he came home, packed up his things, and told Strayhorn he had a chick he was going to live with. He wasn't actually going to live with anybody, and he didn't even tell Strayhorn that he was sick" (Ellington 1974: 165)

Frederick Spencer offered the view that Blanton suffered the recurrence of an infection contracted in childhood, reawakened by lowered resistance due to fatigue. But Eddie Sauter was convinced that he himself caught tuberculosis from Charlie Christian, with whom he came into contact in the recording booths in the Columbia studios (Spencer 2002: 230). In 1941 Jimmy Blanton was a frequent companion of Christian in the after-hours jam sessions at Minton's. According to Allen Tinney, "Christian ... came every night and used to sit right in front of me. ... Christian used to sit his mike right down there, and Jimmy Blanton was there" (Gitler 1985: 81). Roy Eldridge, working at Kelly's Stables in New York, remembered Christian and Blanton regularly showing up together for jam sessions. "Charlie Christian and Jimmy Blanton used to stop by and sit in," he recalled, "and one night they swung so much I felt so good I had to stop playing" (Gitler 1985: 45). It is pure speculation that it was from Christian that Blanton picked up tuberculosis, but if it was feasible on Sauter's limited exposure, it was surely more so for Blanton, the "weak kid" who shared the night-time life with Christian for much of the two-year period in which the signs of the disease were evident.

By the time the Ellington band left California for the East at the end of 1941, Blanton's place had been taken by Junior Raglin. Ellington tried before going to secure the best medical treatment for Blanton, "I found out who the top people on T.B. were in Los Angeles. I made a date and took him down to the big city hospital, where there were three beautiful, young specialists. They all knew him; they were fans of his, and they talked about his music" (Ellington 1974: 163). The band's touring schedule kept them away from the West Coast until their residency at the Trianon Ballroom in April and May 1942. In the meantime Blanton, against Ellington's expressed wishes, was transferred to a treatment center "somewhere near Pasadena, I think it was, somewhere along a railroad siding." Milt Hinton remembered the place, the small town of Duarte, "It was some way out of town, but I went every other day, had to hire a car to get out there" (Gitler 1985: 44). According to Hinton, Blanton "had a lovely room" at Duarte, but by Ellington's account it was a "little square box" without a bathroom and "they had nothing there, no X-rays or anything." Ellington must have seen Blanton in this situation during the stay at the Trianon or at the end of June on the band's return from a tour up and down the West Coast, "there he was, on his cot" (Ellington 1974: 166).

The Ellington band was due to play a residency at the Sherman Hotel in Chicago, and on July 8 they boarded the train for Salt Lake City and Denver. Hinton had continued to visit Blanton and to write and perform music especially for him during regular radio spots, "Every night when we broadcast, Chu Berry[4] and I would sit down and scratch out a little tune, and we'd play it and dedicate it to him on the air. Then when I'd go out to see him—he'd had his radio by the bed—we'd sit down and he'd tell me about the chords. 'Hey, you used a D flat ninth there, you should use this'" (Gitler 1985: 45). Hinton mentioned isolation and loneliness as contributing to Blanton's decline, "He was twenty-two years old, at the peak of his career, and his band was going off and leaving him. He's from Tennessee, and he don't have a friend in California, and his poor heart was broken. . . . You could see the loneliness of it took away his strength and will to live, and he died" (Gitler 1985: 44). Blanton's death occurred, as *Down Beat* put it, "in an institution in Duarte, Calif., in the early morning hours of July 30 as the hot desert wind began to chase away the cool shade of the night" (8.15.42: 12). The news reached the Ellington band via the "musicians' underground" as they entered the third week of their Chicago hotel residency. Blanton's last days had been made "as happy as possible" by the arrival of his mother, herself a musician and teacher, from Chattanooga; visits from the musicians' union Local 767; and chicken dinners sent by Ellington's singer, Ivie Anderson, from her restaurant in Los Angeles.

Down Beat cited a doctor who described Blanton as suffering from "what is frequently called 'galloping consumption,' a type of tuberculosis particularly dangerous to members of the Negro race, who seem to have less resistance to its ravages than whites." The racial angle seems to be *Down Beat* editorializing rather than the doctor's professional opinion, but the article was clear about the significance of Blanton's illness for the community of traveling players, "Like many another musician, he was rendered an easy victim for tuberculosis by the unhealthful conditions which constitute an occupational hazard of the dance business."

The return home of Blanton's body to Tennessee caused *Down Beat* to reference the million-selling hit recording of the previous year, "A 'Chattanooga Choo-Choo' rolled out of [Los Angeles] last week, carrying the mortal remains of a bundle of rhythm that came out of the Tennessee city a few short years ago." The Ellington band accounts for the week of July 23, 1942, during the engagement at the Sherman Hotel, included sums of $106.94, paid to "Rock Island RR, For Mrs. Blanton," and $107.71 for "Expences [sic], For J Blanton, Mother." The account for the week of August 13 contained an item of $76.50, for "Rock Island RR. J. Blanton."

The kind of work that Jimmy Blanton did "takes something out of a fellow," as *Down Beat* said. The trombonist Trummy Young remarked, recalling his days as a traveling musician, hardened to being roused from sleep by the likes of Charlie Christian with a bottle of liquor, "I used to be tired all the time, but I was young, and I didn't pay no attention to it" (Gitler 1985: 30). There was little in the life of the road musician to provide rest and recuperation. George T. Simon, who on occasion traveled with the big bands, wrote, "With so much time spent in traveling and work, musicians' extracurricular activities were necessarily limited. During bus rides, however, in addition to sleeping, they talked, played cards, read and drank" (1974a: 20). The recreational use of alcohol and its effects were attested in scores of deaths. The virtuoso trumpeter Bunny Berigan died on June 2, 1942, as a general result of, in Simon's words, "too many one-nighters and unhealthy living" (1974a: 91), but as a specific result of cirrhosis of the liver.

At this same time, baseball had achieved a greater centrality in American official and popular culture than at any other moment in history. In the first week of the war, President Roosevelt published an endorsement of the recreational and morale-building value of the game (Lingeman 1979:

312). This was also the epoch of such charismatic individual players as Joe DiMaggio and Ted Williams, and the nation's sympathy had been gripped by the illness and the death in June 1941 of the legendary Lou Gehrig. Gary Cooper had been signed to play the role of Gehrig in *The Pride of the Yankees*, the Gehrig biopic that became one of the most successful films of 1942. The 1941 season had climaxed with the famous game 4 of the World Series between the Yankees and the Brooklyn Dodgers. Above all, there was, what Michael Seidel (2002: 193) called the "national rhythmic fix" of Joe DiMaggio's unbroken hitting streak.

Many analogies between playing music and playing baseball were used in the musical press. Fans and players drew parallels between the combinations of team playing and individual skill that were fundamental to both professions. The personnel of big bands were thought of as equivalent to the lineups of baseball teams, with players both in bands and ball teams having specialist roles within the ensemble: the Jay McShann orchestra a band that "has something on the ball," the clarinetist Buster Bailey, who in a 1942 jam session "knocked the cover off the ball" (*DB* 3.1.42: 12).

The rhythm of life on the road in the 1930s and 1940s was similar for musicians and ballplayers, as in this account by the Negro League pitcher Chet Brewer, "We used to ride three or four nights in that big old bus and never see a bed. We'd play in one town at night and then after the game, shower in the shower room, get in that bus, ride all night to the next town and get out and go to some little hamburger joint and have some lunch, go to the ball park" (Holway 1991: 25). As Brewer attested, the worlds of music and baseball also had their racial exclusions. Until the opening up of the major leagues in 1947, black players such as Josh Gibson and Satchel Paige pursued their profession in the segregated environment of the Negro Leagues. The integration of baseball even lagged behind that of the swing bands. There was no equivalent of the hiring of star players such as Teddy Wilson by Benny Goodman and Roy Eldridge by Gene Krupa. The journalist Dan Burley, who wrote extensively about music in the *Amsterdam News*, campaigned for admitting black players into the major leagues, in this 1942 instance perhaps thinking of the black soloists in the big bands, "There is no team playing major league baseball today that would not be improved with the help of a Josh Gibson, a Buck Leonard, a Terris McDuffie or a Buck Easterling" (*AN* 1.31.42: 15).

Negro League ballplayers on the road suffered the same problems as black musicians, "We couldn't stay in white hotels, we couldn't eat in restaurants. In cities there were usually Negro hotels. In those small towns we would stay in family houses, two players here, two players there. Sometimes they'd fix us a meal in the colored church, or we'd bring out food from the grocery store in a paper sack. If we were in Nebraska, we'd ride all night to Lincoln or Omaha. In some of those small towns we couldn't stay, and sometimes we'd just ride all night and sleep in the bus. Then we'd have to play ball the next day" (Holway 1991: 59).

The bluegrass banjoist Earl Scruggs, who from the late 1940s traveled with the Bill Monroe band, described the musicians' therapeutic use of baseball, "Monroe carried two or three baseball gloves and a ball with us. We'd be in the '41 Chevrolet all night and all day, and we couldn't shift our legs, so we'd go out and play catch to loosen up our legs and have something to do until showtime" (Davidoff 1998: 122). Several of the popular white bands played ball games in an informal league, with team titles like Glenn Miller's Millers and Gene Krupa's Kangaroos. Tommy Dorsey and Muggsy Spanier reportedly hired former professional ballplayers to coach their teams. The most committed of the leaders to his bandsmen's baseball activities was Harry James, who is said to have recruited certain players, among them the saxophonist Eugene "Corky" Corcoran, a "terrific third baseman," on the strength of baseball as well as musical ability (Levinson 1999: 102).

Likewise for black orchestras, as Cholly Atkins remembered, "See, all of the bands, Andy Kirk, Count Basie, everybody had softball teams. And all the clubs in all the different cities had squads, too. So whenever a new band came into town, it would make arrangements to challenge local teams, like on a Sunday morning" (Atkins and Malone 2001: 54). Atkins recalled a game in which, while angling for a job with Cab Calloway, he found himself pitching against Calloway for the team representing the Rhumboogie Club in Chicago. Fortunately, Calloway "got a piece of it. So that saved me." The *Chicago Defender* reported on a game in Grant Park in which a team of waiters from the Sherman Hotel "kicked Cab's dog around to the tune of '20 to 4'" (*CD* 7.4.42: 24).

The Count Basie band also ran a team. The saxophonist Earle Warren related that the band, typical of many others, "used to practice on the roadside when we were down south, and all through Texas" (Dance 1980: 79).

The box score of a game between the Basie band and the Benny Goodman band was published in *Metronome*: an 11 to 3 victory for Goodman. What is most surprising to anyone familiar with the reputations of the players involved is the fact that the pitcher for the Basie team was Lester Young. According to Warren, the great saxophonist possessed an effective curve ball, but on this occasion he gave up hits to trumpeter Ziggy Elman and to Harry James, who hit the game's only home run (Simon 1974a: 21).

Writers on certain idioms of music, particularly blues and jazz, have emphasized the separation, the distance between the supposed interests and values of the musicians and those of popular culture and popular taste. By virtue of his achievement as an improviser, a musician like Lester Young has come to be regarded as an art-music or high-art figure, adhering to a set of values that are those of the art form, in its distance from, even its disdain for, popular culture. This is even more markedly the case for bebop players such as Charlie Parker and Dizzy Gillespie, who are represented, as I discuss in chapter 5, as dissident intellectuals whose severance from "mainstream" American popular culture was total, though there is evidence to the contrary. Hence the surprise in finding the proto-hipster Lester Young participating an activity as healthy, as American, as embedded in popular culture, as (in Roosevelt's words) "thoroughly worthwhile," as *normal* as playing baseball.

The conditions in which musicians worked and traveled, however, were not inherent in the music. Despite the later mythologies of the jazz musician as beatnik, given the choice many of them might have preferred an environment other than smoky nightclubs and living out of a suitcase. There were already signs that many musicians were glad to quit the road when it was no longer a necessity and ceasing to be a possibility. As the business tightened through 1942, some bandleaders were sensing a new attitude among musicians that was making recruitment into the traveling bands difficult. Their playing baseball on the road, too, was a sign of a desire for something different, an attachment to the same culture of sport and leisure as the average citizen aspired to, a breath of fresh air, or, as Nicholas Davidoff (1998: 122) expressed it, a way "to feel human again."

The lives of musicians, including their lives on the road, were beginning to be represented in fiction. The film *Blues in the Night* had been released in the summer of 1941 and enjoyed a long run in movie houses.

As we saw in chapter 3, the film introduced a song, the title number of the film, that became popular in a number of versions by well-known singers and bands, and it went on to be nominated for an Academy Award. The film itself creates a strange impression to a viewer more than sixty years later. It introduces a hero, the musician Jigger Pyne, whose motivations are difficult to decipher. As played by Richard Whorf, with a persistent frown and moments of visionary exaltation, it is not clear whether he is to be viewed as a misunderstood hero or as a man whose behavior borders on the sociopathic.

The film is nevertheless important as a text on the representation of American music and, in particular, on the emergence of a special music known as jazz. It was one of a cluster of films made within a year or so that articulated key elements of what was coming to be accepted as the "story" of jazz (the others being *Syncopation* and *The Birth of the Blues*). *Blues in the Night* also treated some topics discussed in this chapter, for example, the young drummer, Pepe, is established early in the film as suffering from a chronic chest problem (possibly hinting at tuberculosis). Like many musicians of the period, the band of which Jigger Pyne is the inspiration and leading light are travelers; but the band's journeys consist of carefree hitchhiking and riding in clean, practically domesticated boxcars. The film established two other important representations of the musician in the newly emerging discourse of jazz. First is the dichotomy between jazz and commercialism, dramatized by Jigger's almost pathological attitude toward money. Second is the devotion of the musician to his music, which was so intense as to drive him to violence, when, for instance, a patron in a nightclub repeatedly asks him to play a pop tune, Jigger punches the man to the floor.

The idealistic light in the eyes of Jigger and his fellow players shows them as true, if implausible, believers in the values of their music and their way of life. They float above the concerns of making a living; they have contempt for money; they travel without cost, strain, or fatigue; and they insist on playing "our own music, our own way." This figure of the supra-commercial musical artist, playing music accorded the title of "jazz," and with a sense of isolation from or even a hostility toward the tastes of "the public," is a new cultural product of the early 1940s.

This chapter showed professional musicians in the first years of World War II implicated in a complex set of relationships with the music business, restrictions of a wartime economy, popular media, and popular culture. *Blues in the Night* and some other texts of the period presented a dream of an ideal music and an ideal musician liberated from all this, consciously and passionately opposed to any limits placed upon his free, unconditioned expression. Jigger Pyne and his comrades are not "popular" musicians, they have the purity of "their own music," and they fear and despise what popularity might tempt then to do with their talents.

At a time when professional musicians all over the United States carried on their working lives in a context of studios, agencies, radio hookups, bus and train travel, hotels, ballrooms, theaters, band accounts, and many other circumstances, the fictitious musicians represented in this movie confront none of these things. They have only a fierce abstract devotion to the integrity of their music. The kind of figure that is produced in such texts, the ideally creative musician-artist free from and disdainful of the contexts that corrupt others, was to become a formative myth in the discourse of American music.

Chapter 5

Disorder at the Border

"I can't get along in a band," Rick said. "It ... I don't know, it sort of
weighs me down."

—DOROTHY BAKER, *Young Man with a Horn*

One evening late in 1941, the music critics Robert Goffin and Leonard
Feather attended a performance by Count Basie's band and a
screening of the film *Blues in the Night*. During the evening, the two men
decided to put into action Goffin's idea of an "officially sponsored course
on the history of jazz." The course they devised, in Feather's view the first
ever study of the music in an academic curriculum, was held at the New
School for Social Research in New York and began on February 4, 1942.
As Richard Peterson noted, "One of the best ways to show that a field
exists is to construct its past" (1997: 199). The initiative taken by Feather
and Goffin began the systematic construction of a past for a music, "jazz,"
whose existence as a distinct entity was at the time not apparent to many
people, including musicians.

"Aside from a few isolated lectures by visiting bandleaders," Feather
later wrote, "there had never been any attempt to offer a serious history
and analysis of the music" (1986: 77). In his estimation, the existing literature on jazz was virtually nonexistent. As precursors to the syllabus

that he and Goffin were setting up, Feather cited Goffin's own book *Aux Frontières de Jazz* (not yet translated into English in 1941), *Hot Jazz* by the French critic Hugues Panassié (1942), and others. Feather did not mention Winthrop Sargeant's *Jazz: Hot and Hybrid* (1938). Sargeant's study, which set out technical analyses of jazz harmony and rhythm, has been reprinted frequently since its original publication. One reason for Feather to pass over Sargeant's book, despite its relevance to the project, was the ideologically problematic way in which it stated the relationship between jazz and popular music.

Sargeant opened his book with the following words, "For at least fifty years, American popular music has exhibited certain characteristic symptoms which have given it a distinct place in the popular music of the world. For at least twenty-five, the popular music exhibiting these symptoms has been known, more or less consistently, as jazz" (Sargeant 1959: 15). This definition identifies practically the totality of American popular music since 1900 as "jazz." This usage might have been acceptable in about 1930, when the term *jazz* referred to a broad range of cultural expression, not limited to music. But by the early 1940s, in the critical circles where its meaning was about to be radically narrowed, Sargeant's conception of what jazz signified was a reminder of a meaning that the new critical initiative was intended to displace.

Rather than a closely defined field called "jazz," contrasted with a broad musical field labeled "popular music," Sargeant's jazz included both as subvarieties, "hot jazz" and "sweet jazz," respectively. Into the latter category fell many popular musicians downgraded by critical opinion and the new terminology. The band of Guy Lombardo, for instance, had become a byword for qualities that jazz artists were presumed to despise (although, contradictorily, Louis Armstrong's admiration for Lombardo was well known). Sargeant stated emphatically that Lombardo's music was "unquestionably a variety of jazz, a hybrid variety that has come as close as anything does to being the folk-music of the great mass of Americans" (1959: 53).

For the later orthodoxies of jazz history and for those formulating them in the early 1940s, Sargeant's views were not congenial. Speaking of this same period, the singer Anita O'Day, then featured with the Gene Krupa band, remembered, "This was the era when jazz and popular music were pretty much the same thing" (O'Day and Eells 1983: 104). But, according to a view that was increasingly propounded from the mid-1930s onward, jazz and popular music were not now and never had been the same thing.

Jazz tends to be seen in isolation from the rest of contemporary culture. This applies also to the criticism of jazz, which has seen itself as being free of outside influence and governed purely by the logic of the music itself. It should be recalled, however, that across a range of art forms and critical writings, the period from the mid-1930s onward was characterized by a flight from the popular. This was the period of the cultural critics of the Frankfurt School, most notably Theodor Adorno (1941, 1989). Adorno's contempt for popular culture extended across the spectrum of what he called the "culture industry," and took in a critique of Hollywood films as well as of popular music. In Adorno's view, each of these American cultural-industrial mediums demonstrated the characteristics of standardization and "pseudo-individualization," the purpose of these procedures being to simplify the production process both for movies and popular songs and to maintain the listener-viewer in passive enslavement to the market. Adorno's article "On Jazz" was published in 1936, and in 1941 appeared "On Popular Music," in which he made it clear that he did not excuse jazz from his excoriating criticisms of popular music. Indeed jazz, for which Adorno had a "visceral dislike" (Jay 1984: 119), was regarded by him only as a more devious form of standardization. He regarded jazz improvisation, its main claim to creative freedom, as itself standardized beyond all possibility of "actual improvisation" occurring. The supposed creative individuality of jazz improvisation was for Adorno merely another set of routines passing itself off as creatively autonomous: in his terms, another instance of "pseudo-individualization."

In the context of this kind of attack and in the climate of opinion that it typified, it is easy to see how exponents of jazz might seek to unshackle it from its idiot companion popular music—even if this was a move that Adorno himself did not allow. It was becoming necessary for jazz critics to insist on the separation of a music called "jazz" and possessing a distinct identity from the deleterious associations of popular music and, beyond that, of popular culture. Beginning to construct a history, as Feather, Goffin, and others were doing in the early 1940s, was an essential step in this strategy of separation.

It is only in the writings of critics such as Scott DeVeaux (1991) and John Gennari (1991) that the idea of "jazz tradition" has come to be recognized as a construct rather than a timeless reality. The history of jazz prior to the mid-1950s has usually been seen as a self-evident continuity; a recent comprehensive history stated, "Up until the 1970s, the story of jazz is a straightforward narrative" (Shipton 2001: 873).[1] This was precisely the opposite of the way that many observers viewed the position even into the late 1940s. Few cultural fields have ever been so bitterly divided. DeVeaux also raised the issue of whether the supposed foregoing clear line of "tradition" was not itself a construct that was the product of much effort, much argument, and an ideological selection from the historical record. One of the arguments of this book is that the so-called jazz tradition and its narrative emphatically was a construct, first formulated during the critical period between 1941 and 1943. At the start of this period it could be said that nobody knew what "jazz" was; at the end, at least the outline of a narrative was in place to support what some people thought it was.

A substructure of publications to support the critical movement had coalesced through the 1930s, with the contribution of European critics such as Goffin and, more effectively Panassié, running alongside new magazines and periodicals in which the territory of jazz was to be mapped out (once it had been viciously fought over). *Down Beat* started publication in 1934, the same year that Panassié published his first authoritative volume, *Le Jazz Hot*. *Metronome* was also an important influence; its editorship was held during the 1940s by Leonard Feather and his associate Barry Ulanov. Shortly after Feather and Goffin set up the first academic course on the history of jazz, they were in negotiation with the editors of the magazine *Esquire* on a related initiative. An annual event in the music calendar was the end-of-year polls conducted by *Down Beat* and *Metronome*, in which readers voted for their favorite musicians in the main big-band roles. An "all-star" band of the *Metronome* poll winners made a special recording session each year until 1949. The band recorded on the last day of 1941 contained such irreproachable jazz names as Roy Eldridge and Benny Carter, but also a scattering of seemingly incorrect choices such as the saxophonists Vido Musso and Tex Beneke. In the 1942 *Down Beat* poll the award for best swing band was won by Duke Ellington, and the "all-American" readers' selections included Eldridge and Ellington's star soloist Johnny Hodges, but also Beneke, the singer Helen Forrest (omitted from Feather's later jazz encyclopedia), and Frank Sinatra.

It was perhaps this *Down Beat* poll that prompted the educational initiative taken soon afterward by Feather and Goffin. Having secured the interest of *Esquire*'s editor, Arnold Gingrich, in giving coverage to jazz, they put to him the idea of a poll conducted along different lines. As Feather expressed it, "We did not want our poll to wind up like those conducted by *Down Beat* or *Metronome*, in which, typically, Charlie Barnet or Tex Beneke would be leaders on 'hot tenor,' followed by Coleman Hawkins or Ben Webster; Ziggy Ellman would win for 'hot trumpet' and Alvino Rey for guitar; Helen O'Connell or Dinah Shore would be elected No. 1 female jazz singer while Billie Holiday went unhonoured" (1986: 79). For this anarchic state of affairs, where the American public could not be trusted to vote for the right candidates, Feather proposed a solution, "The only way out . . . is to put together a panel of experts, rather than rely on the readers." Feather quoted Goffin's response to this proposal, "Right, and we know who the real experts are." Feather related this conversation in his memoir *The Jazz Years* (1986), seemingly without awareness of the presumption it involved.

The twin initiatives of an educational curriculum and an opinion poll judged by a panel of those Feather and Goffin regarded as experts represented a significant stage in the genesis of a jazz orthodoxy: the emergence of a set of standards, established and promulgated by a body of experts, and protected from the uninformed opinions of the public (even the 50,000 readership of *Down Beat*). The board of experts Feather and Goffin assembled consisted of sixteen men. Besides themselves, there was Ulanov, the promoter John Hammond, and various producers and writers. The membership also included Abel Green, editor of *Variety*, on whose presence Feather later commented, "included, against my wishes, for political reasons, and dropped the following year" (1986: 80).

The membership remained "expert" and limited in number, and it represented an emphatic disavowal of mere popularity. The understanding of "jazz" was constituting itself as an expertise, a connoisseurship. It is from this period and this movement in the critical literature that jazz acquired a mystique. Goffin and Feather "knew who the real experts were," a statement that went unquestioned because in jazz, as has become a commonplace ever since, "you either get it or you don't." This new mystique of jazz, which survives in its discourse up to the present day, was inaugurated in fictional texts such as Dorothy Baker's 1939 novel *Young Man with a*

Horn, films like *Blues in the Night,* and in critical texts such as those of Panassié, Goffin, Feather, and Ulanov.

By 1942 even the most charismatic contemporary performers, those that would have lent themselves to the emerging mythology, were not yet possessed of the mystique that surrounded them once this literature had done its work.[2] Even the brilliant soloists in such bands as Ellington's and Basie's, men like Cootie Williams and Lester Young, even the exceptional individualists such as Armstrong or Art Tatum, were still laying their performances before the public without any sense of hip irony or exclusiveness, without an attitude concerning the inability of the public to understand what they were doing. All of these artists were broadcasting their music to as large and inclusive a public as their position in the music business would allow.

It was also in the period between Panassié's first book and the end of the war that the paralyzing dichotomy between jazz and commercialism arose. The bizarre attitude of the jazz genius Jigger Pyne, troubled hero of "Blues in the Night," toward money was noted in chapter 4. But for many musicians, the main problem about commercialism was how to get more of it. This is true for many of those later drawn into the gravitational field of the new, austere concept of jazz. Within reasonable limits, a desire of working musicians is to maximize income. Musicians categorized as jazz artists, however, were presumed by these critics not to share this common concern. Jigger Pyne and the nonfictional musicians fulfilling his archetype would somehow get along without a commercial income and experience the romantic pain that comes with the role of genius in a philistine society—a society in which the artist is sometimes driven to righteous anger against customers who ask him to play "My Melancholy Baby."

The critics in whose work this conception of the jazz artist was being articulated occupied different economic positions from the musicians. None of Feather's sixteen-man *Esquire* panel was a working musician. The background of many of the experts was upper middle-class, or, in the case of John Hammond and Baron Rosenkrantz, patrician. Goffin had been a prominent lawyer, whose departure from Belgium following the Nazi invasion caused him to leave behind a collection of artworks by Gauguin and Matisse; Feather, born in London, came from a family that had servants and a chauffeur.

To state these facts is not to disqualify this group of writers from valid opinions on commercialism in music. Some of them held leftist political views that gave them sympathy with the status of workers in the existing economic order. However, it was not unnatural for men who enjoyed exceptional economic status to project onto the musicians they admired a lack of concern for the economic rewards of their profession. "Commercial music" was opposed to and utterly different from "jazz." This was established as a principle, but it was sometimes difficult to demonstrate in specific cases. Musicians like Ellington were commercially successful to some degree. Did this put them on the wrong side of the jazz-commercial divide?

What was "jazz," anyway? Throughout the 1940s this question was to absorb a great deal of critical energy. The sixteen men on the *Esquire* panel knew what jazz was—but so did other bodies of opinion, and they thought it was something different. Up to 1942 or even afterward, there was never a broad consensus on what jazz actually was. The music's history prior to 1942, supposing it had one, was itself a matter of dispute. In the absence of a clear, uncontentious category of "jazz," the only way to establish one was to compose it by joining together several historical threads. The question then became which threads to use. Do you weave in the thread called "swing," or leave it aside? Do you weave in the threads called "Dixieland," "the blues," "New Orleans jazz"? Or do you, as some other groups of writers were insisting, make "New Orleans" the only thread in the fabric?

A debate began to emerge in which the word *real* was a key value. Hugues Panassié's *Le Vrai Jazz* (*The Real Jazz*) appeared in translation late in 1942. The book was a revision of Panassié's views in the earlier *Hot Jazz*, in particular his opinion on the racial identification of jazz, "throughout, Panassié contends that we should give jazz back to the Negroes, or that it has never been taken from them" (*DB* 1. 15. 43: 23). The reviewer added that "this basic idea is correct," but appears troubled by the raising and lowering of reputations that was an effect of this new critical settlement.

Benny Goodman, as bandleader and clarinetist, had so far been given critical acceptance—to the extent of receiving a Gold Award from the *Esquire* experts. Panassié's revision of the rankings, however, demoted Goodman, putting him below the Chicago clarinetist Jimmy Noone. The *Down Beat* reviewer took issue with this judgment, "True, Benny does not approach Noone as a soloist, but neither is he as bad as Art Shaw, as Panassié insists." What is striking here is Panassié's assumption that Goodman and Shaw, popular bandleaders and virtuoso players of their instrument, represent degrees of *badness*. In his view, the low jazz quality of Artie Shaw's improvisations appears to go without saying.

An ethic of authenticity was beginning to be manifested in writings in the music press at this time, a process of sifting out the "real" jazz. In setting up its criteria of authenticity, the nascent concept of real jazz was embarking on a process that was recapitulated in other American musical fields soon afterward. Indeed, taking some studies of country music and blues together with the 1940s categorization of some jazz as more real than others, it can be taken as an axiom of American popular styles that sooner or later authenticity becomes a dominant issue. But, as Richard Peterson (1997) showed, authenticity in these fields is manufactured. The notion of a "country" or a "blues" performer is conditioned by the model of authenticity imposed upon it. This process is a systematization, a separation of fields of popular music into categories each of which defines, retrospectively, what an authentic artist in each of these categories should be. In 1942 the "real" jazz was at issue; "authentic" blues and "authentic" country would follow a few years later.

An article in *Down Beat*, "Separating the Righteous Jazz" (5.1.42: 14), gave further indications of this direction. However, the categories with which jazz writers operated were not those that later orthodoxy would recognize. In the category of "hot jazz," for instance, were the bands of Bob Crosby and Charlie Barnet, while "swing" (the less favored term), encompassed Count Basie in the same bracket as Jimmy Dorsey and Vaughn Monroe. The redefinition of jazz that was getting underway would shift Basie upward into this category and the others downward out of it.

The conception of a distinct music called "jazz" involved an act of multiple abstraction. Selected musicians and musical forms were abstracted from a complex of contexts in which they had previously existed. The setting up of this new domain was comparable to establishing a political unit such as a state or a nation: you put up borders and begin setting up laws, norms of behavior, and criteria for citizenship. Jazz was the first such category of American popular music to secede from the union, or, to use another historical analogy, to start putting up fences on the open range.

For jazz to achieve its secession, the multiple abstraction required can be summarized as follows: (1) the separation of jazz as a narrative; (2) the isolation of certain features, such as improvisation, as atemporal essences of jazz; (3) the separation of jazz from the performance contexts in which it has subsisted; and (4) the separation of jazz from other musical forms with which it has had some connection. None of these moves was simple.

In the early 1940s, the narrative of jazz was fiercely contested at the very moment when the discourse of jazz was being constructed. Feather and Goffin knew that small-band swing was "real jazz," whereas the revivalists knew that the "real" narrative of jazz actually stopped around 1925. In a year or two, a new form called "bebop" would provoke a further cycle of rejection and fierce struggle over its relation to the narrative. Polemic concerning the true narrative of jazz was vitriolic and prolonged, occupying the whole of the following decade.

Agreeing on the historically immutable essence of this music was not simple, either. Solo improvisation gradually became so central among possible defining features that it has come to be seen as an uncontestable criterion of what jazz is. But a 1942 review of the Nat Towles band could observe, "It is in the ensemble work that the beauty and power of its jazz is recognized" (*DB* 4. 1. 42: 7). It can be shown from numerous reviews and reactions that improvisation was only one among a complex of features considered significant in musical performance, including jazz performance.

The separation of jazz from its performance contexts was another feature of the wartime and post–World War II abstraction. As the prestige of the newly defined form rose, so it repudiated its association with theater, dance, and later ordinary presentational concerns. Jazz was now regarded as inherently separate from its earlier mixed associations, so that a performer like Fats Waller was seen as consisting of two incompatible functions, "serious jazz artist" and "entertainer." In the same way, postabstraction jazz discourse saw the long-time association of bands like Duke Ellington's with entertainers, dancers and on-stage movies as a historic slight upon his dignity. As we shall see later, the immersion of Ellington and others in this unabstracted milieu of entertainment was continuous, and, from the vantage point of the early 1940s, normal. A few years later, jazz as performance would be abstracted from all of this and presented in "pure" form. By the mid-1950s the Modern Jazz Quartet would be presented in concert-hall dress and demeanor and Dizzy Gillespie would be rebuked for failing to suppress his extroverted personality on stage. Jazz players would play "pure jazz" and do nothing else; a little later, blues players would play "pure blues" and nothing else; country players would play "pure country" and nothing else.

Above all, it was no simple matter to separate jazz from the rest of American popular music. The position and nature of its boundaries were not obvious. Categories of music that have come to seem inevitable and natural were not self-evident at the time, and the separation of one music from another was not necessarily easy to negotiate. The first press listings for *country music* (a term that only came into use ten years later) appeared in 1942, but the category they were placed in was "Western and race." These included both black and white performers, linked by a shared difference from the mainstream popular market. This broad category was waiting for further subdivision on racial lines. Country music was, as Richard Peterson related, passing through one of the periodic authenticity crises that affected jazz in a similar way, "In the 1940s 'purists' bemoaned the encroachment of honky-tonkers with electrified instruments who were crowding out the now-established string bands who had been the interlopers a generation before" (1997: 222). In the case of jazz, the most important category separation was that of jazz from popular music. Speaking of his work for bands like Nat Towles and Charlie Barnet, the arranger Neal Hefti said, "I really didn't think of it as jazz. I thought of it as pop music" (Gitler 1985: 190). Hefti's recollection dates from a time before this new category of "jazz" had separated itself. In this new configuration of the field, jazz was emphatically not pop music, and traces of its former identification with that field were reinterpreted or buried.

As we saw in chapter 3, in 1942 as earlier artists later categorized as jazz musicians were still functioning in the popular music process. The repertoire was made up of popular songs and has remained so. There were many such musicians who thought of their activities as happening within a popular-music world. Conversely, some artists who regarded themselves as jazz players have been transferred into other fields by the jazz narrative. The band of Bob Wills, broadcasting out of Tulsa, Oklahoma, until the end of 1942, played a repertoire like that of jazz orchestras, including material by Duke Ellington, and they emphasized swing and improvisation. A 1942 review raised the question of jazz identity, "Don't sniff, pops—this band is the biggest territory band in the world ... this record ought to be under Hot Jazz, if it weren't for the incongruous combination of a good brass section playing against a very loud Hawaiian guitar"(*DB* 10. 15. 42: 8). Richard Peterson confirmed that "western swing was not considered part of country music, nor did its proponents consider it as such. Bob Wills explicitly aspired to be a jazz performer and sought to distance his work from country music" (1997: 265).

Like many other such categories, this new category was normative. It imposed criteria upon artists whose work was never intended to be so judged. It implied a central set of values from which differences were perceived as inferiority within the category, rather than as natural gradations of style and approach. Some musicians' reputations suffered under this system: Louis Jordan, as David Ake (2002) showed, became a victim of the border changes, slipping into the badlands where jazz meets rhythm-and-blues. As we saw above, Benny Goodman as instrumentalist became deficient against the norms represented by Jimmy Noone; similarly, Goodman as bandleader was now perceived as failing to fulfill the norms of jazz as effectively as Duke Ellington. The superb orchestra Goodman led became drawn into a newly devised category in which it could only be classed as a less successful attempt to meet the same criteria. Jazz became a monoculture.

A specific critical dispute concerned the saxophonist and bandleader Jimmy Dorsey. Dorsey was the biggest-selling bandleader in 1941, with recordings such as "Maria Elena" selling over half a million copies (a fact that may have worked against his jazz credibility). Dorsey was a virtuoso instrumentalist, as exemplified by his Pearl Harbor Sunday "Fingerbustin'" and his authorship of books on saxophone technique. His style was relatively "straight," but he had a track record with acknowledged jazz stars and was admired by, among others, Charlie Parker. By 1942 Jimmy Dorsey's playing was a test case in the comparison of "real jazz" players with others. Mike Levin's "righteous jazz" piece of May 1942 offered a faint plea for the defense, "You're tilting at windmills to say that Jimmy Dorsey's alto playing is 'tasteless mush.' It may not be a 'hot' solo, but it is still great technical playing" (*DB* 5. 1. 42: 14).

The community of writers and critics who were establishing the new norms contained members with extramusical political or ethical concerns.

There was the same phenomenon among jazz writers as among codifiers of the blues, "people with progressive political views, who were celebrating the music as a vital cultural expression of black Americans" (Wald 2004: 17). Robert Goffin had been a prominent antifascist in his native Belgium, and John Hammond was well known for his liberal social and cultural views. Leonard Feather held a conception of music conditioned by the experience of the 1930s, in which "in London, Paris and Berlin alike, enthusiasm for jazz had elements in common with membership of a resistance movement" (1986: 7).

The views of these men were honorable and should be respected, but their orientation toward popular culture—and American popular culture, in particular—was not neutral. Through class or national background, none of them was genuinely on home ground with American popular music and popular culture or comfortable with it in political or intellectual terms. There was an overlap with the position of someone like Theodor Adorno. Among these writers, there was a shared desire to advance jazz as art, as a vehicle for the progression of black Americans, and this required them to shuck off its implication in popular culture (Stowe 1994: 50–93; Erenberg 1998: 120–144). The revaluation of jazz, the installation of a narrative of its separateness and its development, derived more from this agenda than from a genuine assessment of its place within American culture.

Under this upward pressure, jazz was in the process not only of separating itself from but also of elevating itself above other varieties of American music. *Jazz* became an honorific term, a term worth fighting over—which is what happened in the 1940s and early 1950s. Jazz ceded a place at the economic center of popular music, but, through its codifiers and critics, began to accrue cultural capital. To assimilate itself to other high art forms, jazz criticism took on the vocabulary and the assumptions of art criticism. It began to formulate stories about its history, its past and future, its progression, and its iconic figures, modeled upon the stories that currently governed other arts.

Though the other popular musical styles that were to undergo their own separations, blues and country, shared with jazz the ethic of authenticity, but neither of them sought to acquire the high-art intellectual status that jazz was beginning to lay claim to. Blues and country music have tended to celebrate instead their folk simplicity, whereas jazz has only done this in its reckoning of how far it has progressed from a deep folk past in black culture to post-1940s modernist sophistication. Jazz, too, in this account was once folk music (hence the narrative of a lineage linking bebop with field hollers).[3] While it never lost the "authenticity" such roots gave it, jazz had equipped itself for the shift into the modern-art narrative of progression.

Progression may be continuous and incremental or sudden and disruptive. The change from one situation to another can be characterized as a natural, inevitable movement toward a historical goal, as evolution, or as the outcome of a struggle between the old and the new, as revolution. In the case of the music that by 1945 was called "bebop" and in 1942 was in the process of formation, revolution is the model preferred by historians. This model dramatizes the activities of the musicians, "plotting" or "conspiring to create" a revolution. Jazz histories use the vocabulary of this model: the musicians were "revolutionaries," "young rebels," "insurgents," and their activity is referred to as "revolution" or "rebellion."[4] New York cabarets, such as Minton's Playhouse on West 118th Street and Monroe's Uptown House on West 134th Street, become cradles of revolution, the only point of change in American music given that title so consistently.

Other periods of change in jazz and popular music have different designations: the sudden emergence of the big-band swing phenomenon in 1935 is sometimes a "craze," and its ten-year period of mass popularity has the bland title of an "era." The unique prevalence of the term *revolution* in connection with bebop implies that its nature as a disruptive break is well defined, that it has the characteristics of revolution in the general sense of the word. In these circumstances, one would expect to find the elements and the conditions of revolution: a situation that provoked it, something to be in revolt against, and, on the part of those making it, a revolutionary intent or a revolutionary consciousness. However, despite the consistency of the labeling, there is little definite evidence of any of these things.

A second model for bebop's coming into existence is the scientific one of experimentation. In this metaphor, Minton's is represented as the site of systematic research and experiment. Ross Russell, the biographer of Charlie Parker, described the club in a phrase that combines both key metaphors, "the laboratory in which musical experiments [were] about to emerge as the bebop revolution began around 1941" (1973: 130). Other movements in the arts had used the same designation for their activities. The usage of *experiment* for the activities in 1941–1942 at Monroe's and Minton's draws on the prestige associated with ideas both in modernist art and in the work of research scientists. The latter domain was at a height of prestige just at this time, when teams of researchers were recruited for projects like the development of atomic fission. Science was creating technologies, concepts, and realities consonant with a modernizing society; on this analogy, bebop was synthesizing in a scientific manner a musical language for use in the modern world. However, as with *revolution*, solid justifications for the description of the Minton's scene as experimentation are difficult to establish from the historical record. It is clear that few participants thought of these musical activities in terms of the metaphors that have become attached to them (Townsend 2000: 51–53).

Charlie Parker arrived in New York with Jay McShann's band in January 1942. Broadcasts of Parker's solos, especially "Cherokee," created a stir of interest among musicians. For reviewers and journalists, Parker's playing was a definite asset to the McShann band, but it was mentioned with no greater prominence than other soloists and received less acclaim than McShann's piano solos and the rhythmic impact of the band as a whole. Parker received no mention in fellow musicians' accounts of the encounter at the Savoy with Lucky Millinder. While in New York early in 1942, Parker began visiting the after-hours jam clubs such as Monroe's and Minton's. It is difficult to establish his whereabouts after this, as his lifestyle was itinerant and chaotic during this period. It may be, as suggested by the personnel listing in the *Amsterdam News* in April, that he temporarily dropped out of the McShann band. The evidence of dates and places is fragmentary and consists of sightings of Parker, such as the incident described by the trumpeter Orville Minor, "My wife once saved him from getting burned up. She looked out the window and said there was smoke coming out of Bird's window. It was 1942, in the Woodside Hotel in New York. They investigated and found Bird asleep in bed with flames all around him. He had fallen asleep with a cigarette and dropped it on the floor" (Reisner 1965: 130). Billy Eckstine, later a bandleader and popular singer, recalled a 1942 contact with Parker at Monroe's, "Bird used to go down there and blow every night when he was with McShann at the Savoy, and he just played gorgeous" (Hentoff and Shapiro 1962: 343).

Parker's deterioration, brought about by his lifestyle and his involve-ment with narcotics, has been described in various biographical accounts. Ross Russell described the hiring of Parker by Earl Hines at the end of the year as a rescue operation. In an interview twelve years later, Parker recalled his 1942 New York sojourn, "New York was . . . well, those were what you might call the good old days." Prompted by his interviewer, the saxophonist Paul Desmond, Parker went on, "There was nothing to do but play, you know, and we had a lot of fun trying to play, you know. . . . I did plenty of jam sessions . . . meant much late hours, plenty good food . . . nice clean living, you know, but basically speaking, much poverty (Vail 1996: 146). Sometime in mid-1942 Parker switched from Monroe's, where he was living off what the customers put in the kitty, to Minton's. He was with the McShann band at a recording session in July, but, except for one short track, there are no known recordings of his many hours of playing at Monroe's, Minton's, and other New York clubs.

Monroe's Uptown House has never achieved the iconic status of Minton's as a revolutionary or experimental site. Both places were low-budget nightclubs with a following among New York musicians for the informal sessions that were at their peak of activity around the time of the attack on Pearl Harbor. There is only slight evidence for a revolution-ary consciousness among the participants at Minton's and Monroe's. Musicians mentioned as regulars included large numbers of the big-band musical establishment. The drummer Kenny Clarke named Earl Hines and his band members; the trumpeters Roy Eldridge and Hot Lips Page, from the Artie Shaw and Gene Krupa bands, respectively; and Shaw's tenor saxo-phonist Georgie Auld. Clarke, credited as the first bebop drummer and an original "rebel," mentioned that when Benny Goodman attended Minton's, "we always got a great deal of pleasure when he came in," and that the Minton's band used to "convert our style to coincide with his" (Hentoff and Shapiro 1962: 329).

This attitude does not sound like that of convinced revolutionaries against the old guard or against the commercialism that Goodman was seen as representing. The rebellion was frequently envisaged, by Ross Russell and other writers, as being directed against the big bands. Time and again in the jazz literature it was stated, on the basis of very slight evidence, that the bebop players were in revolt against the big bands. The word *regimented* and its synonyms were used of big bands almost as frequently as *revolution* was used of the beboppers.[5] Such terms gave the new musical developments a specific grievance—regimentation—and a specific goal of escaping it.

What evidence there is of attitudes toward the big bands among these musicians points, if anything, the other way. After a brief interval, Charlie Parker went from the big band of Jay McShann to the band of Earl Hines. In the words of one of his friends, Parker "loved big bands" (Reisner 1965: 29). In his later career, Parker played and recorded with big bands (and the much-despised string sections) on many occasions. Kenny Clarke went on to play drums in many big bands; after his move to Europe in the 1960s, for the rest of his life he led a band with the French pianist Francy Boland. All of Minton's so-called revolutionaries worked frequently, before and after the Minton's period, in big orchestras. Thelonious Monk's piano style perhaps did not lend itself to the role of big-band pianist, but Monk was organizing and rehearsing a big band contemporaneously with his appearances at Minton's.

Dizzy Gillespie's is the most significant case. A few years after Minton's and the supposed revolt against the big band, Gillespie set up his own big band, which lasted through 1950. He ran similar organizations at intervals throughout the rest of his life. In 1942, having left Cab Calloway, Gillespie wrote arrangements for the bands of Woody Herman and Lucky Millinder, played for a while with Millinder, and then joined Earl Hines's band shortly before Parker got there. It is fair to say that Dizzy Gillespie showed few signs of rebellion against what the big bands offered.

However, the manner of Gillespie's leaving the Calloway band, like other moments in bebop history, has been mythologized into significance. Few practical jokes in the history of American music have been given so much historical significance as one played on the stage of the State Theatre, in Hartford, Connecticut, in the fall of 1941. Gillespie was a practical joker, but on the occasion of someone throwing a spitball during one of Calloway's vocals, he was wrongly taken to be the perpetrator and fired on the spot. There followed a backstage scuffle between Gillespie and the bandleader in which Calloway was cut with a knife. The reason for the standoff was Gillespie's taking the blame for another musician's prank, but the subsequent literature of bebop rebellion reads it as an early act of insurrection against the swing status quo, represented in this case by Calloway.

Because of his symbolic role in this incident, Calloway's reputation has come in for a certain contempt, partly as an embodiment of the discredited values of entertainment and commercialism. The injury inflicted on him by Gillespie is read as an act of revolutionary violence, and this accounts for the exceptional prominence given to a minor incident. Few accounts of the origins of bebop fail to mention the famous spitball; even Scott DeVeaux's *The Birth of Bebop* (1997) has the word *spitball* in the title of a chapter on this period.[6] Gillespie, however, was not the only big-band musician to take violent exception to a sacking. A story in the *Chicago Defender* the following summer gave Gillespie a name-check, "Rumor says Joe [Britton] . . . chased his boss, Lucky Millinder, around the Savoy with his carving weapon when the dynamaestro handed him his notice. An interested bystander was Dizzie Gillespie, who did the same thing to Cab Calloway several months ago" (*CD* 7. 18. 42: 12).

The regimented nature of the big-band musician's world has become an unexamined cliché in the narrative of bebop rebellion. The more regimented the big-band regime, the more laudable and necessary the beboppers' presumed desire to overthrow it. How regimented the situation actually was in any band depended on the leader, the musicians, and the system on which the band was organized. Some bands, such as Bob Crosby's, were cooperatives. In their approach to discipline, other bands were the opposite of regimented: the attitudes of Duke Ellington and Count Basie were relaxed to the point of being careless. Bands like those of Charlie Barnet and Bunny Berigan were noted for wild behavior, descending at times to the 1940s equivalent of partying rock bands. Any organization described by its musicians as "wild" and "a picnic" (Gitler 1985: 95), as Barnet's was, clearly had no problem with too much regimentation.

According to George T. Simon (1974a: 8), the approaches of bandleaders "varied with their personalities and their talents." He cited Miller, Goodman, and Tommy Dorsey as leaders who "knew what they wanted, and knew how to get it." Others' attitudes he summed up as, "You guys are pros . . . so long as you produce, you've got nothing to worry about." However, for the sake of the bebop-as-revolution narrative, all this variation, from the stiff precision of Miller to the drunken chaos of Berigan, is compressed under the description "regimentation." The fixing of this term as a global description of life in the big bands gives bebop revolt an artistic and also a moral justification.

In this view, bebop was a positive or, as it was soon called, "progressive" movement that was opening up a gap between its jazz authenticity and the repressive commercialism of the music-industry bands. For later writers (e.g., Collier 1978: 3), this move became a return to the straight developmental narrative of jazz, after a decade's exile in the land of popular music. The disruptive, revolutionary aspect of bebop was a sign of its transcendence, its progression to a higher cultural level than could be attained within the corrupting swing context, with its fatal attachment to popular music.

Later writers on bebop pointed to specific markers of its progression from other forms. For years afterward, harmony was the preferred domain in which evidence for the accelerated development of jazz was located. The harmonic innovations of bebop were interpreted in ways that exemplified some tendencies of the jazz narrative. For example, their disruptiveness and strangeness were emphasized or exaggerated as corroboration of the ideas of revolt and experimentation. These innovations were also treated as a development strictly internal to jazz. As noted earlier, the abstraction of jazz tended to sever historical connections with other music or other factors in the contemporary context; consequently, the changing harmonic practices could be treated only as an autonomous evolutionary process, with no reference to anything else in contemporary music or culture.

Leonard Feather stressed the centrality of harmony to the developmental process at this moment. In a historical survey in his *Encyclopedia of Jazz*, first published in 1960, Feather described jazz between 1939 and 1942 as, "fighting its way out of a harmonic and melodic blind alley" (1960: 30). The way out of this impasse was then indicated in an instance of the narrative "breakthrough moment" that is a feature both of jazz historiography and the movie biopic, "In California in 1940 Oscar Moore, guitarist with the King Cole trio, ended the group's first Decca record, *Sweet Lorraine*, on a ninth chord with a flattened fifth" (1960: 30). Feather gave no context for Moore's discovery of this lost chord. This example is typical of the jazz narrative's preoccupation with harmony, which represents successive chordal discoveries as a process like that of isolating the elements in the periodic table. The flattened fifth became a fetish of critical writing on bebop and its progressiveness. Feather's *Inside Jazz* (called *Inside Bebop* on first publication in 1949) advised that "the more you listen to bop, the more you will be impressed with the change that has been effected in the whole character and sound of jazz improvisation by the acceptance of this flatted fifth as a 'right' note" (1977: 70). The flattened fifth (sometimes called the "augmented fourth") is the note that lies between the fourth and fifth degrees of the scale: in the scale of C-major, for example, it is the note F-sharp. Its use is allied to functions of the tritone that later players exploited. It is also simply an interestingly discordant note, especially for 1940s listeners whose ears had not become accustomed to it. The technicians in the laboratory at Minton's had now worked out a reliable process for producing it.

If we take Charlie Parker as the bebop musician par excellence, it is notable that, as Thomas Owens's analysis of his style showed, "The famous 'flatted fifth' of bebop played a relatively small role in Parker's playing; many solos contain not a single instance of it" (1995: 33). Schuller commented that as well as being "as old as jazz itself," the note's use in bebop "was overemphasized by writers and press agents," as a musical symbolism equivalent to the eccentric dress codes that appeared during the subsequent publicity for bebop (1989: 365).

On July 14, 1942, the Andy Kirk band recorded a feature number for the trumpeter Howard McGhee entitled "McGhee Special." In Schuller's *The Swing Era*, some harmonic features of this recording are the starting point for six pages of exegesis, including a complex full-page diagram of its theoretical implications (1989: 360–366). The harmonic features that Schuller cited in McGhee's improvisation (the flattening of fifths, sixths, and ninths) are certainly present. In overall effect, however, "McGhee Special" comes across as a classic example of big-band swing trumpet. Traces of Louis Armstrong's style are evident. McGhee admired older players such as Red Allen and Roy Eldridge (Gitler 1985: 28–29), and the piece recalls the styles of both men—indeed, it sounds more backward-looking than Eldridge's playing of the early 1940s. In actuality, the unusual intervals shown in the transcription sound glancing and slurred and do not create an impression of a disruptive modernity set against the conventional swing arrangement. The main feature that prompted Schuller's detailed analysis, however, was that the piece, in F-major, had a bridge in A♭, a minor third above. He saw this unusual relationship as "prophetic of things to come" in jazz, and as opening up the possibility of a new harmonic language. The significance loaded on this one feature of one recording is in the same mode of explanation as Feather's response to Oscar Moore's fateful guitar chord, as if McGhee's A♭ bridge section had suddenly broken the code to a mysterious new world of jazz harmony.

At this point, the abstraction to which jazz historiography is prone reenters as a factor. Where would a musician in 1942 find a precedent for the revolutionary key relationship McGhee used in the Andy Kirk recording? Owing to the theoretical severance of jazz from other musical forms, and especially from commercial popular music, one feasible and obvious answer is cut off from consideration: the influence of popular songwriting. Examples of a similar shift from a major key to one a minor third above include Arthur Johnson's "My Old Flame" and Jerome Kern's "Long Ago and Far Away." Alec Wilder commented on Kern's song that he "was convinced that this device would be too much for the public ear, but not so, for it's a standard song" (1972: 84). "My Old Flame," in G, moves to B♭ in the bridge and has some other unusual chromaticisms.

By the early 1940s popular songwriting had reached a high level of harmonic sophistication. This is an uncontentious point in discussion of the "Great American Songbook," but somehow it has no bearing upon histories of jazz. Searching for flatted fifths, for instance, one could find them as easily in compositions like Joe Bishop's 1932 song "Blue Prelude" or in "The Boy Next Door," written by Hugh Martin for the 1944 musical *Meet Me in St. Louis*, as in the pieces by Ellington and others that are admissible as evidence in a jazz context. Songwriters of the 1930s and 1940s had been making harmonic and melodic innovations that resulted in the situation described by Charles Hamm (1983: 367), in which the full range of chromatic alterations were allowable. This is precisely the stage that jazz reached in bebop; as Schuller put it, "What really happened was that *all* the chromatic alterations, previously more or less forbidden, suddenly sprang into common use" (1989: 366). In other words, as regards progressive harmony, bebop of the mid-1940s was in exactly the same state as contemporary popular songwriting.

Popular songs had been tracing harmonic and melodic patterns that were as complex as those of progressive jazz. The chromaticism of songs like the 1942 "Serenade in Blue" and the earlier "Darn That Dream" was discussed in chapter 3. John Green's 1931 "Out of Nowhere" featured abrupt shifts to a tonality a half-step away from the parent key. Vernon Duke's "April in Paris" had an opening phrase described by Wilder as "melodically and harmonically an extraordinary beginning for a song in 1932, or any other year" (1972: 358). Jerome Kern's "All the Things You Are" demonstrates how sophisticated a popular song could be by 1939, with five different key centers occurring at irregular points within the chorus, without losing melodic or compositional continuity.

A popular song that had particular importance in the construction of jazz history is Ray Noble's "Cherokee." Originally performed as a slow ballad, it was recorded in a successful up-tempo arrangement by Charlie Barnet in 1939 and has since, especially in bebop versions, been played at fast tempo. The harmonic challenge of the song is the sixteen-bar bridge, where the progression shifts from the key of B♭ to a succession of new key centers, beginning on B-natural and dropping a whole tone within each four-bar section, returning to B♭ for the final sixteen bars. "Cherokee" was a song Charlie Parker seems to have been intrigued by—it eventually became the underlying framework of his superb 1945 "Ko-Ko," and it loomed large in his musical activity years earlier. The difficult B section, or bridge, seems to have figured for Parker as a test of technical and harmonic skill.

Parker's encounter with "Cherokee" is another of the founding moments of the bebop narrative, comparable with Gillespie's spitball. The moment in which Parker, working over "Cherokee" in 1939, discovered the secret of his style, is the kind of crisis of invention that had long been a motif in the biopics. This genre was at a historical peak in the early 1940s. For instance, 1942 saw the release of the Lou Gehrig picture, *Pride of the Yankees*, and the premiere of James Cagney as George M. Cohan in *Yankee Doodle Dandy*. Henry Fonda, as Abraham Lincoln in *The Young Mr. Lincoln*, could be seen on the same theater bill as the Earl Hines band. The Lincoln film had a scene in which the future president is perusing Blackstone's *Commentaries*. The words *right* and *wrong* stand out in the text, and Lincoln has a sudden revelation, "By jings! That's all there is to it—right and wrong!" From this moment he is on the road to becoming the Abraham Lincoln of history and legend. The story of Parker's struggle with "Cherokee" has exactly this function in his life story and in the narrative of jazz.

However, the canonical version of the incident, reproduced in virtually all writing on the subject, is a fabrication. The persistence of this version in so many texts indicates that legends are more potent than facts. The
supposed oral-history account by Parker himself is actually a rewriting of a
third-person story by two *Down Beat* journalists in 1949. Parker simply did
not say the words attributed to him in one of the most frequently cited and
most crucial of jazz quotations, "That night I was working over 'Cherokee,'
and, as I did, I found that by using the higher intervals of a chord as a
melody line and backing them with appropriately related changes, I could
play the thing I'd been hearing. I came alive" (Collier 1978: 350). Despite
clarifications published by Thomas Owens (1995: 33) and Scott DeVeaux
(1997: 189), the supposed Parker quote still appears as a pivotal moment in
the story of the genesis of bebop, for instance, with further elaborations in
Ken Burns's 1998 documentary on the history of jazz.[7]

It is difficult to understand why such an inaccuracy could have clung
on for so long, unless it is because of the importance of the narrative in
which it is an essential link. The *Down Beat* journalists wrote, "Charlie
Parker's horn first came alive in 1939" (*DB* 9.12.49: 12). The version that
rewrites the quotation as if spoken by Parker retains the journalists' idea of
coming alive and places it at the climax of the story, where it acquires the
resonance of the biopic moment. Parker has continued to "come alive" for
almost all later writers, in the same kind of revelatory moment as Abraham
Lincoln experienced in his movie incarnation. That the dramatic phrase
in which this breakthrough experience is expressed was never uttered has
made no difference; it was quoted in Collier's *The Making of Jazz* (1978) and
in Gioia's *The History of Jazz* (1997) and, given its persistence, will probably
be quoted to the same effect for the next few decades as well.

But why was Parker working over "Cherokee," a popular song, a hit for
Charlie Barnet that same year? One reason was that it *was* a popular song
that year and therefore part of the professional musician's repertoire. The
song remained important to Parker: it was his live-broadcast "Cherokee"
from the Savoy in 1942 that caught the ear of other musicians. When Parker
made a rare live performance for an amateur recordist in early 1942, possibly at Monroe's, the piece was again "Cherokee." Parker spent much time
over the years trying to find a way of handling the unusual harmonies of
the song's bridge. He noticed that the bridge was a series of II-V-I chords,

and this brought to mind another popular song with a similar passage, Vincent Youmans's "Tea for Two." The outline of the melody of "Tea for Two" is audible in places in both the 1942 Monroe's solo and the 1945 "Ko-Ko." Parker used the harmonies of one popular song to help him negotiate the harmonies of another.

The challenge was the popular song, and the source was the popular song. Parker was not researching in the abstract, exploring chains of II-V-I sequences descending in whole tones, he was trying to play "Cherokee." The harmonic challenge for any bebop player, or indeed any musician, was embodied in the popular song repertoire. After all, this repertoire already contained the harmonic elaborations that jazz styles were using. Each of the innovative songs mentioned above became part of the repertoire of bebop and have since acquired the status of (note the phrase) "jazz standards." Parker, Gillespie, Monk, and Miles Davis recorded "All the Things You Are," and Parker, Monk, and Bud Powell recorded "April in Paris." "Out of Nowhere" exists in a version by Kenny Clarke and five separate recordings by Parker; "Cherokee" had seven recordings by Parker and three by Powell.

Players such as Parker, Davis, Monk, and Gillespie worked in a musical world saturated with the popular music of the day. From their early playing years through big-band employment to the end of their musical lives, their jazz playing would be thoroughly conditioned by popular music. The jazz narrative, however, holds that jazz players managed prolonged exposure to popular music without taking any material or influence from the music that permeated their working lives. Thus, when jazz players considered harmony, they are assumed to have done so entirely from within jazz. This narrative, were we not accustomed to it from half a century of denigration of the popular, would surely strain credulity.

Even a writer like DeVeaux, however, can adopt this position of territorial separation. He credited Thelonious Monk with introducing to jazz the half-diminished chord, "then still a 'freaky sound' on or beyond the boundaries of most musicians' knowledge" (1997: 223). Monk represents aspects of bebop, particularly its "weirdness," more fully than either Parker or Gillespie. Consider, though, Monk's relationship to the popular song repertoire: among many such titles he recorded are Irving Berlin's "All Alone," Jimmy van Heusen's "Darn That Dream," the 1920s Harry Akst song "Dinah," Gershwin's "Nice Work If You Can Get It," and Harry

Warren's "Lulu's Back in Town." Monk's own compositions use the chord progressions of popular songs, with his 1948 "In Walked Bud" having the harmonic structure of Berlin's 1927 "Blue Skies." Monk had a wide, though idiosyncratic, acquaintance with the popular song and its harmonies. At the sophisticated end of the popular song harmonic vocabulary, the half-diminished chord was not unknown. Monk could have derived this chord from, among other possible examples, the song "I'm Getting Sentimental over You." Monk was still playing and recording the song in the 1960s (as were Duke Ellington and Bill Evans). In the third bar the song's melody traces the notes of a half-diminished chord and is usually harmonized with this chord. It is an attractive and unusual song, and, being the theme song of the Tommy Dorsey band, was among the most radio-played of all songs in the late 1930s and early 1940s. Like other Americans, Monk had plenty of opportunities to become acquainted with it.

The question of where bebop derived its harmonic practices from is not usually considered, as it is supposed that, like other actors in the jazz narrative, bebop got it from within itself or by pure, abstract speculation. The resistance to the idea that bebop got its harmonies from popular songs has been immense. Leonard Feather wrote of jazz as possessing an almost elemental antipathy to popular music; his 1960 encyclopedia referred to "rock 'n' roll and other pap fed daily to the American public," while jazz itself "has retained the elusive essence that separates it from so-called popular music" (1960: 61).

On the other hand, critics including Feather remarked that harmonic developments in jazz carried it to the level of early-twentieth-century European classical harmony. This is regarded as a mark of cultural achievement by jazz, which is commended for having reached this height more quickly than classical music managed it. This is a curious idea—as if harmonic development were a process akin to physiological development, gone through by each musical form independently of the others. Jazz was said to be recapitulating this process entirely on its own, racing through the phases of European harmony in a fraction of the time.[8] Change and development in jazz were again seen as entirely internal processes; nothing entered from outside sources to lead or influence its development. According to this line of argument, jazz was deriving its advanced harmonic language entirely from its own resources.

Since as early as the 1910s, however, writers of popular songs had been incorporating expanded classical harmonic language into compositions and arrangements. Some were accomplished composers whose work was consistent with classical practice of the period. George Gershwin remains a canonical American composer. Vernon Duke, writer of "April in Paris," had a parallel career as a classical composer. Jerome Kern was a notable writer for the theater; in 1942 he joined Copland and Virgil Thomson in writing for concert performance musical tributes to notable Americans, when Kern chose Mark Twain. There is no doubt that the harmonic sophistication of these writers derived from experience in the classical as well as the popular field. However, it is not claimed for Broadway and Hollywood writers such as Kern, Duke, and Gershwin that they derived their harmonic devices through a process internal to the "Great American Songbook." It is only historians of jazz who insist on the idea of completely autonomous and internal processes of development. Jazz, in this scenario, is beholden to nothing. Serious European music can be likened to it, as a comparable classical idiom, but is not offered as a source or influence.

Rather than allow the possibility that jazz took any of its content, especially its much-prized harmonic development, from popular music, jazz writers have had to hypothesize an abstract course of development that would be recapitulated by any music of real value. Jazz could not have derived its harmonies from Kern, Gershwin, and the rest, because they were popular songwriters. This was to ignore a series of facts about such writers: that all were as harmonically sophisticated as any jazz player, including the beboppers; that the "advanced" harmonies of bebop are all found some years earlier in the work of these writers; that jazz musicians played a repertoire consisting largely of popular material; and that the songs the jazz/bebop players were particularly interested in were precisely those in which these writers had used striking harmonic devices.

In retrospect, it is hard to see how the direct influence of popular song harmony on jazz harmony could have been denied. The motivation seems to have been ideological opposition to popular culture on the part of the early proponents of a separate jazz identity. In the early 1940s, Theodor Adorno, recently arrived from Germany and meeting American popular culture with uncomprehending horror, was propounding the principle that anything that is touched by commercialism loses all value. From the late

1930s, jazz writers were beginning to articulate within a broadly Marxist framework the narrative of jazz as a folk music with a classical destiny, untouched by popular music, which for them was tainted by commercialism. There was a sustained effort to separate jazz from any connection with the world of the popular songwriter.

Bebop was viewed by a section of the jazz critical community as the transcendence of the popular, as well as having revolutionary and experimental aspects characteristic of modernist art discourse. In parallel with this, there was an effort to enlist practitioners of the style into an ideology of modernist avant-gardism consistent with its historical progressiveness. During these years, jazz had its manifest destiny mapped out, namely becoming a quasi-classical form. The musicians themselves were characterized as modernist figures in their tastes and attitudes. Some accounts of Charlie Parker emphasized his interest in modern composers such as Stravinsky and Hindemith. Leonard Feather described the singer Leo Watson as "The James Joyce of jazz," and later "the Gertrude Stein of jazz" (Feather 1986: 95). These descriptions are as accurate as calling James Joyce "the Leo Watson of the Irish novel," but both Joyce and Stein are definitively modernist artists, and this connection was the point of Feather's comparison. In actuality, Watson's vocalizing was linked with Louis Armstrong's scat style or with other popular vocal acrobats; he had been a member of The Spirits of Rhythm, a music and comedy troupe with a large following in Harlem and on 52nd Street. Watson went on to appear in movies, including the feature film *Panama Hattie*. Watson's milieu and potential audience was not dissimilar to that of Slim Gaillard or Louis Jordan, both of whom were making inroads commercially by 1942. Like these men, Watson was an entertainer. But Feather's description achieves two ideological aims: it ignores any implication in entertainment and the popular arts, and it turns Watson into a modernist artist. It also, like Feather's later reinterpretation of Fats Waller, turns the wild, hilarious Watson into a "serious" figure.

Some dysfunctional aspects of Parker's personality, later made him an available subject for appropriation by Beat ideology. More significant in jazz historiography was the emphasis on Parker as a modernist artist. The most thorough account of this kind to date is in Ted Gioia's jazz history, in which Parker was straightforwardly called a modernist and a "highbrow" (1997: 205). Since the 1940s, Parker's image has consistently been shifted in this direction. From the Parker biographies, however, we can glean the information that Parker "loved big bands," while the prevailing discourse claimed he was in revolt against them. One of Parker's friends recalled an occasion when he was delighted to get a free pass to a Benny Goodman performance, and sat there listening raptly (Gitler 1985: 156). This was also a man who "loved movies, good and bad" (Reisner 1965: 33), and made frequent references in his conversation to the cartoon character Popeye. Parker's love for hillbilly music is also on the record; he is said to have selected country songs on jukeboxes (1965: 117) and to have commented on them, "Just listen to the stories." These seem to be closer to the tastes of a typical consumer of American popular culture than to those of a "highbrow."

A frequent proposition among writers on some American music forms is that the performers in these styles share their own detachment from the tastes of the general public. This is particularly prevalent where this involves racial as well as musical categorization. Elijah Wald wrote of this attitude among the post-1960s audience for the blues, "Hard as it is for modern blues fans to accept, the artists we most admire often shared the mass tastes we despise" (2004: xiv). From this springs a sense of anomaly when facing, for instance, Muddy Waters's enthusiasm for the cowboy singer Gene Autry, which ignores barriers of race and musical style. For as Wald wrote of the ideological effort expended on blues a little later than the critical initiative on jazz, "A great part of the battle was to separate important 'folk art' from disposable everyday entertainment" (2004: 235). Thus, it was confusing and a setback in the battle if the honored "authentic" artist claimed to enjoy the entertainment alternative or even to prefer it to the "real" version, as when, for the black Mississippi teenagers encountered by Alan Lomax on a fieldtrip in 1941 had to be persuaded to record a traditional song instead of the Mercer-Arlen "Blues in the Night," which was their first choice.

This sort of contact with or participation in mass taste is even more anomalous in a putative modernist like Charlie Parker. Jazz-narrative writers have sometimes responded to this with an argument akin to the Marxist notion of "false consciousness." This is typified by a particularly patronizing explanation by Joachim Berendt of Parker's admiration for fellow altoist Jimmy Dorsey, "Charlie Parker, for example, always had praise for Jimmy Dorsey—with that touching tendency to overrate technical ability so frequent among musicians" (1976: 203). A similar forbearance was extended to Louis Armstrong's liking for Guy Lombardo (e.g., Schuller 1989: 170). These artists, it is presumed, can only admire such noncanonical and deprecated players for odd reasons, through misunderstanding, or on account of personal foibles that are excusable in geniuses.

The same attitude was generalized on behalf of entire social or racial groups. Blacks, above all, were assumed to have a race-specific purist disdain for the products of mass popular culture. Since black culture is viewed as the source for several varieties of authentic music, namely jazz and the blues, it necessarily draws the same distinctions of value as the critical community. As Elijah Wald commented on some views of John Hammond, "this contention—that black audiences expected straight music, whereas white audiences liked cheap entertainment—has no basis in fact, but fits perfectly with the idea of 'primitive' genius as opposed to polished theatricality" (2004: 314).

Black Americans are typecast or pigeonholed as being confined to musical and artistic tastes prescribed for them by the narratives of authenticity. For other forms of popular culture such as films, the same kinds of assumptions would be made. But black Americans of the period saw the same movies as other Americans, and they cannot be assumed to have reacted to them in any specifically different way. The black publication the *Amsterdam News* commented on Disney's *Bambi* as follows, "It is the story of high romance and thrilling adventure told through the medium of animals living in a forest" (9.19.42: 17); the tear-jerking story of the indomitable British middle classes *Mrs. Miniver* was described as "the greatest heart-thrill of all time" (9.26.42: 17). This sort of statement, even in newspaper copy, should act as a check on assumptions about predictably pure tastes of blacks en bloc, as should the fact of Bing Crosby's "White Christmas" topping the "Harlem Hit Parade" and the 1941–1942 selections on the jukeboxes in the Delta-blues territory of Clarksdale, Mississippi (to be discussed in chapter 6). As not only a black American but also an exemplar of "revolution" and an "experimental" modernist to boot, Charlie Parker's allegiances were supposed to lie with the cultural forms that embody these categorizations. Muddy Waters wasn't supposed to sing "Red Sails in the Sunset"; even more so, someone in Parker's position wasn't supposed to like hillbilly music.

It is not clear at what point in 1942 Parker departed the McShann band altogether. Some accounts suggest that it was soon after the recording date on July 2, others that he stayed with the band until offered a job in another. It is possible that Parker was the unnamed "ace sax man" caught by *Billboard* in a McShann performance at the Paradise in Detroit in October, "taking numerous mike passages" (11.14.42: 16). In December 1942, however, Parker certainly had taken a job in the orchestra of Earl Hines.

When the Hines band played the Apollo Theatre in October, the performance included material from the current popular song repertoire, with Madeleine Green singing "He's My Guy" that was a hit for Helen Forrest with Harry James. The other band singer, Billy Eckstine, sang the Mercer-Carmichael "Skylark," "Take Me" (recorded earlier by Frank Sinatra and Dick Haymes), and the dreaming song "Just As Though You Were Here" (*Var.* 10.14.42: 22). Shortly after this, Hines heard a young female singer, Sarah Vaughan, in a talent contest at the Apollo and hired her to sing alongside Eckstine. There were no recordings of the 1942–1943 Earl Hines band; histories of jazz often regret that an organization that brought together Parker, Gillespie, and other "revolutionaries" left no recordings. But, given the presence of two such vocalists as Eckstine and Vaughan and the repertoire the band was playing as late as October 1942, it is likely that any missing recordings would present the popular song repertoire as much as any signs of incubating bebop. Parker had quit the "routine swing" of McShann, but he had not left behind the world of popular music.

To view Charlie Parker as a man involved in popular music and popular culture is not to diminish him. This view is at least as consistent with what is known of his life as is the concept of Parker as a "highbrow," a high-art figure, a modernist in the line of Pablo Picasso, James Joyce, or Arnold Schoenberg. The critical discourse that has promulgated the high-art Parker has itself been hostile to popular culture, in the manner of Adorno, or at least convinced of its inferiority. If, however, we accept that there can be value in the products of commercial popular culture, it is no discredit to Parker to place him in this context.

It is possible to hold the view that Parker was one of the greatest of twentieth-century musicians without needing to convert him into a self-conscious artistic modernist and without denying his working in the popular art of music. The consensus around jazz, however, was formed at a time when there were persuasive critical forces denigrating popular music and culture. Jazz criticism did not in the 1940s, and has not since, come to an accommodation with popular culture, as has the study of film, which is comfortable with the idea that there can be great creativity and power of expression within popular forms. For writers on jazz, there has been no way of taking a popular form like jazz seriously without taking it *seriously*.

Fats Waller was the first jazz artist to have his talents presented in Carnegie Hall in 1942. Waller was a composer of numerous popular songs, a brilliant pianist in the Harlem style, and a powerful and distinctive singer. He was also a great impromptu comedian with a charismatic personality, which he projected in clubs and theaters, in recordings, and in movie appearances. The stage of Carnegie Hall, however, represented none of these familiar settings for Waller's musicianship and individuality.

A parameter used by ethnomusicologists in the description of a musical event is "context of performance." Carnegie Hall was for Waller, twenty years into his musical career, a radical change of context. Such was the intensity of Waller's performance style (depicted in Eudora Welty's story "Powerhouse"; 1943: 184–197) that there was a possibility that he could impose himself upon this new context. But Waller's style was founded on warm rapport with an audience. It was not one to translate easily to a venue where classical protocols were in place. Waller, who had a solid knowledge of the classical piano repertoire, must have been conscious of the norms that applied in the new setting in which he had been placed.

Although Waller harbored side-ambitions as a performer of classical music, the initiative to present him at Carnegie Hall on January 14, 1942, was taken by the promoter Ernie Anderson. It was not by chance that the auditorium on 57th Street and Seventh Avenue was the one chosen: Carnegie Hall had long represented for the popular musician an idea more than a real place. As a symbol of a higher level of professional esteem, a dreamed-of ultimate destination, Carnegie Hall remained in the popular musician's mythology for many years. A musicians' joke about the way to get to Carnegie Hall ("Practice!") was current into the 1960s. In the 1954 film *The Benny Goodman Story*, his 1938 concert in Carnegie Hall functions as the narrative triumph, in accordance with its place in the prevailing myth of final artistic recognition. Carnegie Hall reflected the popular musician's awareness of the existing hierarchy of musical forms and symbolized what they called "legitimacy."

Fats Waller was performing in an unfamiliar context that put constraints on qualities of his performance identity that made him outstanding. He was also coping with the weight of social and artistic myth. Further, although Waller was used to playing with his regular band, and lately with his big band, he played most of the Carnegie Hall concert completely solo. If not quite a disaster, the concert fell short of the triumph Waller and Anderson had envisioned. Waller seemed hesitant and uncertain of his material and understandably "overawed." Dan Burley's review in the *Amsterdam News* said, "whether he laid an egg on this, his first appearance as a concert artist, is open to question." Burley described Waller as seeming "lonely as he faced the massive Steinway . . . Carnegie Hall, it seemed, had awed the great Fats Waller." Another phrase succinctly expressed the sense of two distinct identities coming into conflict, with one subduing the other, "In a word, Fats Waller went 'Carnegie Hall' instead of making Carnegie Hall go 'Fats Waller.'" (*AN* 1.24.42: 1).

Even if the concert had been a success, in what sense was Waller better presented in Carnegie Hall than in the theater and club dates he was doing at this time? Supposing Waller had succeeded in making the transition to classical concert venues, in what sense would this represent the best outcome? If Waller had transferred his style and presence intact into the concert context, nothing would essentially have been gained; if he had permanently "gone Carnegie Hall," then much of what had previously made him original would have to be abandoned. Waller was a performer whose style had many facets; to isolate the "pure" musical element among the complex flavors of his style would be another instance of the abstraction that was being required of jazz as a cultural form. Waller would have to shed the entertainment function if he was to be accorded the esteem that was denied to popular musicians by jazz critics. In Waller's case, this imperative seems particularly destructive.

Other artists took to the Carnegie Hall stage later in the year. A few weeks after Waller's concert, groups of traditional or Dixieland players organized by Eddie Condon began a series of appearances that were more successful. This was perhaps due to Condon's energetic approach to promotion and publicity and the strong group sense of the bands he put together. From February 21, a similar aggregation of players began a series of performances in New York's Town Hall. This was an offshoot of a longstanding jam-session establishment at Jimmy Ryan's on 52nd Street, as Condon's was of a regular series at Nick's. The trumpeter Max Kaminsky was one of the participants in a wave of renewed interest in older styles, and he was a regular at Ryan's and the Town Hall concerts. Both venues were successful, but it is noticeable that Kaminsky reserved his praise for the more vernacular club setting, "There was a moment there, in 1941–1942, at the Ryan's sessions, when hot jazz seemed at its purest" (Kaminsky and Hughes 1965: 122).

But if hot jazz or other popular styles were to move to the new performance context of the concert stage, they could not be unaffected. The musicological notion of performance context is not merely descriptive of circumstances around an existing musical form, it is a *defining* factor. Context, together with other factors, creates the character of the musical event; that is, context changes it, makes it different from how it would otherwise be. If jazz or any other popular form were to shift to the concert-hall context, this would inevitably change its nature. Presenting jazz in concert would not be simply putting the same picture in a different frame—the jazz that would be performed would be a different jazz from the one that first entered the concert context. Thus, concert presentation was not a way of showcasing jazz to better advantage, it was a way of changing its character.

For a musician like Benny Goodman, this shift had some personal coherence. In early 1942 he was on a tour that alternated classical concertos accompanied by a symphony orchestra with sets by his big band. The two strands were kept separate, however, with no indication that Goodman wished to shift his big band to a classical context. But some other musicians were showing themselves amenable to jazz undergoing the change of identity that would flow from concert-hall ambitions. Such progression was in accordance with the conception of a serious high-art jazz that was beginning to be promulgated by such critics as Feather and Ulanov. Among 1942 contributions to *Metronome*, at this time coedited by Ulanov, there were disparaging references to nonmusical performers appearing on theater bills with jazz players. A reader's letter complains of "stage shows in which you expect to see some name band—what do you hear or rather see? Vaudeville singers, dancers, comedians and jugglers" (*Metr.* 1.42: 5). Several months later, Ulanov sympathized with Andy Kirk's sharing the stage at

Loew's State with "a couple of acrobats, some ballroom dancing, and like as not, a dismal comedian" (8.42: 16). Does the description "vaudeville singers, dancers, comedians and jugglers" apply to such outstanding performers in their fields as Marie Bryant, White's Lindy Hoppers, Jackie Mabley, Honi Coles, Scatman Crothers, Cholly Atkins, Bill Robinson, Ethel Waters, and other black or white practitioners of these skills?

Stan Kenton was the musician whose conception best matched the prospect of a classical future of jazz and who was favorable to a change in its performance contexts. The arrival in New York in early 1942 of Kenton's orchestra was one of the most anticipated events of the year. As *Down Beat* commented, "Kenton and his spectacular ork have rolled up an amazing record on the coast in the last six months" (2.1.42: 1). Kenton's band had been resident at the Rendezvous Ballroom at Balboa Beach in Los Angeles; an engagement at Glendale Auditorium had seen fans virtually out of control and a near-riot taking place. Kenton's repertoire already had incidental clues to his conception of classical status: song titles and radio links make use of some of the vocabulary of classical performance, "opus," "concerto," "setting," and "elegie."

When Kenton opened in February at the inappropriately conservative Roseland Ballroom, *Down Beat* reported that his was "a band that shapes up as one of those sensations.... Stan Kenton is going to be a great big name one of these days." But the reviewer, the jazz-oriented critic George Frazier, went on to clarify his reaction, "To me, it's terrific in a revolting way" (3.1.42: 11). This was an early instance of a response that some jazz writers were to have to Kenton for his entire career. In the review, Frazier set out specific antipathies to the band's style: "it's much too pretentious, much too much out for Significance rather than for the natural flow of the music," and "I cannot stand performers who take themselves too seriously, and it is my impression that practically everyone in the Kenton band owns a complete set of Aeschylus." This is certainly not a high-art criticism, as Frazier's preferences leaned toward hot jazz; in this instance it was the artist whose high-art demeanor challenged the sympathies of a more vernacular critic.

In a July review of a Kenton radio broadcast, referring to a tendency toward loudness, the reviewer commented, "that's what Kenton does, whether playing a ballad or a novelty, his band pounds and pounds." For this writer also, this musical fault was linked to a problem of attitude, "The fault seems to lie in a complete lack of humor. We never knew music could be a matter of such dead seriousness. The result, of course, is diminished appeal as far as the general, unappreciative public is concerned" (*BB* 7.18.42: 22).

Kenton's orchestra was still playing for dancers at Roseland and the Meadowbrook, but its heavy dynamics were not what most dancers were accustomed to. There was some strain in the relationship between the public entertainment function and the different orientation apparent in Kenton's music. During 1942 there were reviews of Kenton performances that seem to represent stages in a struggle between these two forces. The band could swing effectively for the audience at the Savoy, where, after microphone problems had hampered earlier acts, "'twas okay when Stan Kenton and crew took over and the house rocked" (*AN* 10.31.42: 16). A review in *Variety* detected a softening of attitude on Kenton's part. Of a performance at the New York Strand Theater in which Kenton appeared with the tap dancer Doreen Russell and The Three Stooges, the reviewer commented that "Kenton has straightened out, at least for stage purposes, his seeming aversion to commercial music" (*Var.* 10.21.42: 52).

But a backstage interview with Kenton in St. Louis a few months later found him in an uncompromising visionary mood. He told *Down Beat* that, "Someday—and that day is not very far off—millions of Americans will pay big money to attend jazz concerts in stadiums from Cape Cod to San Diego" and that if he failed in achieving this goal he would go back to playing in saloons (*DB* 2.1.43: 15). Kenton's vision of a postwar America of jazz played in settings resembling the Hollywood Bowl is grand scale; it was only by the 1960s that stadiums were filled by popular musicians, and then it was for rock concerts. It is significant, however, that in this vision jazz becomes a music relieved of responsibility for entertainment and dance and assuming the classical model of composer, orchestra, and listener.

Kenton later spoke of jazz as not needing to swing and not needing to feature improvisation (Hentoff and Shapiro 1962: 369, 372). It is clear that what Kenton had in mind was that jazz should become "America's classical music" in a literal sense. This would require a continued application of an abstraction that was being formulated in the critical writings and initiatives of those years, jazz as a music with a specific essence that should be presented intact and unmixed, removed from the performance contexts in which it had operated, from the world of entertainment it had somehow become involved with, and, above all, from any association with popular music. Kenton was categorical on this last point. In comments published in Hentoff and Shapiro's *Hear Me Talkin' to Ya*, he said jazz should never have been "mixed up with popular music" (1962: 372).

Kenton's views are consistent with the new conception of jazz that was synthesized and articulated by others during the early 1940s: jazz needed to be lifted into its rightful place above surrounding American musical forms. Jazz would be autonomous, independent of the lower forms of musical culture with which it had been mistakenly implicated. It would begin to look and behave like classical music. Jazz would reestablish the creative freedom it had lost by surrendering its essential nature to the world of entertainment, especially during the preceding decade of swing. Jazz would also discover the dynamic of progress—it was essential to jazz, as it was to science, to surpass in each period the ideas of the one before. Jazz had, for instance, "conquered" the chromatic scale (Green 1973: 129). According to Kenton, it was facing a utopia of vast stadiums dedicated to the notions of progressive jazz composers.

But in the vitriolic critical atmosphere of the later 1940s, for many other parties, including a sizeable sector of the jazz community, this was such a misguided conception as to represent the enemy. Simultaneously with Kenton's arrival on the scene and the progressive projection of a classicized jazz future, an exactly opposite philosophy, "revivalism," was being formulated elsewhere. Rather than seeking a vindication of jazz in the future, revivalism held that the essence of jazz lay, partly concealed, in the past. As a cultural phenomenon, revivalism was complex, but by the end of 1942 the forms in which it was emerging primarily consisted of several distinct groups of musicians rediscovering older styles and a critical literature giving the rediscovery its rationale.

A taste for small-group hot jazz played in a style that predated swing was being catered for by groups such as the Condon musicians at such places as Jimmy Ryan's and Nick's. This was a relatively nonideological wing of the movement, musicians who a few years earlier had been playing this kind of music in any case. In California, white bands featuring such musicians as Lu Watters and Turk Murphy were more consciously recreating older styles and rejecting newer ones. The most critically significant movement among the revivalist tendency, however, was the group of writers and researchers who were literally recreating the music of 1920s New Orleans, writers such as Frederick Ramsey Jr. and Charles Edward Smith (1958), who had actually searched the Deep South for the old-time players and were relaunching them in authentic revivalist ensembles. The most celebrated returnee was the cornetist William "Bunk" Johnson, reclaimed from rural obscurity and supplied by revivalist fans with the means to begin a career as a recording artist at the reported age of sixty-two in November 1942.

This tendency could hardly have been more different in outlook from Kenton's. An early 1942 review of a recording by Lu Watters predicted correctly that its approach would "split the country's jazzophiles into warring camps" (DB 2.15.42: 12). The two camps held incompatible versions of the narrative of jazz. For the revivalists, it was a story of expulsion and diaspora from the spiritual homeland of New Orleans, followed by years in the wilderness before the current revival. For them, the only future was a return to the paradisal past—no progression was possible or desirable. In any case, they did not regard later forms as jazz at all, and Kenton's music in 1942 would have struck them as outlandish. Yet, the progressivist-modernists and the revivalists shared some axiomatic views of the nature of jazz. For both parties, jazz was a pure music, in the sense of being music only and of being free of corrupting outside influences. Both held that jazz, however differently they conceived of it, stood against the values of entertainment and was not in any way to be confused with popular music. Both groups believed that jazz needed to be extricated from involvement with these things not essential to its nature.

Despite vast ideological differences in other respects, a musician like Kenton and the revivalist promoters of musicians like Bunk Johnson insisted alike that the music be presented in concert format. Among the revivalists, respect was paid to the diverse functions of music in New Orleans society, in particular the funeral parades (Blesh 1976: 170–172), but when Johnson and George Lewis were presented on the nation's stages, the typical performance was as classicized as Kenton's were. For both parties, the performance of jazz called for seriousness in the performer and respectful attention in the listener. By the 1950s, this new self-conception of jazz and its norms of performance would be permanently established. In the first years of World War II, however, the effort of separation from popular culture and elevation of jazz above other American forms was just gathering itself.

Chapter 6

The Avenue

Simplicity was the way out of isolation for the contemporary composer.
—AARON COPLAND (Copland and Perls 1984: 279)

The summer of 1942 saw a series of premiere performances that had a strong reference to the United States in wartime and secondarily to some iconic figures of American popular music. George M. Cohan, writer of the songs of the last war, was celebrated in June with the opening of the film *Yankee Doodle Dandy*, in which the part of Cohan was given an energetic performance by James Cagney. Cohan had died in May, having given his imprimatur to his film representation. Irving Berlin, whose career also went back to the early years of the century, appeared in person in his new hit show *This Is the Army*, which opened July 4. Berlin used his own small voice to sing the title song, but the rest of the cast and personnel were drawn from the U.S. Army. As *Variety* commented, "The 1942 saga of the American soldier playing theatre is not only great propaganda, tremendous Americanism and an excellent example of American democracy in practical work—it's an extraordinary, superb entertainment" (7.8.42: 24). On the same day, Aaron Copland's *Lincoln Portrait* was performed in Washington, D.C. The players were stationed on barges on the Potomac, in the presence of senators, congressmen, and members of Roosevelt's cabinet. A year earlier, Copland had written that it was unreasonable to ignore the audience that "had grown up around the radio and the phonograph" (1941: 229). The *Lincoln Portrait* was an accessible work that has remained the most performed of all Copland's works.

During that same week in July, features on stage at the Apollo in Harlem included Benny Carter's big band and the dance team Tip, Tap, and Toe. In Chicago, attractions were Horace Henderson's band at the Rhumboogie Club and Louis Armstrong's at the Regal, where the movie was *Shanghai Gesture*, starring Victor Mature and Gene Tierney. In Pittsburgh, at the Stanley Theatre, *Variety* caught the Tommy Dorsey band and devoted much space to a secondary attraction, "Unusual for a band vocalist to get the closing spot, but that's the lot of Frank Sinatra; he fills it—and how! Crowd simply wouldn't let him get off and ran the opening performance overtime by at least 15 minutes" (*Var.* 7.8.42: 48).

Under the headline "Orks Drop Like Flies," *Billboard* listed "bands which have ceased existence since the start of the war: Terry Shand, George Olsen, Red Norvo, Will Bradley and Larry Clinton," all of whom had "soured on bandleading's headaches" (7.18.42: 19). The same issue struck a positive note reviewing Bing Crosby's recording of a country song (then known by *Billboard* as "hillbilly" or "American folk"), "Walkin' the Floor over You." Ernest Tubb's composition joined two other Western-flavored songs, "Deep in the Heart of Texas" and "(I've Got Spurs That) Jingle Jangle Jingle" among the successes of the middle of the year. Giving a favorable notice to Crosby's less authentic version, *Billboard* lent support to the genre as a whole, "Like most of the hillbilly music, this close-to-the-good-earth ditty is even more free in spirit and spontaneous in expression. The charm, of course, lies in its naturalness and simplicity" (7.18.42: 22).

A prospect of relief from a problem facing record manufacturers came in June, "Ersatz Shellac Hopes High." Efforts to produce a substitute for shellac had issued in a material that lacked durability, but *Billboard* theorized that "for average home consumption, a 30–50 performance per platter is adequate, and even if it gets a little muddy or scratchy with repetitive playings, the average home owner won't squawk" (6.3.42: 39).

The middle of 1942 was not a favorable time to be starting a record company, but the year saw the launch of several independent labels, the most successful of which was Capitol, inaugurated in Hollywood in April.

From the start, the Capitol management adopted a defiantly upbeat attitude. *Down Beat* quoted one of the founders, Glen Wallichs, "We're going into the open market for the best songs and the best performers we can give the public. We plan a complete catalogue that will offer sweet music, swing music, Hawaiian, hill billy and race music" (4.15.42: 12). Capitol already had access to good material, as two of its founders were the songwriters Buddy DeSylva and Johnny Mercer, whose writing career was at its peak. Mercer also worked as talent finder and recording producer, and some of the freshness of Capitol's output was due to his judgment of popular material. The new label received good press in part because of sheer nerve. "What gets me," said a *Down Beat* writer in July, "is that with everybody else in the business putting up the shutters, these guys are setting out full of drive and confidence that they can make a go of it" (7.15.42: 10). When the first Capitol issues appeared, *Down Beat* headlined them "Splendid," with "Quality, Choice of Material Both Excellent." The first issues included two immediate successes, the novelty Mercer song "Strip Polka" and a boogie-woogie number given a cowboy lyric and sung by Ella Mae Morse, "Cow Cow Boogie."

DeSylva and Mercer also were involved in the movie industry, and the company benefited from Hollywood connections and talent. Another advantage was the economy of southern California and the West Coast. California had run an expansive economy even in the late 1930s, and with the approach of war defense industries such as aircraft and ship construction moved into high gear. By the early 1940s, white Southerners were being encouraged to take jobs in the Douglas and Lockheed aircraft plants, the Kaiser and Long Beach shipyards, and in other industries that served war production. The situation was as found in cities such as Detroit or Buffalo but on a larger scale. The war produced a historic shift in the population of California—of a magnitude unmatched in other parts of the nation and permanently affecting the cultural character of the Golden State.

The wartime growth of the West Coast economy and its function as a magnet for workers from across the nation had a significant effect upon American popular music. Until the eve of war, the influx of a black population had been held back by restrictive employment practices in defense and other industries. Even without the black presence, which grew only gradually before 1942, the massive shift of white Southerners and Westerners had already brought about a displacement of white working-class musical culture. Hillbilly music was receiving press attention at a national level. Traveling country spectaculars and radio shows with huge territorial coverage, such as the *Grand Ole Opry* and *National Barn Dance*, were making a broad and deep impact. In June a major venue for the music of transplanted Southern-white culture was opened at Venice Beach pier near Los Angeles. Massive ballrooms such as this gave country music some of the force and the celebratory qualities that many Americans enjoyed in big-band swing.

The West Coast industries continued to need additional workers, and Executive Order 8802 largely outlawed the restrictive practices familiar before the war. By the late summer of 1942, the majority of defense industries in the West were at last open to black Americans. With income in the defense industries 40 percent higher than the national average—and most blacks accustomed to something below the national average—the economic incentives to travel west were strong. Black Southern migrants also found the racism of California relatively slight, though incidents such as the 1941 segregation of Duke Ellington from his musicians in an Oakland restaurant have already been noted and witnesses to the period have their own instances. Some Los Angeles areas did not accept black residents, and trouble was taken to exclude them even as visitors. Virtually all entertainment venues were in effect segregated. The Trianon Ballroom, for instance, where the Ellington band played a summer residency, was for white patrons only.

The black musical culture that grew with immigration was associated with the section of Los Angeles around Central Avenue, a corridor running south of downtown into which the majority of the black population, hemmed in by residential restrictions, were concentrated. Other areas had sections where black music flourished, but "Central Avenue" became a metonym for black Los Angeles as "Harlem" had for black New York (and for black culture generally). The San Francisco area had a focus of black music in Oakland, where blues was a specialty, and other West Coast cities had their own "Central Avenues," for instance, in Seattle the area around Jackson Street.

Los Angeles's Central Avenue was a long strip of hotels, theaters, clubs, bars, restaurants, and places of entertainment. Its peak years began in 1942 and extended into the late 1940s. By 1942 there were establishments such as the Cotton Club, the Lincoln Theatre, and Club Alabam, as well as informal places like Lovejoy's, where Art Tatum played with a crate of Pabst beer on top of the piano. From 1941 to late 1942 Lester Young was in his brother Lee's band at the Trouville, described by Lee Young as a "gorgeous" place and owned by the entrepreneur Billy Berg (Bryant et al. 1998: 62). Berg's clubs featured some of the most remarkable musicians of the time, from Benny Carter to Charlie Parker, singers such as Joe Turner and Billie Holiday, and musical entertainers such as Leo Watson and Harry "The Hipster" Gibson. Upscale places like Berg's attracted a racially mixed crowd. With some of his clubs situated in Hollywood, Berg's clientele was drawn from the movie industry, including Humphrey Bogart, Lana Turner, Ava Gardner, and the black performers then featured in film roles.

By the start of the war, Central Avenue had known prosperity as well as slump and shutdowns motivated by the city authorities' sense of racial morality. Musicians fondly remembered the main period of Central Avenue's ascendancy, beginning in mid-1942. "Everything worthwhile happened on Central or close to Central," said the trombonist Jack Kelson. "Central Avenue had any and everything you might want" (Bryant 1998: 232). The pianist Fletcher Smith, who played there with the Les Hite and Lionel Hampton bands, drew comparisons with other locales of the period, "I've been to all those places that were supposed to be swinging, like Kansas City, Chicago and New York, and all those places. But they didn't swing like Central Avenue" (1998: 87). By the early 1940s few well-known musicians had emerged from the California scene, and these usually originated elsewhere, such as Lionel Hampton from Chicago and Charles Mingus from Arizona. After 1942 there were others who rose to success through associations with the Avenue and its music outlets: Nat "King" Cole, Dexter Gordon, Slim Gaillard, T-Bone Walker, Joe Liggins, Charles Brown, Johnny Otis, Wynonie Harris, Jimmy Witherspoon, Roy Milton, and Big Jay McNeely.

From the point of view of most histories, this list is mixed. It throws in blues artists such as Walker and Witherspoon; jazz players such as Gordon; jazzman-turned-pop-singer Cole; rhythm-and-blues performers Harris, Milton, and Liggins; and Otis, whose later career is linked with rock and roll. But, as we have seen in other domains, the mixed environment is more frequently encountered than is the pure. In the early 1940s categories of music were intermingled, not perceived as distinct, or not perceived at all.

Even though we now see Dexter Gordon as belonging to a separate cultural formation from, say, T-Bone Walker, it is likely that all pairings from the above list were acquainted, worked in the same venues, and saw themselves as sharing the same musical culture. In the real context of a specific place like Central Avenue, the elements that have since been separated were part of a single field.

At this point, we again run into the different and competing musical-historical narratives, primarily that of jazz. The received view in these sources of the progress of black popular music is that, from the mid-1940s, a large number of musicians and a majority of the public abandoned jazz for a style described as "rhythm-and-blues" (e.g., Stearns 1956: 218). Whereas blues, in the older rural forms, is classified as a part of the prehistory of jazz and as therefore a thing of value, rhythm-and-blues is generally looked on as a degenerate form not associated with the jazz narrative at all. There are several reasons for this. First, jazz was seen as progressing to a plane of greater complexity in the mid-1940s, and the simplicity of rhythm-and-blues represented a failure to cope with its intellectual and technical demands on the part of both players and the public (Schuller 1989: 391). Second, rhythm-and-blues was seen to represent a further stage of commercialized decline, coming on the heels of the discredited swing period, and now pulling previously uncorrupt black culture into its orbit (Schuller 1989: 391). The fact that, on the whole, the black American public voted for this music was problematic for critics of jazz.

Rhythm-and-blues could not be incorporated into the jazz narrative because it was contemporaneous with progressivism. Logically, the only place for a less complex form was as a forerunner, as in the case of blues. Yet, here was rhythm-and-blues—simple, direct, and mostly in classic twelve-bar form—developing at the same time that bebop was being installed as the appropriate form in the narrative. As David Ake (2002: 42–61) showed, a widespread critical assumption was that jazz should now develop along the parameters of complexity and classicism and shed the entertainment function—and with it sacrifice the expectation of a mass audience (except in Kenton's vision of jazz stadiums). Black music or not, rhythm-and-blues was doing none of these things and was consequently to be excluded with prejudice from the jazz narrative. This exclusion, however, was not a fact of musicians' experience on Central Avenue or elsewhere.

T-Bone Walker was born in Texas and had early associations with Blind Lemon Jefferson, thus giving him credentials as a blues player. By the late 1940s his music, while not actually changing, would be classified as "rhythm-and-blues." In the meantime Walker acquired a claim to jazz status through his stay in the Les Hite orchestra, in which he played alongside Dexter Gordon. This candidature for three different genres is confusing. What Walker was doing, in fact, was essentially one thing, and it is the categorization that produces any difficulties. Jimmy Witherspoon could also be divided between the same three categories. The rougher styles of Roy Milton and Joe Liggins are not distinct from the work of Walker and Witherspoon, but their rhythm-and-blues categorization suggests that they were.

More than any of the others, Johnny Otis exemplifies the difficulties and distortions that can be provoked by categories and purism in a field as complex as musical culture. Johnny Otis, a Greek-American raised in Oakland's black community, became a drummer and later an entrepreneur and bandleader. His first top-level jobs were in the Omaha territory bands, where he worked with Buddy Tate and Preston Love in the Lloyd Hunter and Nat Towles bands. Otis was an admirer of the Count Basie band, especially its brilliant and influential drummer, Jo Jones. Otis later wrote of a 1941 Basie performance, "Preston Love and I haunted the Orpheum when the great Black bands played there. During one Count Basie engagement, we sat through almost every set, every day. It was just as thrilling during the final show as during the first" (Otis 1993: 120). Thus far, by experience and taste, Otis fits the profile of a jazz musician.

After his return to California, Otis became house drummer at the Central Avenue spot Club Alabam. In this capacity, he was continuously in contact with styles of music heard within the Los Angeles scene. Naturally, Otis was aware of stylistic changes taking place. Some of the artists playing the spectrum of styles were later classified as jazz musicians, whereas others acquired other designations. The Kansas City orchestra of Harlan Leonard, for instance, comes under consideration in the jazz narrative; others, such as Wynonie Harris, are classified as rhythm-and-blues performers. But for Otis, "from my vantage point on the drummer's stool in the Club Alabam," there was no cutoff point between the styles of these and other performers he names; "I could see the music that was to be named rhythm and blues taking shape" (Otis 1993: 46). At this point, we fall off the edge of the jazz narrative into the lower regions. But for Otis, this new music had its inspiration and origin among musicians whose place in the jazz narrative is partly secure, "These new show stoppers grew out of the Lionel Hampton, Louis Jordan, Ray Nance, Jimmy Rushing, Illinois Jacquet tradition" (1993: 46). For critics this is another problematic list: Hampton, Rushing, and Nance were associated with such axiomatic jazz figures as Duke Ellington and Count Basie, whereas Jordan was a casualty of category disputes. Illinois Jacquet's case is a particularly interesting one; an excellent conventional jazz saxophonist, his reputation among jazz critics was tainted by "exhibitionistic" playing that hinted at rhythm-and-blues allegiances (Schuller 1989: 398).

For Otis the black performers he encountered were "demonstrating that artistry, energy and fun could coexist in Black music without sacrificing artistic integrity" (1993: 46). More and more, however, a self-conscious jazz aesthetic was requiring the separation of these qualities. For Otis (1993: 46) bebop was not revolutionary but rather "conservative." For the jazz critical community, conversely, the music called "rhythm-and-blues" was exhibitionistic and vulgar. These two bodies of opinion moved apart. For jazz critics, rhythm-and-blues represented a vulgarization of black music; for a working musician such as Otis, the same music demonstrating that "the jazz and the blues elements were coming together" (1993: 46). These were two incompatible narratives of the Los Angeles scene. For jazz critics, rhythm-and-blues was neither an acceptable variation upon jazz nor an embodiment of blues, and thus not deserving the cultural value attached to either of these forms.

In retrospect, it is difficult to see compelling reasons for separating these styles of black music from the stream of jazz or vice versa. Like jazz players, rhythm-and-blues musicians improvised. Louis Jordan, for instance, was a skilled saxophonist and had in his playing Southwestern blues inflections. Rhythm-and-blues swung. It had deep connections with the blues, but jazz writers were unwilling to credit rhythm-and-blues with the "folk" virtues that the blues possessed.[1] Rhythm-and-blues could be bawdy and celebratory, or in Otis's terms "down-to-earth, uninhibited." It should have been possible to see a likeness between the music of Joe Liggins, Wynonie Harris, and T-Bone Walker and that of earlier black performers such as Ma Rainey, Bessie Smith, and Louis Armstrong.

Early performances within the jazz narrative were sometimes praised for their simplicity. In rhythm-and-blues, however, simplicity became a failing; and there were further contradictions. The jazz tradition was seen as deriving much of its value from its status as the music of black Americans. Yet, a music such as rhythm-and-blues, which by the mid-1940s demonstrably had a mass audience of black Americans, derived no value from that fact. Among other things, rhythm-and-blues was entertainment, a fatal flaw from the perspective of jazz critics. At a time when jazz was accruing value in proportion to its distance from the entertainment function, the rhythm-and-blues idiom could only forfeit value because of its closeness to entertainment.

Finally, for the jazz narrative, the progressivist agenda was an obstacle to a rapprochement between this emerging black music style and jazz. If high complexity was the goal of any worthy musical tradition, there was no direction for the critical status of rhythm-and-blues to go but downward. Rhythm-and-blues improvisers whose blues playing clung to simpler pre-bebop harmonies were not eligible for the critical approval of the jazz community. No matter that earthy simplicity had been admired in blues artists and in jazz players such as Johnny Dodds and would be again, in the twist in the jazz narrative that approved of the "funky" jazz of Horace Silver and Cannonball Adderley, rhythm-and-blues players were doing simplicity at the wrong time.

Dismissive critical comment on rhythm-and-blues styles is found in the jazz literature up to the present day (Ake 2002: 42–61). However, the critical orthodoxy that fixed this separation was not in place by the first years of World War II and was not in evidence in the day-to-day traffic of the music scene in places like Central Avenue. Johnny Otis worked with performers such as Count Basie, Earl Hines, Jimmie Lunceford, and Lionel Hampton (all jazz) and T-Bone Walker, Louis Jordan, and Wynonie Harris (all rhythm-and-blues), but Otis's experience was not one of switching between two separate idioms of music. Contemporary listeners could recognize differences between the playing styles of Teddy Wilson, Slim Gaillard, Johnny Hodges, and Charles Brown without assigning these artists to separate musical categories, with all the attendant distinctions of value and esteem.

The American popular music audience of 1942, whether black or white, did not operate with the criteria that were fixed by postwar critical orthodoxies, with jazz as the predominant mode of valuation. Like the musicians who came and went from the Club Alabam, the featured artists in 1942 at the Apollo Theatre demonstrate an absence of separate categories. Bands at the Apollo from the week of Pearl Harbor onward included Jimmie Lunceford, Count Basie, Earl Hines, Louis Armstrong, Ella Fitzgerald, Fats Waller, and Andy Kirk, all of whom were classified as jazz artists. But other headliners were the bands of Tiny Bradshaw, Louis Jordan, and Eddie Vinson, who represent a shift toward rhythm-and-blues. Others, such as the Ink Spots, the Mills Brothers, and Louis Prima, seem to us more like popular-music acts. But can we suppose that the Harlem audience of 1942 thought of these performers as constantly shifting between "jazz" and "nonjazz"? Can we even assume that when the Ink Spots made their regular appearances, the Apollo audiences thought of them as categorically different from, say, Lucky Millinder, who was due up the following week? Bands like Millinder's exemplify the nonseparation between what later became codified as jazz and what became known as "rhythm-and-blues." In fact, Millinder's band seems to have acquired a place in the jazz narrative only because for a few weeks in 1942 it featured Dizzy Gillespie. The Millinder band's book otherwise leaned toward a style that might demote it into the rhythm-and-blues category. It featured many blues numbers, with vocals by Trevor Bacon or Sister Rosetta Tharpe, whose powerful voice and electric guitar could be classed as proto-rhythm-and-blues.

Tharpe's equivalent in the Les Hite band was the sensational T-Bone Walker. Walker, an excellent and original blues guitarist, was also a spectacular entertainer who performed stunts such as playing the guitar behind his back. (To the discomfort of many jazz purists, two decades later Walker was featured in Norman Granz's "Jazz at the Philharmonic" tours.) A 1942 report from the *Amsterdam News*'s Chicago correspondent has Walker as "the sensation of the west chirping nothing but the blues" (9.12.42: 8). At the Rhumboogie Club, Walker was billed as "Hollywood's Famous Blues Shouter." Featured together with another band with a rhythm-and-blues tendency, Milt Larkin, Walker received rave notices in the *Chicago Defender*, "the applause is tumultuous at the conclusion of each Larkin rendition and unbelievable when Teabone [sic] Walker departs" (8.15.42: 12).

It is noticeable that in 1942 other black bands were performing and recording strongly rhythmic numbers that emphasized the blues aspect of their styles. Bands like those of Kirk, Lunceford, and even Basie were using a riffing, jivey style that recalled what Louis Jordan was doing in small-band format. The Kirk band, notwithstanding the so-called revolutionary "McGhee Special," was recording pieces like "Take It and Git" and blues vocals by June Richmond. The Lunceford band had a hit with a song that was even more successful for Louis Jordan, the blues number "I'm Gonna Move to the Outskirts of Town." Basie's recordings in the summer of 1942 used his singer Jimmy Rushing in a series of blues and jive numbers. Southwestern bands like Basie's and Kirk's had come out of a background deeply marked by the blues; in the jazz aesthetic, that was definitely a good thing. But by mid-1942, without realizing it, these bands were straying dangerously near the edge of rhythm-and-blues.

Another popular band in which the same recessive tendency was noted by later jazz writers was Lionel Hampton's, the "mad, super-talented" band that had set Harlem "back on its haunches" (*AN* 12.6.41: 20). Hampton had a good track record as a jazz player, with the Goodman band and many well-regarded small groups. But from its inception in 1941, his own band emphasized rhythmic excitement. A *Variety* reviewer witnessed the band at the Earle Theatre in Philadelphia in May. The repertoire included two Johnny Mercer ballads, "Skylark" and "Tangerine," but what caught the reporter's ear was a feature for the tenor saxophonist Illinois Jacquet, "last, but by no means least, is the band's finale 'Flying Home.' It's one of the hottest hunks of jive scattered around these parts in many a moon. ... Both the bandsmen and the audience are limp when the curtain falls" (*Var.* 5.20.42: 23). Hampton was in the habit of extending this number to fifteen or twenty minutes, driving the rhythm onward and calling on Jacquet to take chorus after climactic chorus.

Hampton's band was involved in two sensational "battles of bands" in Harlem in the spring of 1942, the first against Erskine Hawkins, "whether Hampton 'took' Hawkins or whether the Hawk 'cut' Hampton was a moot question and one still being debated in the candy stores, drugstores, hotel lobbies, school locker rooms and on the street" (*AN* 3.28.42: 16). Within days of the Philadelphia date in May, Hampton was involved in a second battle, this time at the Savoy in competition with Count Basie's band. According to the *Amsterdam News* Harlem was "still buzzing" a week later. The Savoy somehow accommodated 6900 paid admissions, with crowds lining up four blocks along Lenox Avenue. The Basie orchestra was celebrated for its rhythm playing, and yet Hampton seems to have come out best, thanks to the unmatchable impact of their finale, "Lionel, whose band had already been established at the Home of Happy Feet, had the crowd with him from the start, and when his boys came through with their 16 minute arrangement of 'Flying Home,' there was nothing Basie could do to top it" (*AN* 5.23.42: 17).

On May 26, ten days after this triumph, the Hampton band put "Flying Home" on record. Though the time limitation of a disc reins it in to about one-fifth of live-performance length, "Flying Home" is an exciting recording. It was an immediate success, with six-figure sales by early August. The recording has a brief introduction by Hampton on vibraphone and a chorus in which the saxophone section plays the main riff. It ends with a rousing chorus including a call-and-response riff by Hampton and the trumpeter Ernie Royal. In between come the two thirty-two-bar choruses of Jacquet's saxophone solo.

Despite the renown of Jacquet's improvisation on "Flying Home" and its place in the literature of the tenor saxophone (to this day, many players memorize it), it attracted opprobrium among some jazz critics, and Jacquet's reputation never quite cast off its shadow. For Gunther Schuller, it was "a frantic tenor solo ... which became the model for hundreds of later honking rhythm-and-blues and rock-and-roll tenor players" (1989: 398). Schuller also noted that Jacquet later made reparations, "In fairness to Jacquet, although he continued to feature his squealing high-note and honking low-note style through his tenure with Jazz at the Philharmonic, he adopted a less exhibitionistic manner when he joined Count Basie in 1945 and is playing in a fine matured style to this day" (1989: 398 n). Compare another valuation by the jazz critic Leonard Feather, "His fast tempo solos, when not spoiled by unmusical gimmicks, are often genuinely exciting and show a fine sense of construction and climax" (1960: 266).

The solo put down by Jacquet at the Decca studios in May 1942 does not seem to deserve what Feather called his identification with "freak high notes and other artificial effects" (1960: 266) and it is a moot point whether it merits Schuller's term "frantic." Given that the solo's function is undoubtedly to raise the excitement level, it seems a controlled affair. There is virtually no distortion of the saxophone tone, no unusually high or low notes;

the solo is played within the compass of an octave and a half. The first chorus opens with a rolling glissando that settles on the third of the chord, and there follows a series of steadily rocking phrases that fall away to a conclusion at the end of each eight bars. The bridge features some looping rifflike phrases that might have been played by Charlie Christian. Only in the second chorus, with the tonic note rhythmically repeated twelve times in each of the first two eight-bar sections, does Jacquet do anything that might remotely be considered rabble-rousing—but it is actually rather calm and controlled—and the solo ends with a neat final phrase leading into the final full-band chorus. It is a well-paced, well-controlled, and at the same time a very exciting improvisation. Its reputation for frenzy is as exaggerated in the jazz narrative as the reputation of bebop for iconoclasm.

For Schuller, such a recording as "Flying Home" became successful because it located "the public's fevered pulse" in these days of early wartime, in the atmosphere he described as "the mounting pitch of war frenzy" (1989: 398). Yet, this so-called frenzy was also producing "Dearly Beloved," "I'm Old Fashioned," and "'I Left My Heart at the Stage Door Canteen." The idea of bad taste is invoked, in conjunction both with Jacquet's playing and with the wartime public's judgment. From this perspective rhythm-and-blues, which this solo is seen as foreshadowing, is a corruption of jazz, a falling away from its standards under the pressure of commercialism or the fevered circumstances of wartime, when the public's judgment had deserted it. Illinois Jacquet's so-called frenzied exhibitionistic solo of May 26, 1942, becomes one of the signals, if not one of the causes, of the forthcoming decline represented by the musical style rhythm-and-blues.

There were indications of a renewed taste for blues-based music, especially among black audiences. In addition to those mentioned above, there was the "jump" style of players like the saxophonist Pete Brown. This movement must have been apparent in the Central Avenue environment. But those involved in the music scene did not conceive of a music called "jazz" being degraded into a distinct music "rhythm-and-blues." As the saxophonist Buddy Collette recalled, "We didn't have the categories as much as we do now. T-Bone Walker and Pee Wee Crayton, all of them played at the Last Word and the Downbeat" (Bryant 1998: 148). Ralph Eastman, another writer on the California scene, said, "The strict compartmentalization of musical styles (bop, rhythm and blues, swing) that became common among critics, musicians and fans during the postwar period was not yet ingrained" (Cogdell Dje Dje and Meadows 1998: 96). In the words of Buddy Collette, "It was all a pretty good mixture" (Bryant 1998: 148).

The historical process by which swing gave way to rhythm-and-blues was gradual, without any moment of schism or abandonment of one in favor of the other. For instance, the Houston club run by Don Albert in the 1940s booked jazz players and rhythm-and-blues players without discrimination: Jay McShann, Earl Hines, and Louis Armstrong intermingled with Louis Jordan, Eddie Vinson, and Joe Liggins (Wilkinson 2001: 216). It is hard to believe that patrons of the Keyhole Club conceived of its booking policy as an alternation between different categories of music or different levels of taste. A broader, more inclusive continuum of musical culture than jazz surely encompassed all of these. All these performers represented expressions of black musical culture. This, however, was no proof against the disapproval of later jazz critics. The jump style of Pete Brown, for instance, was for Eric Hobsbaum, "a honking, jumping sometimes tasteless style *much appreciated in Harlem*" (1961: 155; emphasis mine). Compare this with a comment by Barry Ulanov in a review of a performance by the Les Hite band, on "two anguishing demonstrations of the falsetto tenor *that Harlem loves so much*" (*Metr.* 5.42: 21; emphasis mine). The good taste of "Harlem" could evidently be just as faulty as that of the American public at large.

From this moment, the values of the jazz critical community and those of the previously talismanic black audience diverge. An explication of the significance of this moment came in Marshall Stearns's authoritative *The Story of Jazz* (1956). By the early 1940s, according to Stearns, jazz had acquired enough "momentum and maturity" to experience a revolution "more or less within itself" (Stearns 1956: 218). This was bebop, "a quick and logical eruption within jazz" (note the stress on internality). For Stearns, this moment marked a stage of development in jazz at which it no longer had any relation to "new movements from the South." In other words, jazz in the form of bebop no longer had any necessary connection with a working-class black community; it had moved into a realm of virtually complete autonomy. Stearns mentioned the music (rhythm-and-blues) that "is heard on jukeboxes in black neighbourhoods." This was the music of the black working class, which could be omitted from the jazz narrative and taken no account of in assessments of musical value. Jazz now inhabited an art world, whereas other popular forms languished in the realms of entertainment and vulgarization.

What are we to make of phenomena such as the popular success of recordings like "Flying Home," the black music scenes of places like Central Avenue, the testimonies of such writers as Malcolm X and LeRoi Jones on the "artistry, energy and fun" of rhythm-and-blues? (See Malcolm X's description of seeing "Flying Home" performed at the Savoy one night in 1942; X and Haley 1965: 74). The question arises retrospectively in trying to deal with the dead hand of the jazz narrative. In the war-boomed economies of Los Angeles, San Francisco, Detroit, Boston, and elsewhere, there was the immediate experience of a musical idiom fluctuating, changing, and adapting, as musical cultures inevitably do. For Johnny Otis, in the thick of Central Avenue, the changing style was indicative not simply of a music but of an entire urban context and a way of living at a particular moment of history.

One of the changes Otis witnessed was that, "In the early forties Black entrepreneurs discovered that being a record manufacturer was not an unattainable ambition" (1993: 42). The growing and unprecedentedly well-off populations of southern California tilted the calculation in any potential record entrepreneur's favor. Capitol's success was one sign of encouragement, and there was an outbreak of small independent record labels for the first time in the long reign of the big-three companies, Columbia, Victor, and Decca. The classically jazz label Blue Note had begun recording in 1939, and Savoy was launched in Newark late in 1942.

A San Francisco company, Rhythm, had an isolated success in 1942 with the first California blues release, "S.K. Blues," by locally known artist Saunders King. Historically, independent labels have sometimes had difficulties with unexpected hits. Rhythm's problems with "S.K. Blues" recall the problems wartime brought with it: the record sold in tens of thousands and the company "had difficulty meeting demand for the record because of the wartime shellac shortage" (Cogdell Dje Dje and Meadows 1998: 105). Otis's remarks apply more to the end of the war, when companies like Exclusive and Excelsior were setting up around Los Angeles; within a few years, the Aladdin, Modern, Specialty, and Imperial labels were set up in Los Angeles, Chess in Chicago, King in Cincinnati, Atlantic in New York, and many others. Despite the outstanding launch of Capitol, conditions in 1942 were problematic for record companies to an extent unequalled in popular music history.

Shellac, the basic material in the manufacturing process, was in critically short supply. Companies tried to stockpile it, recycle it, or develop a substitute. Quotas had been imposed by government agencies on production of recordings, phonographs, and other materials. On the other hand, demand was buoyant, and sales were higher than they had been for many years. The record business had weathered the 1941 ASCAP dispute, which had shown how much the recording industry was dependent on the songwriting industry. Adding to all these other factors, a new crisis was about to demonstrate how much the songwriting industry was dependent on the record industry.

Dissatisfaction had been growing in the AFM, represented by James C. Petrillo, over the increasing use of recorded music in place of live musicians on radio stations and in other places where musicians found work. At the outbreak of war, Petrillo issued a statement that the AFM would take no strike action "for the duration." But by the time of AFM's convention in Houston in June 1942, the view was strongly held by Petrillo and others that musicians needed to be compensated for loss of employment and that the record companies should have a levy imposed to pay the compensation. When the record companies refused, Petrillo ordered that licenses they held with the AFM should not be renewed after July 31. This meant that no AFM member would make commercial recordings until the companies accepted the AFM's terms—in effect no professional musician in the country would be allowed to record. There were six weeks between Petrillo's announcement and the start of the recording ban. Some early press response to the proposed ban was sympathetic. *Variety* quoted Petrillo's motive as trying to ensure that "our people eat instead of starving." "Vivid in the struggle" a second article said, "is the now-old story of men against machines" invoking memories of the past troubled decade, in "a nation that has had 12 years to learn what not having a job means" (6.17.42: 41).

During this grace period between mid-June and the end of July, the record companies worked out strategies in the event of the ban being confirmed. The next edition of *Variety* reported, "The interim will probably be used by phonograph record and transcription makers alike to stock up on as many masters as possible" (6.24.42: 1). Transcription companies, which made recordings for broadcast by radio stations rather than for sale to the public, were equally affected by the ban. The jukebox operators were unrepentant, at least at first. Their customers, they declared, had been "spoiled by the finest music from the best bands," and would not happily revert to listening to local musicians in their place (6.24.42: 45).

As the negotiations and opposing press statements continued, the record companies began to stockpile recordings. By mid-July there was "day and night activity in the phonograph recording studios" (7.15.42: 41). During July 1942, virtually all American recording artists of any commercial viability went into the studios. Singers like Bing Crosby, the Andrews Sisters, the Mills Brothers, Carmen Miranda, and Tony Martin and the bands of Count Basie, Duke Ellington, Glenn Miller, Tommy Dorsey, Jimmy Dorsey, Cab Calloway, Jay McShann, Gene Krupa, Jimmie Lunceford, Charlie Barnet, and Guy Lombardo were in the studios during the push to get recordings in the can before a strike that might go on for many months. By mid-July it was estimated that the companies had stockpiled enough material to last through December. As July moved to a close, the tempo of activity speeded up even further. Between July 29 and the close of business on July 31, the following artists had recording sessions in New York and California: Connee Boswell, Dinah Shore, Kay Kyser (twice), Tony Pastor, the Casa Loma orchestra, Ella Fitzgerald, Benny Goodman, Woody Herman (twice), Harry James, Buddy Johnson, Andy Kirk, Mary Lee, Lucky Millinder, Dick Robertson, Fats Waller, and Teddy Wilson.

One of the immediate effects of the ban on the songwriting industry was an interruption in the exploitation profile of songs that had just become available—what was referred to in chapter 3 as the "cycle" of a song. A piece like "Blues in the Night" enjoyed a life of about six months in the recording studios, with big-name bands and singers attempting versions and the companies spreading these across their issue schedules. With recording ending on July 31, a number of promising songs were not allowed to complete their cycle. Particular casualties were the songs Irving Berlin had written for his July 4 all-Army show, including "I Left My Heart at the Stage Door Canteen," a song about a wartime romance that Kenny Baker and Charlie Spivak managed to put on record before the ban. The first success for the new Capitol label, "Strip Polka," was covered only once each by the three majors, with the Andrews Sisters recording it for Decca, Alvino Rey for Victor/Bluebird, and Kay Kyser making a version for Columbia on the last possible day. Another war-themed song, "When the Lights Go on Again," was recorded in several versions in the July rush by Lucky Millinder, Les Brown, and Vaughn Monroe before the lights went out on it. The film *You Were Never Lovelier* contained commercially promising material by Johnny Mercer and Jerome Kern, but it also came too late for a full cycle of recording life. Two of the songs were recorded in haste in the June–July siege of the studios, "I'm Old Fashioned" and "Dearly Beloved," in four versions each between July 24 and 31, by Benny Goodman, Dinah Shore, and Woody Herman, among others.

Songwriters and the industry were even more concerned over the longer-term prospects. These songs were denied full exploitation opportunities, but there were films and songs still unreleased that would not benefit at all from the exposure that a song such as "Blues in the Night" had. In August the Glenn Miller picture *Orchestra Wives* showed off some exploitable songs by Harry Warren, which only the Miller band recorded. The film *Star Spangled Rhythm* was in production, with a score by Arlen and Mercer and songs like "That Old Black Magic" waiting to be recorded. If the ban went on into 1943, songwriters would find themselves devoid of means of publicizing their work and multiplying their incomes—the recording fees, royalties on recordings, and sales of sheet music that would decline without the stimulus of recordings.

The recording ban would also have an impact on musicians, the record companies, and the public. It was not likely to improve James Petrillo's already unfavorable image, particularly in view of the earlier statement on the suspension of industrial conflict. Apart from other arguments, the AFM's move could be perceived as unpatriotic. *Billboard* asserted that Petrillo, who tended to be seen as the sole architect of the ban, "could hardly have picked a worse time," what with "recorded music doing such a yeoman job over the radio lanes as well as on automatic machine network in helping to keep the morale of everyone at key pitch" (7.25.42: 92). Petrillo was accused of putting "a straitjacket on American music" at a "singularly poor time" (*Var.* 7.22.42: 33). Late in July came an intervention by Elmer Davis, who made "a dramatic appeal, in the name of the Army, Navy, Marine Corps, Coast Guards, Treasury, Office of Civilian

Defense and his own OWI" to Petrillo, to "call off his ultimatum" (*Var.* 7.29.42: 1). *Variety* carried Petrillo's reply, "After weighing the report for three days, Petrillo last week replied to Elmer Davis, Director of the Office of War Information, that in essence he did not know what he was talking about" (8.5.42: 1).

The ban came into force on August 1, with a total blanking out of recording studios. For the duration of the ban (which for Victor and Columbia lasted until November 1944), practical, political, and legal efforts would be made to resolve or defeat it. In the fall of 1942, Petrillo and the AFM overcame a claim for an injunction against the ban, sought on the basis that the issue was an antitrust and not a labor dispute. But in October in Chicago's District Court, "before an audience of radio and union officials, musicians and others," Judge John P. Barnes handed down a ruling to the contrary. *Variety's* headline was "Petrillo Is Victorious" (10.14.42: 39).

Some accounts of the Petrillo affair suggest that the record companies simply switched their focus from bands to singers, who were not affected by the ban. Since singers required accompaniment, however, this was not easy. The companies tried a variety of strategies as the ban went on. Victor stated in August that they would continue to record, without specifying how they would do this. While other companies, as *Variety* put it, "elected to stand pat on huge stacks of masters they turned out before the ban," Victor was thought to be planning to record in Mexico or to use "an elaborate voice group" to give "the effect of an instrumental ensemble" (8.26.42: 43). Both of these tactics were employed during the ban; for instance, in October there was a report of a minor company, Continental, recording six discs in Mexico (*Var.* 10.14.42: 39).

It was the jukebox operators who turned out to be the most vulnerable and the most willing to talk terms with the AFM. The jukebox operators' body, the Association of Coin Machine Operators (ACMO), was sensitive about their public image. They frowned on the use of the term *jukebox* and, according to *Variety*, once requested the singer Dick Todd to drop "King of the Jukebox" from his billing for that reason. In October the Glenn Miller recording "Juke Box Saturday Night" was issued by Victor, despite worries about the objections of the ACMO, which was unhappy about such public use of the word. Incidents such as one reported in October did not help the self-assurance of the ACMO: "A mob of 125 Detroit hoodlums—which the newspapers swiftly tagged as a 'Juke Box Mob'—headed out in suburban St. Claire and smashed up a juke spot there known as The Sugar Bowl . . . the mob got out of hand, spread terrorism in the suburb before police, bolstered by citizens, finally clapped 22 uninhibited zoot suits into jail" (*Var.* 10.28.42: 1).

The "coin machines," as the operators called them, depended on a supply of discs to stock them. In normal times, discs were replaced as recordings of new songs came on the market. From August 1942, however, new songs could be heard only in movies and in unrecorded performances on radio. The jukeboxes stood a good chance of falling behind. "It's only a matter of time," *Variety* advised in October, "before the estimated 400,000 jukeboxes in the country can become depreciated stock." It was not surprising that from the ACMO, "overtures have already been heard that they'd be amenable to paying some royalty per jukebox machine and/or per recording, to the American Federation of Musicians, so long as they could replenish their stock" (10.14.42: 39).

In October 1943, Decca was the first of the big-three companies to sign an agreement with the AFM. According to William Kenney (1999: 192), part of Decca's motivation might have been to gain an advantage over the non-signers Victor and Columbia. For these two, the ban resulted in a twenty-seven-month suspension of normal recording activities. The 1942–1944 ban was an event of some significance in the history of recorded music in the United States. A good deal of music that would otherwise be preserved in recordings was lost. Some critics have argued that what is missing is of particular historical importance. Stanley Dance contended, "The union recording ban . . . prevented the preservation of many important musical developments" during a crucial time in jazz history (1980: 200). For Leonard Feather, "The progress of jazz may well have been impaired" by the ban (1960: 30). Others suggested that the careers of players, especially the emerging beboppers, were held back by the ban (with Charlie Parker, Thelonious Monk, and Bud Powell reaching the ripe old ages of twenty-four, twenty-three, and twenty, respectively, by the end of the ban in 1944).

The tone of discussion in relation to jazz history is "tragic," in Gunther Schuller's expression. Echoing Feather, Schuller referred to the view that the ban "broke the momentum of jazz's progress" (1989: 847). From other writers one has the idea that the chronology of the ban was particularly untimely, that it occurred in synchronicity with a "break" in jazz itself. The discographer Brian Rust (1977) asserted that by 1944, "jazz had branched off in a new direction" (Rust and Debus 1973: i). The break in recording, therefore, covered a transition of which there is no aural record. The ban is perceived as depriving historians of information that is more significant than if some other periods had been blanked out. It seems quite coincidental that James C. Petrillo should have taken industrial action just at a moment when an unprecedented change, even a "revolution," was on the point of happening.

A group of hypothetical recordings mentioned with particular regret are those that might have been made by the Earl Hines band during the period. Schuller noted, "How wonderful it would be to hear recordings of the young Parker and Gillespie in Earl Hines's 1942–43 band" (1989: 847). This statement, however, assumes that such recordings would furnish clues to the development of bebop. But it is possible that the output of the Hines band continued much as it was in its last recording session or in live performance late in 1942, with frequent ballad features for Billy Eckstine and the new discovery Sarah Vaughan and plenty of space for the piano solos of the leader. There is an assumption in speculation about the recording ban, as Scott DeVeaux noted, that the purpose of recording is "documentation," that because music is of interest to historians, it somehow automatically becomes recorded and preserved for historical research purposes (1988: 133). But recording companies are not the Census Bureau; recordings are made because there is some possibility that they may be commercially profitable.

The recording ban of 1942–1944 became a "convenient cut-off point for the discussion of further developments in jazz," (Schuller 1989: 844) or a "convenient watershed in the history of jazz" (DeVeaux 1997: 296). Its place in the jazz narrative is a prominent one, as if the ban struck jazz with particular force. Its effect upon jazz, however, was just an aspect of its impact upon the larger field of popular music. But, as I noted in chapter 3, popular music does not *have* a narrative for the period concerned. The jazz narrative also represents its music as "progressing" or having a "revolution" in 1942–1944, a responsibility no other music was burdened with. The ban, in this view, simply mattered more to jazz than to other forms.

The ban has also given grounds for historical generalizations about the demise of big-band music and the rise to prominence of the individual vocalist. For some, this is a simple deduction from the fact that instrumentalists were not allowed to record while singers were. In this view, the musicians were guilty of leaving the field empty for the singers to occupy it. Schuller spoke of "hundreds" of vocalists continuing to record during the ban, the recording industry's "total embrace of singers" during this period: "Many singers acquired the status of stars almost overnight, an advantage over instrumentalists they were never to relinquish" (1989: 847).

To examine the evidence against this would take this discussion away from the circumstances of the recording ban. However, it is necessary to adopt a broad historical perspective on the relative prominence of singers and instrumentalists. Even in the early days of recording, singers enjoyed massive popularity: the first million-selling recording was by the operatic tenor Enrico Caruso, and singers such as Caruso and John McCormack continued to sell copiously into the 1940s. Prior to Glenn Miller's "Chattanooga Choo-Choo," the all-time best-selling recording was the 1927 "My Blue Heaven" by the Texas singer Gene Austin. In the 1920s and 1930s singers such as Al Jolson, Russ Columbo, and, above all, Bing Crosby enjoyed popularity beyond the dreams of any instrumentalist. Crosby had the biggest recording sales of 1942 as well. The popularity of singers needs no special explanation at any time: if the singers returned to a greater relative prominence during and after the 1942–1944 ban, this was a reversion to the historical norm rather than an unfortunate side-effect of a temporary recording ban.

There is plenty of evidence from recordings made prior to the ban that singers were already central to band performance. This can be exemplified from discographies of almost any band. For instance, Benny Goodman's recordings from December 1941 to July 1942 consist of thirty-two tracks with singers and twelve without. During the two years before the ban the Andy Kirk band made seventeen of twenty-three tracks with vocals. Gene Krupa had Anita O'Day and Roy Eldridge as vocalists, Glenn Miller had Ray Eberle and Tex Beneke, Harry James had Helen Forrest, and Tommy Dorsey had Jo Stafford and Frank Sinatra. Many bands had vocal groups, such as the Pied Pipers with Tommy Dorsey and the Cab Jivers with Cab Calloway.

A band like Ellington's made more consistent use of singers than is usually acknowledged; their 1942 recordings featured vocals by Ivie Anderson and Herb Jeffries. After the start of the ban and Anderson's retirement, the vocalists Ellington was using became a talking point, as in this *Chicago Defender* item, "When Duke plays theatre he rotates his trio of girl vocalists, Phyllis Smiley, Joya Sherrill and Betti Roché . . . Flash! different days you see and hear a different girl" (8.29.42: 11). There were also many individual singing stars active in 1942 not waiting for a break in the instrumentalists' hegemony: to name only the best-known, Judy Garland, Deanna Durbin, Alice Faye, Jeanette McDonald, Lena Horne, and Dinah Shore. For decades country music had been based around songs and singers and increasingly so in the early 1940s, from Jimmy Rodgers in the 1920s to Roy Acuff, Ernest Tubb, and others whose popularity was established at the national level. Even in country music the historic preference for individual singers was reaffirmed; after a period of interest in singing groups, "vocal soloists starting to come back into the spotlight" (Allen 1994: 22).

The popularity of singers in 1942–1944 does not require explanation by special circumstances. It is the relative prominence of the instrumental music of the big bands between the mid-1930s and the mid-1940s that is a historical exception. Big-band performance itself was more thoroughly characterized by singers than jazz writers have acknowledged. The recording ban did little to change the historic prominence of vocalists one way or the other. Singers have been marginalized within jazz discourse: critics turned a blind eye to the swathes of band discographies which are, track for track, much more concerned with songs and singers than with improvisation and "hot" playing or of elements that make up jazz.

The effects of the AFM ban upon the direction of popular music or of a subsection such as jazz are open to interpretation. One possibility is that its effects were not very great. The ban had concrete effects upon the working situation of musicians and the music business. However, although it has been looked upon as a major blow to the economic circumstances of musicians, the loss of income from royalties and session fees was much less important than the increasing traveling restrictions, with their impact upon the more lucrative live engagements. Recordings were more important as publicity than for the direct income they produced, except for top-selling bands such as Glenn Miller's.

The *Amsterdam News* anticipated that the ban "will work a greater hardship on Colored bands than on White" (7.18.42: 15), because white bands secured more live radio time, while black bands were heard on radio largely through recordings. The suspension of recording also meant a stop to occasional breakthroughs that came to black artists via successful recordings, "Lil Green zoomed from the relief rolls to a star now earning several hundred dollars weekly on the strength of one recording 'Romance in the Dark.' Louis Jordan is currently drawing crowds because of the popularity of his 'I'm Gonna Move to the Outskirts of Town' while Erskine Hawkins was greatly aided by 'Tuxedo Junction'"(*AN* 7.18.42: 15). The implication is still that recordings benefited artists by increasing opportunities to secure live engagements. For both black and white musicians, the effect of the ban was added to the other difficulties that were beginning to pile up at this time—another source of income, if a lesser or more indirect one, was drying up. For many hundreds of bands in existence in 1942, the opportunity to record was a distant dream in any case, and so the ban had no material effect upon their fortunes.

The two-year hiatus in recording caused the disruption of a well-established system. The AFM ban came less than a year after the end of the ASCAP dispute, another event that interrupted the link between songwriters, recording companies, and artists. In the earlier dispute it was the songwriters who broke the supply line to the recording industry; now the songwriters were supplying a flow of material to an industry that was temporarily unable to exploit it. The greatest effect of the ban, as of the earlier ASCAP dispute, was destabilization of the system. This accelerated some processes of change in popular music that were already active.

The ASCAP dispute opened the way to nonestablished song producers and song types, whereas the recording ban opened the way to independent record companies. Both of these changes favored country or folk music over the Broadway-Hollywood idiom of popular song that operated under the old system. Music from folk sources, both white and black, was making inroads in record sales and getting a favorable reception in the press. The longer the flow of "normal" music was disrupted, the longer these nonstandard forms and supply routes had to establish themselves. As Bill Malone pointed out, the major companies learned that the independents were supplying something the public wanted. When they came back on stream, companies like Decca were ready to supply their own versions. Capitol, with typical promptitude, rapidly acquired a stable of hillbilly singers. The Capitol recording of "Jingle Jangle Jingle" by the cowboy singer Tex Ritter was top of the record charts as the recording ban started and stayed in that position for seven weeks.

In the first two weeks of July 1942, the Glenn Miller orchestra played a residency in the Hotel Sherman in Chicago. The Sherman engagement was a prize as valuable as residencies at New York locations such as the Pennsylvania and the New Yorker. Such places were often lavishly decorated, and the Panther Room in the Sherman had a touch of the exotic—photographs show it apparently draped in leopard skin. For the Miller band to make recordings in the hectic month of July, they had to record in the Victor studios in Chicago. There were recording sessions over three consecutive days, just before the end of the Sherman Hotel job.

Duke Ellington's was the next band into the Sherman, opening on July 17 for four weeks. Away from usual recording centers in New York and Los Angeles, it was necessary for Ellington, too, to record in Chicago, given the imminent start of the ban. The last commercial session that Ellington made until December 1944, the Chicago recordings of July 28 are notable for war-tinged lyrics, including a rousing marching number "Hayfoot Strawfoot," the last recording Ivie Anderson made with Ellington. After the month at the Sherman, Anderson left the band, as had the long-serving clarinet virtuoso Barney Bigard a month earlier. It was during the stay at the Sherman that Ellington and his musicians learned of the death of Jimmy Blanton.

An important visitor to the Sherman Hotel residency in late July was the jazz writer-critic Leonard Feather. As well as editing *Metronome*, organizing recording sessions, and taking initiatives such as the jazz history course in New York, Feather worked as a publicist. Beginning in the summer of 1942, one of his clients was Duke Ellington. Feather's first contact with the Ellington band in this capacity was the July visit to the Sherman Hotel, when the band "had recorded a few sides just under the wire" (1986: 71). Feather was to remain press agent to the Ellington band during this time of instability and change and to stay on into 1943. Feather, whose views on the destiny of jazz were discussed in chapter 5, was in a position to contribute to decisions that Ellington took before the end of the year.

In his autobiography, Ellington recalled that another visitor during the Sherman engagement was Frank Sinatra. As Ellington correctly perceived, in the summer of 1942 Sinatra "was ready to split the Dorsey gig." Ellington says he knew this "by the way Tommy said goodnight to him." Sinatra had already made his last recordings with Dorsey and would announce his departure for a solo career the following month. This meeting was one of three occasions before the end of the year when Ellington's path would cross Sinatra's (Ellington 1974: 238). Both men, in common with other recording artists, were locked out of the studios. This was possibly a less weighty matter for Ellington, who had been recording since 1923, than for Sinatra, who was on the verge of a new career as a solo artist, with as yet few recordings away from the Dorsey band.

The music of late 1942 is not a complete recording void, and a few recordings of radio shows exist for both Ellington and Sinatra for this period. There are three dates from the Ellington band during the last months of the year: a broadcast from the Palace Theatre in Cleveland in August, in which the band played the hit tunes "Tangerine" and "I Don't Want to Walk Without You"; a show for an audience of soldiers at Fort Dix, New Jersey; and a broadcast from a college prom in Providence in December. Some of Sinatra's last shows with Dorsey were recorded during broadcasts of Raleigh-sponsored shows on NBC. Two of these in August, from theaters in Washington, D.C., and Youngstown, Ohio, still showed Sinatra limited to one or two songs per program.

These were unofficial recordings of radio broadcasts. The only remaining official location where recording could be done was the sound stages of the movie studios. Six weeks after closing at the Sherman, the unending itinerary of the Ellington band carried them to the MGM and Columbia studios in Hollywood, where they would be recording for two films in the last week of October. Sinatra, who had made an uncomfortable departure from the Dorsey band, would cross paths once more with Ellington in the same movie studio. Neither for Sinatra nor Ellington was this the first experience of Hollywood. With the Dorsey band, Sinatra had sung three numbers in a lightweight MGM production *Ship Ahoy*, and Ellington had made appearances in films since 1929. Appearing in movies was one of the things a successful singer or bandleader did. Films were an integral part of the system that linked the music industry, musical performers, and the public.

In the last few days of September the Ellington band appeared on the lot at MGM to record and film two numbers for the movie *Cabin in the Sky*. Ten days later they recorded and shot at Columbia a cameo appearance for a second film, a wartime music compilation named *Reveille with Beverley*. Ellington and his orchestra were not prominent in either movie. *Cabin in the Sky* was one of the first products of the celebrated Freed-Minelli production unit at MGM. It had an all-black cast including the singer Ethel Waters, who premiered the Vernon Duke song "Taking a Chance on Love," Louis Armstrong, Lena Horne, and comedians and actors such as Eddie "Rochester" Anderson and Butterfly McQueen. On *Reveille with Beverley* Ellington and his band were in the company of white stars such as Anne Miller, who played the lead role of a disc-jockey, and other musical performers including the Count Basie, Bob Crosby, and Freddie Slack bands; the Mills Brothers; and Frank Sinatra, in a minor role. Ellington's band played their new signature tune, "Take the 'A' Train," and Sinatra sang one number, "Night and Day." The Freddie Slack band accompanied Ella Mae Morse singing "Cow Cow Boogie," as on the successful Capitol release. For two days of filming, Sinatra was reputedly paid barely enough to pay the expenses of the trip from New York.

Typically, Ellington and his musicians were busy elsewhere during the spell of film work. Between the sessions at MGM they appeared at the inauguration of a new club, the Hollywood Canteen, set up for the benefit of service personnel and located in Sunset Boulevard. At the opening broadcast on the night of October 3, Ellington's orchestra appeared on the same bill as Eddie Cantor, Abbott and Costello, Dinah Shore, Rudy Vallee, Eleanor Powell, and Bette Davis, who had originated the idea of the Canteen. A few days later, the band played at the first edition of an important wartime music and entertainment show, *Jubilee*, at the NBC studios in Los Angeles.

Once again, Ellington and his orchestra were performing with dancers, singers, actors, and comedians. Histories of jazz and biographical work on Ellington and comparable musicians rarely juxtapose their names with those of performers like Eddie Cantor, Rudy Vallee, or Bette Davis. The star of melodramas like the 1942 *Now Voyager*, Davis was noted as rejecting a "race slur" at the Canteen, when objections were raised to its policy of allowing racially mixed couples (*AN* 2.1.43: 16). The incongruity of placing Ellington alongside Bette Davis is not primarily racial. It has to do with a hierarchy of cultural esteem, in which it is perceived as being beneath the dignity of such a musician as Ellington to be associated with these artists. Ellington's presence in such contexts as a Hollywood musical is perceived not as a benefit of success within an entertainment world, but as a historical offence against a performer whose destiny was higher. In this view, as extended, for example, by the British critic Spike Hughes (Shipton 2001: 276), Duke Ellington should not have been obliged to associate himself with comedians, actors, and dancers.

However, Ellington was doing what other musicians and bandleaders were doing at this same time—and had always done. Harry James, whose popularity was reaching its height, made appearances in two lightweight films in 1942, *Private Buckaroo* and *Springtime in the Rockies*. Benny Goodman had made numerous film appearances and was to go on to limited speaking roles in later films. Leaders and musicians Artie Shaw and Glenn Miller were also frequent movie presences. The Miller-based film *Orchestra Wives*, released in August, was one of few movies where the working life of the big bands was a central thread of the story. More often bands were shown on in the night-club and stage-show settings that conventional films included.

At this period in American popular music, players, bands, and singers appeared in films more frequently even than at the height of rock music. This was indicative not only of how easily a musical scene could be fitted into a scenario, but also of the centrality of popular music in the cultural frame of reference. In the 1942 Bob Hope feature *My Favorite Blonde*, the name of Benny Goodman crops up naturally in the banter between Hope and an English secret agent, played by Madeleine Carroll. The bandleaders were as comfortable and as welcome presences in films as were cameo appearances by personalities such as Hope, Crosby, or Durante.

Not only the top line of musicians and bands found places in the Hollywood output of the time. The Woody Herman band appeared in the 1942 comedy *What's Cookin'* and later in *Wintertime*, a 1943 vehicle for the ice-skating queen Sonja Henie. Black bands and musicians were also featured, though not at the same levels of budget and publicity. In addition to Ellington's long run of appearances, such performers as Cab Calloway, Fats Waller, and Louis Armstrong were regularly featured in films. Count Basie and his orchestra also appeared in *Reveille with Beverley* and in *Hit Parade of 1943*, *Crazyhouse* (a sequel to the very popular *Hellzapoppin'*), and the Donald O'Connor musical *Top Man*. For Basie this inaugurated a career of involvement with film that culminated in his unexpected appearance in the 1974 Mel Brooks comedy *Blazing Saddles*. In 1942 Duke Ellington was doing nothing anomalous by appearing in the same categories of films.

This is not to say that musicians and fans were necessarily satisfied with the kinds of exposure that films gave. The 1942 "Band Year Book" published in *Billboard* asked whether Hollywood "Is doing the best possible job with name bands." It is apparent that the presence of a "name" band in a film was considered to add drawing power, to the extent that producers made only minimal efforts to integrate the bands into films, owing to "that absolute and sudden faith a film executive can place in the marquee value of a big-name band, to the point where the maestro is handed the worst stories to play with." The Harry James feature in *Private Buckaroo* was cited as an instance, "a botched script, low-budget execution, and neglected trifles" (*BB* 9.26.42: 43). It is difficult, though, to detect in the commentary on music and film any sense that Hollywood was an unsuitable environment for musicians or any seeking after an ideal, "authentic" presentation. If anything, the expressed wish was for more complete immersion in the film-industry machinery. The trade press reported on musicians being signed for film deals and taking part in productions; rarely was there comment on any sense of anomaly that artists such as Basie or Ellington should be participating in mainstream films in the usual Hollywood manner.

Throughout this book, I have noted that musicians, in stage presentations across the nation, shared bills with movies, such as Count Basie or Glenn Miller with *Blues in the Night*, Woody Herman with *They Died with Their Boots On*, and Louis Armstrong with *Shanghai Gesture*. The movie attraction with Duke Ellington at the Oriental in Chicago in August, was a film entitled *Sabotage Special*. Examples can be drawn from hundreds of stage shows across the United States. Audiences experienced bands as part of entertainment packages together with films, films together with bands. From the perspective of our own time, there is a sense of disjunction in a performance that juxtaposed these elements, which for us have been rigidly kept apart. The consumption of an Ellington band performance followed by a Hollywood movie would require for us a difficult conceptual adjustment from one mode of spectating to another. For instance, in the case of Ellington and a movie, this would involve a shift from high-art mode to popular-culture mode. These different levels of culture are not normally placed so closely together (and we now have the word *postmodern* for a certain kind of odd situation in which they do occur together).

But for an audience in 1942 there was no postmodern incongruity, nor any sense of different categories having to be reconciled. The Woody Herman band offered one kind of popular entertainment, and the audience moved on to experience another kind, a Western movie, and then on to comedians, dancers, and other musical performers. In between a performances by the Ellington band, the comedian Dusty Fletcher, and the dancer Baby Lawrence, an audience could enjoy a wartime espionage movie, then, if they wished, sit through the Ellington band's set again. This coexistence of what we view retrospectively as disparate performances was characteristic of the way in which music was experienced by American audiences for many years.

This is not to say that all the elements so combined were of equal quality and equal interest to a given audience. In the above example, it is likely that the Ellington band was a stronger attraction than the film; had the movie been a popular film such as *Mrs. Miniver* or *My Favorite Blonde*, the balance might have been more even. There was a payoff between a band's performance and the film with which it was coupled. Some reviews describe a weak film being salvaged by a popular band, as when Jimmy Dorsey's band "bounced" the film *Ghosts* to a "Smash $32,500 in Philly" (*Var.* 6.17.42: 13). The trade press commented on the policies of some theaters, "When playing a Harry James [performance], the Adams, Newark, to draw a hypothetical case, will buy a film for $300 to $500 and leave the box office entirely up to the power of the band to pull them in" (*Var.* 10.7.42: 41). The managing director of the Paramount in Times Square, Bob Weitman, credited the name band "with nearly 30% of the grosses at his theatre when the house is playing a strong picture." In the case of a weak picture, the band earned a higher proportion of the box office pull. In either situation, it is apparent that theaters had some notion of the relative power of the band and the movie. For, say, a Duke Ellington theater performance the band might represent somewhere in the range of 30 to 50 percent of the package's appeal. Whether this implied that a section of the audience was bored by or inattentive to such performances is impossible to determine, but there is no reason to suppose that they were. It is hard to see how this kind of package could have been universal in the nation's theaters if a large percentage of audiences were antipathetic to major elements of a show or incapable of appreciating them.

In the early 1940s, bands appeared in films and with films. Film was also the medium through which many newly published songs were given their first exposure; writers like Harry Warren worked largely within and for the movie industry. Musicians and singers of all styles launched new songs through performances on the screen, after which the songs entered the usual cycle of exploitation, being picked up and covered by record companies and other musicians. At least, this last stage occurred when the process was operating normally, as it was not after July 31, 1942. For the rest of the year and for the duration of the AFM ban, new songs that were heard in films like *Star Spangled Rhythm* had a more limited scope of exposure. The same was true of the batch of seasonal Irving Berlin songs written for the film *Holiday Inn*, which had its premiere four days after the start of the recording ban. Fortunately for Berlin and Decca records, before the ban began Bing Crosby had already made a recording of the song "White Christmas," which was released concurrently with the film.

Films were part of the popular music process, and popular music was part of the movie process. Each supported the other by enlarging the circle of publicity. Musicians were both agents and beneficiaries of this circle. For a few musicians, including Ellington, feature films distributed by major studios were not the only means of being seen by a broader public. A growing business in the early 1940s, one that did not outlast wartime, was an early video-jukebox format called "soundies." Ellington and his musicians made several soundies in California shortly before the attack on Pearl Harbor, following the 1941 run of "Jump for Joy" in Los Angeles. Soundies enabled appropriately equipped jukeboxes to show short programs of visual clips of artists including musicians, singers, and dancers, with the jukebox providing the audio track. One program containing two of the five soundies made by the Ellington band includes six clips by other artists, among them comedy numbers, a band-vocal number, and a patriotic song evidently recorded in immediate post–Pearl Harbor mood, "Well Slap the Jap into the Laps of the Nazis." The Ellington soundies were strongly related to the recent "Jump for Joy" revue. The Lindy Hoppers dance troupe, who feature in one soundie, had been in the show. Ivie Anderson sings "I Got It

Bad," and the singer-dancers Marie Bryant and Paul White perform the comedy number "Bli-Blip," as in "Jump for Joy." Many prominent players never made soundies; Ellington did so through being in Hollywood, where productions were made.

The significance of soundies for later writers is that they document some jazz artists who are otherwise underrepresented on film. Otherwise, in the view of one writer, of 2000 such recordings made, "only a small percentage are of interest today," as all that they preserve are "bad singers, untalented dance groups, comedy acts, vaudeville performers such as jugglers and the like" (Stratemann 1992: 180). It should be remembered, however, that the Ellington performances were programmed among those "bad singers . . . and the like," within the soundies. Further, Ellington's soundies performances were shared with such nonmusical artists. Whitey's Lindy Hoppers danced to "Cottontail," the song "Flamingo" was shot with a dance troupe on screen, "Bli-Blip" was a broad comedy-musical number with dancing and facial contortions by Bryant and White, and even "Jam Session," where the focus was on the band musicians, adorned the set with dancing extras.

As we have seen, the historiography of jazz has tended to abstract the music from all of this context. This is especially the case for an artist such as Ellington, who enjoys high status as a serious composer on the classical model. Yet, it is a fact that by 1943, in every medium in which his work was disseminated apart from sound recordings, Ellington was associated with performers other than jazz musicians, whose presence has been written out of jazz-based history but whose work was integral to the experience an Ellington performance offered. In movies and soundies Ellington was accompanied by singers, dancers, and actors. In the majority of the live performances on the orchestra's touring schedule, there was again a troupe of these other performers presented in variety format. When in 1941 Ellington devised the first major stage production of his career, "Jump for Joy," it made use of the same singers, dancers, and actors that accompanied him elsewhere. Virtually all of the Ellington band's performances were accomplished in the company and the format of a variety show. Song, dance, and comedy were what an Ellington audience got, and this had been the case throughout twenty years of his career. Jazz historians barely refer to this.

As I discussed at length in chapter 5, the new discourse of jazz that would detach musicians like Ellington from the context of entertainment, not only theoretically but also in fact, was in the process of being created at this time. The narrative of jazz's nature and of its history was emerging early in this process. By 1942 it was entering into the repertoire of stories out of which Hollywood films were constructed. There was a series of films from 1941 onward that paralleled the work of the jazz critical writers in setting out a discourse of jazz as history. *Blues in the Night* and *Birth of the Blues* were released in late 1941 and *Syncopation*, a more concerted telling of the jazz narrative, in the middle of 1942. *Blues in the Night*, as we saw in chapter 3, brings the tortured antihero over from the jazz novel to the jazz film. It also establishes for the first time a distinct jazz knowledge; in the character played by Elia Kazan, we meet an aficionado who declares that he "has read everything from *Down Beat* to *Le Jazz Hot*," and that he "knows the anatomy of swing." The sequence that underlies the title song enshrines the story of the movement of jazz up the river from New Orleans, an element of the jazz narrative that had become mythic in less than twenty years. *The Birth of the Blues*, as its title indicates, also offers a myth of origin; but as *The New Grove Dictionary of Jazz* noted, its plot "was riddled with distortions and errors" (Kernfeld 1994: 377). *Syncopation* also traced "the rise of jazz" from New Orleans, but its plot, too, "bore little resemblance to reality" (1994: 378).

On the release of *Syncopation*, *Variety* observed connections between this and the previous films: it had "something of the same appeal . . . having to do with modern syncopation as derived from the levees of old New Orleans" (5.6.42: 22). Each of these films has much to say about the relationship between a black community that originates a musical style and individual white musicians who acquire it. *Syncopation* received careful consideration in a review in *Amsterdam News*. The previous week, the paper noted signs in Hollywood of "an effort to present colored people in a more favorable light" (6.6.42: 17). Todd Duncan, as the New Orleans trumpeter Rex Tearbone, "definitely isn't an Uncle Tom . . . and neither is Jessie Grayson as Aunt Dinah." The review concluded that the film was "really worth seeing, folks," despite mistaken details that the review was at pains to point out, such as "the salient fact that in Chicago in the early 20's people were not using the jive expression, 'solid'" (*AN* 6.13.42: 16). On its opening in Chicago, *Syncopation* received a less ambiguous endorsement by the *Chicago Defender*: it was "groovy" and "right hot" with its "aggregation of musicians destined to send the boogie and jive addicts into that brand of tuneful trance known as out-of-this-world" (8.29.42: 13).

A fourth, and by all accounts a more substantial, film might have added to this 1941–1942 sequence, *It's All True*, the conception for which originated with Orson Welles in the aftermath of his historic first feature *Citizen Kane*. Welles introduced himself to Duke Ellington during the run of "Jump for Joy," and plans were made for a film tracing the history of jazz and making prominent use of both Ellington and Louis Armstrong. Ellington's function within the project, however, fluctuated in response to Welles's frequent changes of plans, while he received a salary of $1000 a week for researching the picture and writing the score. Armstrong sent Welles a written account of his early life that was to be the basis of the jazz portion of the film. This portion, however, declined from being the entire film to being one of four episodes to being omitted altogether when the project turned into a film about Brazil. Ellington, by his own account, wrote twenty-eight bars of music for the film (1974: 240). RKO finally put an end to the project in any form by sacking Welles for his extravagance. By the summer of 1942 all prospect of what might have been another text in the emerging narrative of jazz had disappeared.

Chapter 7

The Street

Maintaining the sense of authenticity takes work.
—RICHARD A. PETERSON (1997: 223)

In a study of the legendary blues artist Robert Johnson, Elijah Wald (2004) argued that the term *blues* has such variable meanings that the question of its origins has no single or useful answer. Wald's view should be seen against the idea that blues is actually one thing and that it has one point of origin. The blues, like jazz, has become a monoculture. It is a music played in a single form, with lyrics restricted to a limited range of subjects. Attempts by writers such as Albert Murray (1978) to show the historical diversity of style and mood in blues have done little to shift the conception of the music that took root sometime in the 1960s.

A determinate music must have a determinate point of origin, and for the blues that has been the Mississippi Delta. Wald provided ample evidence that among pre–World War II blues players a minority were of Mississippi provenance. However, the notion of this geographical location as the music's birthplace (as Alan Lomax [1993] titled it, "The Land Where the Blues Began") is mythological. The Mississippi Delta occupies in the historiography of the blues the place that is occupied in jazz by New Orleans. The origins of the blues are lost in the mythic land of the Delta in the late nineteenth century, just as those of jazz are lost in the slums of New Orleans around the same time. Two initiatives were active in the summer of 1942 that, in part, took their rationale from this view of musical traditions. First was the project that sent field researchers from Fisk University and the Library of Congress to southern locations including Coahoma County, Mississippi. The second was the work of jazz revivalists, such as William Russell and Frederick Ramsey Jr., tracking down and relaunching the careers of veteran New Orleans musicians, most notably the cornetist William "Bunk" Johnson.

To motivate the efforts of the jazz revivalists, two beliefs were required: that there existed "some central essence named *jazz*" that was possible to isolate (DeVeaux 1991: 485) and that cultural traditions have a past in which they had a pure form. This latter belief was so widespread in the nineteenth and early twentieth centuries that it was regarded as common sense. To find out what a tradition truly is, you trace it back to its pure point of origin. This lay behind the search for the original Indo-European language and the study of local dialects across the globe; in the study of folklore, scholars such as Krohn and Aarne were continually searching for earlier and purer forms of folktales and customs. Therefore, it is not surprising to come across the belief in the 1940s that if one could discover older texts, one would find what jazz or blues was before it lost its original purity. The black citizens of Coahoma County and men like Bunk Johnson were assumed to be these older texts.

A supporting principle was corruption: folk customs are corrupted by influences that surround and infiltrate them, and they lose their original pure identity. For jazz and blues, the signs of this corruption, modern means of communication, were everywhere: music on radio, with KFFA pumping out 50,000 watts from Helena, Arkansas; the *Grand Ole Opry* audible all over the South; Hope and Crosby movies playing in local theaters across the United States. To locate the essence of a black musical tradition like jazz or the blues, it was necessary to go back beyond this, to seek out a rural county less exposed to the modern world, an individual whose memories stretched back to the uncorrupted past. The idea of corruption by modern popular culture was also a commonplace: it provided the foundations of "cultural studies" for the first twenty years of its existence. It is tied to arguments over authenticity in country music, definitions of the real jazz, and the idea "that some blues singers were 'realer' than others" (Wald 2004: 232).

The belief that these musical forms had an essence is of particular interest in relation to the early 1940s. DeVeaux (1991: 528) described this view as holding that the essence of jazz "remains constant throughout all the dramatic transformations that have resulted in modern-day jazz." Gunther Schuller said, "it will be abundantly clear that jazz is a grand historical continuum" (1989: 845). For a more recent historian, Ted Gioia, jazz is "a chameleon art, delighting us with the ease with which it changes colors" (1997: 395). These views are close to a current consensus on the nature of jazz, but they are not those of the revivalists. For them, jazz was a music of the past that needed to be rescued from the neglect into which it had fallen. Its essence was located in the collectively improvised music of the pre-1925 New Orleans small band and not anywhere else. For the revivalists, to know what jazz really was, it was necessary to return to this source. If it was not possible to recreate the musical world of early New Orleans, one could at least find eyewitnesses—or better still, real surviving practitioners.

In comparison with the more recent inclusive theory of the history of jazz, the revivalists can be regarded as narrow and inflexible in their definition of jazz. But their viewpoint was reasonable from a semantic point of view—a narrow definition is not worse than a broad one, only different. In addition, their view of the history of popular musical forms was not distant from a widely shared popular perspective. The lyric to "The Old Music Master," a Hoagy Carmichael–Johnny Mercer hit song of 1942, includes the lines, "Along about nineteen-seventeen, / Jazz will come upon the scene, / Then around nineteen thirty-five, / You'll begin to get swing, boogie-woogie and jive." This lyric uncontroversially assumes that jazz came to an end a decade or so earlier and that swing and boogie-woogie are separate from it. It is likely that the contemporary audience did not find this thumbnail history objectionable and the views of the revivalists to that extent unobjectionable, too.

The narrative of a grand historical continuum of jazz is relatively new. What it amounts to is another semantic decision, to use *jazz* as an umbrella term covering the entirety of a disparate and once fiercely divided field, rather than just a part of it. It is not reasonable to blame the revivalists of the 1940s for a failure to grasp the grand perspective that emerged only later. Today, the rather mystical consensus is that jazz is a single music with a continuous hundred years of history behind it (e.g., Schuller 1989; Gioia 1997). This view was not found in the early 1940s, except embryonically in such places as the Feather-Goffin syllabus—and they, too, were participants in the bitterly polarized arguments about jazz that characterized the later 1940s. The protagonists in the jazz definition wars that raged during the 1940s, revivalists and their opponents, would be astonished to find themselves dissolved with their opponents into the vast melting pot the jazz narrative now subsumes.

The narrative that informed the revivalists' views was one of loss, corruption, and rescue. In less purist forms, the same kind of view was articulated elsewhere in the early 1940s, in movies like *Blues in the Night* ("That's the real misery, boys!") and in several written studies, most prominently Ramsey and Smith's *Jazzmen* (1946). In a later book about the rural South, Frederick Ramsey Jr. set out the motives of this kind of work, "I took it upon myself to uncover any trace of musical activity, past and present, that I could find. There was only one way to do this: to rely on the memories of living persons who could recall the past—to go 'way back then and bring it on up to now'"(1960: xi). The Coahoma County researchers had the residents of existing communities to involve in their study. For a time in 1942 the activities of the revivalists centered on one living person who could recall the past, Bunk Johnson.

Johnson seemed an ideal candidate for the position. His memories of New Orleans went back to the nineteenth century, he had played with the mythic Buddy Bolden, and he claimed to have taught Louis Armstrong to play the trumpet. At the time of his resurrection by Ramsey and other enthusiasts, Johnson was working as a field hand in New Iberia, Louisiana. He had quit music years before, and at over sixty years of age he was not in shape to begin playing trumpet again. Through the help of local enthusiasts, in early 1942 Johnson was fitted with new teeth and provided with an instrument. Shortly afterward he made a demonstration recording that he sent to revivalists on the West Coast (California, especially San Francisco, was a center for revivalism, represented by bands like those of Turk Murphy and Lu Watters). The response was to send a team of specialists to Louisiana to record Johnson, late in 1942, for an independent label. This set of recordings, made under difficult conditions, "a makeshift studio, intense heat, and through the windows, sounds of automobile horns, streetcars' bells and barking dogs" (Williams 1967: 234), led to Johnson's being presented in appearances in New York, and from there to a second musical career that lasted until his death in 1949.

In some respects, however, Bunk Johnson was a disappointment to those who sponsored his comeback. He had seemed to represent the black rural proletariat that were believed to be the true audience for this music, but Johnson was well-educated, even urbane, and highly articulate. He had an attractive but difficult personality. More significantly, he did not fulfill the cultural dimensions of the role of classic pure New Orleans jazzman. At the first meeting with the recording team, Johnson surprised them by wanting to play "Deep in the Heart of Texas," the current hillbilly hit by Tex Ritter, instead of classic New Orleans repertoire. This confrontation between the preconceptions of jazz theorists and the current tastes of the musician is one of a long series of such moments of surprise and disappointment. Examples of this are frequent in jazz and blues, where the gap between the notions of the (generally white) enthusiasts and those of the (generally black) musicians tends to be wider. Wald gave another example from the blues context, "In the 1960s Chris Strachwitz was horrified to find that most of the rural musicians he recorded for his Arhoolie roots label, from blues singers to Tex-Mex bands and Louisiana zydeco outfits, were enthusiastic fans of Lawrence Welk" (2004: 97).

Bunk Johnson's post-1942 career featured other such moments, "Johnson would shock the fans who thronged around him to voice endless requests for 'High Society' or 'When the Saints Go Marching In' by saying that he certainly did enjoy Louis Jordan's record of 'There Ain't Nobody Here But Us Chickens'" (Williams 1967: 224). When Johnson played concerts in San Francisco, his fellow musicians were shocked when he wanted to play "Mairzy Doats." Similarly for another New Orleans veteran, the clarinetist George Lewis, "fans and champions of his authenticity would probably be surprised that he has named Artie Shaw as a favorite clarinetist, and shocked to learn that his 'St. Philip Street Breakdown' is actually an attempt to play Woody Herman's 'Chips Boogie Woogie' plus the Count Basie–Benny Goodman 'Gone with the Wind'" (Williams 1967: 247). These so-called authentic musicians were not behaving in the ways prescribed by the exponents of their purity, who were "shocked," "surprised," and "horrified." The boundaries within which musical traditions supposedly operated were not being observed.

The researchers in Mississippi also were encountering cultural disjunctions in 1942. The blues performers around Clarksdale were able to perform traditional songs of blues and other authentic types, but they did not necessarily share the frame of reference—even of the black researchers in the team. The prime discovery among Mississippi players was McKinley Morganfield, a farm worker already performing under the name he was to make famous, Muddy Waters. On a previous visit Alan Lomax and his team had been impressed by Morganfield's singing and guitar playing, and at the end of July Lomax returned to the Morganfield home to interview and record him again. These July 1942 recordings were issued on a Library of Congress album early the next year. On receiving two copies of the disc, Morganfield had one installed on the jukebox of a local tavern and was photographed, in an elegant suit, holding a disc on his knee like a trophy.

Muddy Waters remains one of the most revered figures in the blues tradition. In 1943, encouraged by the enthusiasm of Lomax and the Fisk University researchers and these first recordings, he moved to Chicago and became a progenitor of the "urban blues" style. But the 1942 interviews and other data include indications that Waters did not match the profile of the purist blues player. His repertoire contained what Robert Gordon called "pop pap," songs like "Red Sails in the Sunset," "Dinah," and "Bye Bye Blues" as well as cowboy or hillbilly tunes like "Home on the Range," "You Are My Sunshine," "Boots and Saddles," and the same current hit "Deep in the Heart of Texas" that shocked Bunk Johnson's recordists in New Orleans a few months earlier (Gordon 2002: 59). Waters sang traditional blues numbers, his own compositions, and those of Walter Davis, but also "Dark Town Strutters' Ball" and two contemporary tunes that cropped up in all contexts in 1941–1942, "Chattanooga Choo-Choo" and "Blues in the Night." Waters also told Lomax that his favorite artist on the radio was Fats Waller.

Some members of the Fisk team, more sociologically oriented than Lomax, made efforts to construct a broader picture of musical activities and tastes in their chosen region of Mississippi. The researcher Samuel Adams made lists of favorite radio artists for many of his informants and of records on the local jukeboxes. The radio lists disconfirm any idea that a black rural community in an area of the Deep South had any exclusive affinity with blues music or black artists in general. Among the names of Sister Rosetta Tharpe (with Lucky Millinder) and Duke Ellington were Glenn Miller, Artie Shaw, Benny Goodman, and country singers Gene Autry and Roy Acuff. On the Clarksdale jukeboxes, which contained some blues material and selections by Louis Jordan, were all the above white artists plus Bing Crosby and the "sweet" bands of Eddy Duchin, Larry Clinton, and Sammy Kaye (Wald 2004: Appendix).

A common explanation of this phenomenon has been a reiteration of the narrative of purity and corruption. Bunk Johnson, Muddy Waters, the black citizens of Clarksdale—all had already surrendered their purity by the early 1940s. The simple integrity of the popular traditions they came from was already compromised. It had been presumed that blues artists like Muddy Waters would feel disdain for contemporary commercial music. Instead, like many of his fellow black Mississippians, like the New Orleans veterans, not only was Waters found not disdaining popular music but he was actually playing it and expressing enthusiasm for it.

Such information was not easy to assimilate into the model of musical culture that Lomax, for instance, took down to Mississippi, nor does it seem to have affected his views afterward. In general this relationship between "pure" black jazz and blues musicians and popular music has been suppressed. Charlie Parker liking country singers, Louis Armstrong enjoying Guy Lombardo, Bunk Johnson wanting to play "Mairzy Doats," the black jukebox customers of Clarksdale voting for Eddy Duchin's "Maria Elena"—for the received narratives of American musical forms, these have been moments of embarrassment and denial.

These narratives were predicated on the idea that mainstream popular music was a low-grade product with which proud indigenous traditions had nothing to do. If, however, a New Orleans jazzman like Johnson enjoyed a current cowboy ditty, if a solidly rooted Delta bluesman like Muddy Waters not only played "pop pap" but appeared to enjoy it, this posed problems for the construction of folk monocultures. One response was to ignore the unwelcome anomaly and to omit it from histories of the music; another was to dismiss it as the product of individual quirks in otherwise "pure" artists; and a third was to regard it as an indication of how far the corrupting influence of popular music had spread.

At a later stage, through the power of the prevailing narratives and the canons they have constructed, there was a tendency for these artists to become confined within stricter boundaries, even in performance. The separate musical forms have moved off to separate territories, so that someone like Muddy Waters finished by becoming an exclusively "blues" performer. The identification of a distinct musical tradition, such as jazz or blues, functions as self-fulfilling prophesy. The critical discourse of blues or jazz creates the conditions in which artists work. It would have seemed strange to the audiences that went to see Muddy Waters packaged as a blues artist in the 1960s and 1970s to hear him launch into "Dinah" or "Red Sails in the Sunset." However, it would have given a better account of his range and versatility as a musician than these audiences were actually getting. Such was the normative effect of the label "blues" and the critical discourse that supported it.

Bunk Johnson's 1942 recordists wanted him to play blues tunes, but as Martin Williams recalled, "Bunk felt the blues was one number, and there was no point in doing it twice" (Williams 1967: 232). In a sense the blues is one number; it has a single form and one set of changes. It is not surprising, even on the principle of avoiding repetition, for Waters to play popular material outside the prescribed diet of twelve-bar blues. A common principle in all performance is to introduce variety, as between tempos, keys, types of material, different performers or voices, humor and seriousness, and so on. But for these newly codified musical forms of blues and jazz, limits were imposed upon this fundamental practice and upon the versatility of the musicians themselves. Listeners coming to blues later would have had difficulty in finding out that blues players had once used varied popular repertoires, so total was the exclusion of this fact from the prevailing narrative. Few blues players ever made recordings of this material.

The 1942 expeditions of Russell, Ramsey, Lomax, and the Fisk researchers to the South helped to advance the construction of boundaries between American musical forms. The researchers were dedicated to rediscovering the essence of two separate musical forms, as was happening elsewhere in critical debate. This laid the groundwork for a post–World War II settlement in which there has been a territorial separation between styles and categories of music. The most prominent, although not the only, criterion for separating one tradition from another was race. Henceforth, it was understood that white musicians played "white" music and black musician played "black" music. This reflected obvious social realities, but it also imposed assumptions that were, in effect if not in intention, racist.

While this musical segregation had limiting effects upon all musicians, it placed the greater restriction upon black musicians. Whites could, with some difficulty, achieve acceptance in a designated "black" field such as jazz. Black artists, however, were by definition exclusively representative of traditions with which they were connected. There was inequality of access to the music of the other racial category, which was the cause of the sense of anomaly experienced when a black musician enjoys "white" popular music. In a sense, these musicians were not allowed to appreciate such music. Music, however, is made out of harmonic, melodic, and rhythmic features, and the ability to respond to these is given to any listener. To do so, even when the music concerned was not of a kind that the critical narrative would find acceptable, is an aspect of Muddy Waters's, Charlie Parker's, or Louis Armstrong's musicality and musicianship that has been suppressed.

Bunk Johnson's post-1942 experience was "unique in jazz history," not only for his rediscovery and second career but also for "the fact that the nature of that rediscovery was determined by a group of jazz fans and scholars" (Williams 1967: 247). We have seen in other contexts in 1941–1943 the growing presence of a theorized view of a determinate music called "jazz," with an aesthetic and a historical narrative. We see jazz becoming the domain of experts. When Bunk Johnson left Louisiana in 1943, it was to appear in the setting of a lecture series given by the critic Rudi Blesh at the Museum of Modern Art in San Francisco.

In the same months as Johnson was recording, there took place what *Down Beat* called "two final blows" to the business of transporting bands (10.15.42: 1). From October, train schedules would be frozen, with no additional services and no new trains for hire. The following month, nationwide rationing of gasoline was brought into full effect. If a band had been displaced from buses to trains and then from trains to private automobiles, there was nowhere else for them to turn. There was still strong demand for bands that could stay on the road. *Billboard*, in its annual bands issue in September, reported "a general increase in both business and attendance figures" as compared with the returns for 1941. "Boom towns" in particular, "have been offering top money for one-nighter favorites. Jimmy

Dorsey averaged $1500 per night for dates in Iowa, Minnesota and Kansas" (*BB* 9.26.42: 91). The article also mentioned one-nighters for which Dorsey was offered even more money had he been able to reach them.

There were some bands touring on the same schedules as before. Duke Ellington's band kept up its constant movement, running one-nighters through the fall across the Midwest and down the East Coast. Returning from the film work in Hollywood, the band played a week in St. Louis and one- and two-nighters in Omaha, Storm Lake, Fort Dodge, St. Paul, and Madison. The first week in November at the Regal Theatre in Chicago was followed by one-nighters in Toledo, Cincinnati, Youngstown, Toronto, Kitchener, and Buffalo. Each of these transfers, difficult enough in peacetime, was more complicated and more costly under the conditions that applied one year into the war. The Ellington accounts do not indicate a sudden jump in transportation costs, but a piece in *Variety* detailed the convolutions bands went through in negotiating the schedules, "Let's use an example, a tentative route laid out for one band between Binghamton, N.Y., and Pottstown, Pa., a distance of perhaps 180 miles and roughly five hours by car or bus. Outfit would have finished at Binghamton barely in time to catch a 2:25 a.m. train to Scranton, arriving at 4:05 a.m., then the men had a three-and-a-half hour interval to sleep on the station platform awaiting a 7:25 train to Reading, where they had to change again for Pottstown, arriving at their destination at 3:31 in the afternoon. That allowed a few hours for sleeping, eating and cleaning up" (10.14.42: 42). There was extra cost in fatigue and general wear and tear, but there was a more decisive pressure on the financial costs. The new government restrictions on travel had not yet been "two final blows," but the margin was getting narrower all the time.

In October Vic Schroeder, an Omaha ballroom operator, was quoted as saying that "there are going to be changes none of us like. In addition to rationing and other curtailment, it looks like fewer bands and higher costs." In illustrating what he viewed as "the worst crisis in history," Schroeder set out the financial calculations, "From many years of operating experience, a band's minimum fixed costs, according to Schroeder, include—on a weekly basis, $15 for depreciation, insurance, maintenance of transportation equipment, $35 for arranger and library costs, $5 for stands, lights, depreciation and maintenance, $10 for telephone and general expenses and transportation costs based on an average of 250 miles a week, $25"

(*Var.* 10.21.42: 44). These figures may mean little to a present-day reader, but they represented heavy overheads in 1942 for a band on a modest budget. Schroeder's concluded that "the situation has gotten around to where every cent counts," and bands were forced to "cut to the bone." Schroeder reported that "many bands in this territory are quitting the business."

The music press was carrying frequent items about bands and leaders quitting the business. The draft, as well as financial pressure, was multiplying the problems of maintaining a band in proper condition. "There have been persistent reports," said *Variety* in October, "that Jack Teagarden was about to break up his band for the duration because he has lost or is losing men to the armed forces." Attached was a secondary rumor that Teagarden and his musicians were planning to enlist en masse, something the band of Clyde McCoy had already done (10.21.42: 44). Artie Shaw had made a typically sudden decision to sign up in January 1942. The bandleader and pianist Claude Thornhill, despite breakthrough success early in the year, volunteered for the service. Benny Goodman had been rejected as a 4-F, on the grounds of a back problem. Count Basie and Duke Ellington (who, at forty-three, was almost at the age limit) were awaiting the call from their draft boards. The press continued to post reports on the drafting of name musicians, for instance, the *Amsterdam News* reported in September "Kansas (drum) Fields is solid Navy blue, and is getting his three a day from Uncle in that killer tar tog" (9.19.42: 16).

The most publicized induction of a name bandleader was that of Glenn Miller into the army at the end of September. In view of Miller's actions and statements in support of the war effort, his joining the armed forces was not a surprise. After being turned down for the navy during the summer, Miller wrote to General Young, promising to help "streamline" military music if he were offered a commission. The farewell performance of the civilian Glenn Miller orchestra took place in an emotionally overwhelmed atmosphere at the Central Theater in Passaic, New Jersey, on September 27. This last show "never finished—the curtain was rung down while the band was still in the middle of its theme, with Miller and Marion Hutton no longer on the stage. Vocalist Hutton broke down in the middle of 'Kalamazoo,' started crying, and ran off the stage. Most of the brass section weren't doing much better in the start of the theme that followed—this was one case of the 'choke-up' being no alibi. Miller, famed for his taciturnity, turned away from the band to keep from cracking up himself—only to face rows and rows of kids bawling their eyes out" (*DB* 10.15.42: 1). Miller's departure for the service was seen in some quarters as marking the end of an epoch. The band was at the height of popularity, with only the rising Harry James as a contender, and only a few months from the historic golden disc for "Chattanooga Choo-Choo." Unlike some musicians and leaders, Miller was not quitting because of a lack of commercial success, as he pointed out in his letter to General Young.

Miller's music has come to be seen by later generations as a sedate, middle-aged affair, but some audience reactions in theaters were as frantic as those of the rock-and-roll audiences of the 1950s and 1960s. According to a Cleveland reviewer, in early 1942 the band had created, "frenzy and ecstasy in the auditorium" (Flower 1972: 404). A Detroit theater date saw "the kids practically getting out of hand" (1972: 407). In Pottstown, Pennsylvania, at a dance date in February, "State Troopers had to be called to preserve order" (1972: 420). The Miller band was not alone in generating wild responses; the Goodman band, at the Stanley Theatre in Pittsburgh, faced an "uncontrollable" audience, "cops were stationed everywhere to keep the jitterbug hordes from following the dictates of their feet and tribal spirits, but it was no use" (*Var.* 5.20.42: 23).

When the Miller band broke up, most of its players quickly found jobs elsewhere. High-grade musicians were in demand, despite the diminishing number of bands, as the draft was causing the pool of good musicians to shrink even more quickly. A piece in *Variety* asked its readers, "Did you ever circulate around rehearsal studios and watch new bands go through their paces? You wonder where most of them dug up the personnel. In many cases the guys behind the instruments look like they're doubling from elementary school" (10.7.42: 41).

Many professional musicians were discovering that they might be better off in the service. Musicians joined the armed forces for the same reasons as other Americans, and some, like Claude Thornhill, insisted that they receive no special treatment. The army, navy, and air force wanted musicians, however, and some prospects they held out to professional players were especially attractive in the insecure condition of the business. In July the *Chicago Defender* reported on auditions at the Savoy Ballroom for a U.S. Navy band. Among "some of the country's leading musicians," recruits would be "inducted, taken to Great Lakes for four weeks and then shipped to San Francisco, where they will remain for the duration. Best thing about the band is the pay, which is $56 per month" (*CD* 7.25.42: 11). By November, Artie Shaw, now a captain in the navy, was recruiting musicians in New York, "The outfit will begin rehearsals in a training ship moored in the Hudson River, for an eventual tour which might take it as far as Pearl Harbor" (*Var.* 11.11.42: 39).

The United States was less than twelve months into the war, and already the conditions of everyday life—let alone those in the music business—felt its pressures. Rationing of gasoline, which had reached across the nation by the fall, affected everyone. Other items, from household appliances to staple foods, were coming under stricter control: coffee was by then rationed, at the rate of about three ounces per person per week. These were the early stages of a long struggle, the war itself, and it was difficult for professional musicians and others to take an optimistic view of the short and medium term. By late fall of 1942 there was news from some theaters of war that indicated an upturn, even a turning point: the combined American and British armies had won a brilliant victory in North Africa, and within a year the way would be open for an invasion of Italy. The advance of the German army had been halted in the bitter stalemate of Stalingrad. Even in the Pacific, after crucial victories at Midway Island in the summer, there were signs of improvement. It was nevertheless clear in all these zones of war that there was a long way to go.

The music that the war was producing was still the object of some scorn. The ambitions of songwriters such as Oscar Hammerstein and Hoagy Carmichael, and of Aaron Copland in a different field, to produce music expressing the feelings of a population at war had not been realized to critics' satisfaction. The first rush of material after the attack on Pearl Harbor had provoked the *Down Beat* verdict that they "stank." In March *Variety* conveyed the opinion of jukebox operators that "all of the stuff written since Dec. 7 was found wanting with the exception of 'Remember Pearl Harbor.'" The operators found that "Standard numbers like the 'Marines Hymn' etc, were okay," but these were songs of World War I and the military past (*Var.* 3.25.42: 8). As we saw in chapter 2, bands such as those of Gene Krupa and Bob Crosby made a specialty of playing these tunes in contemporary swing arrangements. Even at the end of the year, in a broadcast from Williamsport, Pennsylvania, the Crosby band was featuring a Dixieland treatment of "It's a Long Way to Tipperary," announced as "this war's top version of one of the last war's top songs."

The idiom that remained popular and had some relation to the fact of wartime was the romantic ballad. The songwriting industry had found that the situation of wartime could lend extra poignancy to familiar styles and suggest motifs of separation, longing, dreams, and reunions that took additional resonance from the common events of the time: men being drafted, sent overseas, returning on temporary leave, and so on. Some of these songs subsequently lost much of this added meaning and were not perpetuated in peacetime. More significantly, songs of this type suffered from later deep-seated changes in the conventions of popular song.

By the late summer of 1942, current styles and moods of popular song were perceived in some quarters as problematic for the ongoing war effort. In August it was announced that the government was considering giving financial help to songwriters, "to aid in and encourage the writing of rousing war songs" (*Var.* 8.26.42: 3). The absence of songs with the qualities of those of the recently deceased George M. Cohan, such as "Over There" (another World War I anthem revamped by the Bob Crosby band), was one cause of official dissatisfaction. Even more strongly regretted was the nature of the songs that had been produced over the preceding year. By October 1942 there existed a governmental Music Committee, headed by Jack Joy, an official of the Office of War Information. As *Variety* explained, "the trouble, from the viewpoint of America's Ministry of Propaganda, is that everything is too saccharine" (10.7.42: 2).

A term that was becoming current for music perceived as unduly "sweet" or "saccharine" was *slush*. For the Office of War Information, among the slush pile were many current popular songs, even those with a direct war reference, "Even our war ballads are nothing but love songs with a once-over-lightly war background. 'Johnny Doughboy Found a Rose in Ireland' is just boy-meets-girl; so is 'He Wears a Pair of Silver Wings.'" Even Irving Berlin's patriotically minded July 4 show had come under the opprobrium of the committee, "'I Left My Heart at the Stage Door Canteen' has been questioned by the OWI in light of its punchline 'A soldier boy without a heart, Has two strikes on him from the start,' and 'I Threw a Kiss in the Ocean,' also Berlin's, is deemed too ballady" (*Var.* 10.7.42: 2).

Songs with a "more martial spirit," of the same type as the immediate post–Pearl Harbor songs, were still being written. In August the poet Langston Hughes wrote with the veteran blues composer W. C. Handy "Go-and-Get-the-Enemy Blues." But there were no signs of a definitive song to fulfill the same function in this war as the still-serving songs of the last. There also were concerns about the effects that the genre of romantic songs might have upon morale, fighting spirit, and moral fiber. Slush might be dangerous; with its air of melancholy and longing, it might sap the strength needed to get the job done. The noticeably slow tempos in which some songs were performed did not suggest the required energy and urgency. The Tommy Dorsey band was using unprecedentedly slow tempos in recordings that featured singers, including Frank Sinatra, backed by vocal groups and a string section. Recordings such as "There Are Such Things" do not evoke the atmosphere of a military march, still less the "mounting pitch of war frenzy" (Schuller 1989: 398).

With the genre of the ballad and its questioning in wartime, we come up against ideas of gender. In the cinema there was a view of a certain genre of films, those dealing with romantic love, as the "woman's film." A similar identification with female audiences and tastes was made, less explicitly, for the genre of the romantic-sentimental song. The unease of the military and the Office of War Information about the song output of mid-1942 implied an idea of masculine values threatened by the weakening or debilitating effects of the feminine love song. In all cultural fields, especially in a time of armed conflict, "masculine" values are elevated above "feminine" ones; this led to a disparagement of the genre of the romantic love song as a whole: not worthy of great respect at any time and dangerous in wartime to the necessary "masculine" values.

Love ballads lost popularity and critical respect within the next two decades. Later references to "sentimental" popular songs of the era are always unfavorable (e.g., Gillett 1971: vi). The word *sentimental* itself has come to mean "addicted to indulgence in superficial emotion" (*Shorter Oxford Dictionary*). This was not previously its meaning and seems not to have been a widely shared usage in 1941–1942. In earlier uses, through Sterne's novel *A Sentimental Journey* and Flaubert's *Sentimental Education* and into the twentieth century, the word referred to a positive refinement of the emotions, a capacity for feeling and expressing emotion.

The word was still found in a positive sense in songs of the 1930s
and 1940s, for instance, "In a Sentimental Mood" by Duke Ellington.
"Sentimental Lady" was recorded by the Ellington band at the last session
before the recording ban. In the lyric of a song from "Jump for Joy," we hear,
"My poor heart is sentimental, Not made of wood." There was the 1944 hit
"For Sentimental Reasons" and in 1945 "Sentimental Journey." The theme
song of the Tommy Dorsey orchestra was "I'm Getting Sentimental over
You"; one of Dorsey's small-band units was called The Sentimentalists and
his nickname (despite his pugnacious personality) was "The Sentimental
Gentleman of Swing." Modern uses of the word *sentimental* to describe
songs of this period tend to be dismissive or apologetic, as if some songs
can be good despite being sentimental. For audiences in 1942, it was just as
possible for songs to be good *because* they were sentimental.

Sentiment, romance, and their associated images were coming to be
stigmatized, however. The ballads of the period were perceived as embody-
ing feminine concerns and emotions and as representing feminine tastes.
But there are many indications that these tastes were shared by much of
the male audience. It appears that this feminine aspect of popular song
was not repudiated by male listeners. A letter from a soldier, published in
Variety in September, stated firmly that slush was just as popular with soldiers as other types of music. "If you don't believe me," the writer insisted,
"hop out to some army camp some night and keep a box-score on the
tunes played on any of the boxes. You'll find the slush tunes getting as big
a play" (9.2.42: 13). This is borne out informally by the request numbers
on Glenn Miller's radio programs, with the soldiery of camps and training
bases voting for tunes like "Moonlight Cocktail" (played in June for the
soldiers of Fort Benning, Georgia). From the point of view of the Office
of War Information committee, the fact that American soldiers seemed
to enjoy slush was a problem. But their enjoyment also provides a deeper
understanding of popular tastes during this period.

As I noted in chapter 3, one of the difficulties in discussing American
popular music of the pre-Presley periods is the lack of respect that it is
afforded by music historians. This applies most strongly to the genres
of romantic-sentimental popular song. Many critics and listeners react
to them by withholding the close and balanced attention they might
give to other material. The entire idiom can be bypassed by naming it

"sentimental," thus placing it in a category beneath serious consideration. The American sentimental love song, however, was an active and extremely popular genre. There is a body of writing that honors the achievements in World War II of what is called "the greatest generation," the Americans who were of draftable age in the 1940s. At the same time, historians of popular music show a consistent disregard for the musical tastes of the same people. Many Americans went through the war listening to and enjoying romantic and sentimental love songs. It is certain, at any rate, that the soundtrack of the war had a remarkably different character from those of Vietnam and the Gulf wars.

The romantic-sentimental love song could be read as a literary convention equivalent to pastoral conventions of the sixteenth to eighteenth centuries. For instance, when John Milton's friend Edward King was drowned, Milton's elegy for King was expressed through that convention, with King becoming the shepherd Lycidas and his life and death translated into the vocabulary of "swains" and "nymphs." This did not mean that Milton's perception of death and loss was unreal or sentimental. Similarly, the love songs of the mid-twentieth century, using the language of roses, cottages, and moonlight, did not necessarily offer these images as real elements of sexual relationships. The language was that of a lyrical convention to which listeners were able to attach their actual emotions, without necessarily taking its images as pictures of the real lives they aspired to. The millions of buyers of "My Blue Heaven" in 1927 did not necessarily expect whippoorwills and roses as a part of the marriage contract. The critical literature on the superior reality of blues lyrics, for example, has closed off consideration of popular song genres of this type (Charters 1963). However, it is debatable how much more real for a middle-class white audience the imagery of a Southern prison blues is than that of comfortable suburban monogamy.

The love songs of the 1940s spoke a language that has lost its resonance over time. Even the lyrics a writer like Johnny Mercer was producing in 1942 are largely made up of a language that is sentimental in present-day terms, "Somewhere in heaven you were fashioned for me." The opening line of a 1942 Jimmy Van Heusen song, "Moonlight becomes you, it goes with your hair," addresses the loved one in a style that is no longer viable in popular music. It is impossible to imagine a twenty-first-century U.S. Army base voting for a song whose lyric begins "Start with a jigger of moonlight."

But in the early 1940s it was still permissible for songs, performers, and audiences to communicate through a stylistic language that was sentimental, even feminine. There are examples among the songs that Frank Sinatra recorded with the Dorsey band. Later writers on Sinatra (Lees 1987; Clarke 1997: 149) and his later publicity favor the aggressively masculine persona he acquired in the 1950s, for example, in recordings that swung with a big band, and, in the personal sphere, his rumored associations with organized crime, his fisticuffs with photographers, and the "Rat Pack" with whom he consorted in Las Vegas. In 1942, however, Sinatra's repertoire, vocal style, and band arrangements were in keeping with a soft presentation, with the appurtenances of the romantic and the sentimental. The more expressly masculine baritone singers such as Dick Haymes and Vaughn Monroe also drew on the same repertoire, but Sinatra's persona was lighter, softer, more feminine. Some of the songs he recorded at the time suggested passivity: notice the fragility of the protagonist of "Be Careful, It's My Heart" and the song "Take Me," which could have been written for a female singer.

Sinatra's vocal quality, more easily endorsed by critics in its harder post-1950s sonority, is a conspicuously beautiful one in these early recordings. The voice is lighter and softer, with a well-controlled violinlike vibrato, and it recalls the aesthetic of the *bel canto* lyrical tradition. The orchestral arrangements are from the sweet end of the spectrum, with rich harmonies and full sonorities, and from mid-1942 onward, to the disgust of jazz writers, a string section. Even Donald Clarke, a critic responsive to these earlier recordings, described Dorsey's hiring a string section as a "disaster" (1997: 71). Gunther Schuller praised some white bands on the basis of resistance to what he calls "the string temptation" (1989: 690 n.). String sections were suggestive of the sweet ethos and the romantic-sentimental love ballad, and as one of Sinatra's 1940s fans said, "Ballads were for girls" (Petkov and Mustazza 1995: 52).

The 1930s and 1940s divide between "swing" and "sweet" bands has to do with images of gender as much as with anything objectively present in the music. Subsequent jazz history was built around the swing half of this dichotomy—or rather it distanced itself from the sweet side. In actual practice, though, all bands played a mixture of swing and sweet material. The bands of Glenn Miller and Duke Ellington were highly placed in readers' polls in both categories. The sweet (sentimental/ballad) material that all bands played has become the submerged portion of their discographies. Little account is taken, especially in the histories of jazz, of the existence on record and in performance of this material, plentiful and significant as it was.

As far as governmental agencies in late 1942 were concerned, the popular yet martial piece it was looking for might have been "Praise the Lord and Pass the Ammunition," the song by Frank Loesser that was recorded by Kay Kyser just before the Petrillo ban. The Kyser arrangement combines vigorous choral passages with interpolated swing passages for the band. Loesser's lyrics had touches of cynicism ("You can't afford to be a politician"), but their message in relation to the war effort was unmistakable. By early November the recording, eventually to sell over a million copies, was "riding the crest of ballyhoo" (*Var.* 11.11.42: 41).

At about that time, Frank Sinatra's career as a solo artist was proving unexpectedly difficult. With the Dorsey band his popularity had climbed to poll-winning levels, but his position was subsidiary. A review of a theater date in Chicago mentioned Sinatra only in the last paragraph, where he was described as "Poised and nonchalant, with a definite appeal to the ladies" (*Var.* 7.22.42: 39). In Cleveland a week later, "Frank Sinatra's singing and ingratiating vocal harmony by the Pied Pipers were other terrifically applauded highlights" (*Var.* 7.29.42: 46). At the Earle in Philadelphia on August 1, "Frank Sinatra's melodious voice nets him plenty of kudoes" (*Var.* 8.5.42: 56). In Washington, D.C., Sinatra's cancellation with tonsillitis caused an audience reaction, "Jitterbugs took the indisposition announcement with a chorus of groans, indicating that Sinatra, were he present, could have had the nomination by acclamation" (*Var.* 8.19.42: 40).

By late fall, Sinatra had left the Dorsey band and was out of the national limelight. A recording by Bing Crosby of a song from the recently released film *Holiday Inn* gave further evidence of public taste for what the press referred to as "slush." "White Christmas" reached the top of the sales charts in October and stayed there for eleven weeks. It is interesting to note, too, that for several weeks the song was at the top of the "Harlem Hit Parade." Crosby's recording was the single biggest commercial success of 1942. Its nostalgic sentimental lyric, with Yuletide imagery of children listening for sleigh bells in the snow did not identify it as a song of wartime, except by implication. "White Christmas" was escapist, and its great popularity with servicemen as well as with Americans on the home front made it an exhibit in the case against the effects of slush upon morale.

Despite the pessimism and the sense of failure expressed in hillbilly songs such as Ernest Tubbs's "Walking the Floor over You" and Ted Daffan's "Born to Lose," music from American folk sources was not accused of injuring fighting spirit. In part this was because these emerging styles had not fully registered as a force in national musical culture. It was possible, however, for the eastern music press to pick up signals of country music's increasing impact at a national level. There had been big recording successes in 1941 and 1942 derived from the music of the Southwest or from movie cowboys such as Tex Ritter and Gene Autry. Bing Crosby had covered "Walkin' the Floor" and was to pick up several more country hits. "(I've Got Spurs That) Jingle Jangle Jingle," a piece by Frank Loesser no more authentically cowboy than Cole Porter's "Don't Fence Me In," was successful in versions by Kay Kyser and Guy Lombardo.

One of the most popular songs of the year was "Deep in the Heart of Texas," a 1941 composition by Don Swander. Lombardo and Kyser recorded versions of this, too, as did Bing Crosby, Wayne King, Horace Heidt, and the vocal group the Merry Macs. It was reported as the favorite sing-along piece for factory workers in England, perhaps because of the opportunity for rhythmic clapping on the four beats before the title phrase. As noted earlier, the song was in the 1942 repertoire of Muddy Waters and was requested by Bunk Johnson at his first recording session. By mid-1942 the cultural reach of country styles of music, and equally of the image of the cowboy, was extensive. This was aided by the long-established film genre of the Western, which made stars of singing cowboy performers like Autry. By 1936 the song genre was well enough established for Johnny Mercer to parody it in "I'm an Old Cowhand." Mercer's company, Capitol, had its first success in summer 1942 with the song "Cow Cow Boogie" sung by Ella Mae Morse over a swing-boogie accompaniment. The lyric tells of a lone cowboy on the plains whose singing is a blend of cowboy ballad and black boogie-woogie. The character brings together two symbolic figures of popular song, the cowboy and the hep-cat, in the words of the song, "a swing half-breed" whose speech combines "a knockdown Western accent with a Harlem touch."

In 1938, Aaron Copland composed the first of his cowboy ballets, "Billy the Kid." Characteristically, Copland worried about his qualifications for this project until he discovered that the historic Billy the Kid was, like himself, a New Yorker. Copland had no qualms about the artistic quality of the cowboy ballads he was working from; in his view, "The words are usually delightful and the manner of singing needs no praise from me" (Copland and Perls 1984: 279). The ballet, which received good reviews, was performed several times in 1938–1939 and revived in 1941 and 1943. In the spring of 1942, Copland was working on the patriotic *Lincoln Portrait* when he was approached by the choreographer Agnes de Mille, who asked that he compose another piece for the Ballet Russe. Copland was reluctant to do another cowboy ballet, but agreed to do the piece de Mille had sketched out. She appealed to Copland on the grounds of "Americanism." In a phrase that recalled Willa Cather, her scenario noted "one must always be conscious of the enormous land on which these people live and their proud loneliness." de Mille's appeal to the Ballet Russe was on similar grounds, "it was wartime, and they wanted an American ballet on an American theme by an American" (1984: 356). Copland began work immediately on the new cowboy ballet, at first simply "An American Ballet," but later retitled *Rodeo*. He had the work planned by mid-May, aiming at rehearsals in July and a premiere in the fall.

The welcome extended by the music press to cowboy and country music was also conditioned by Americanism. The most receptive of the magazines was *Billboard*, the first to set up a popularity chart for music in this new domain. Critics' attitudes toward the audiences could still be patronizing, as in a *Variety* review of a Renfro Valley Barn Dance package in Indianapolis, "This hay-flavored bill has little appeal to smartened showgoers, but it is getting a nice play from defense workers and the rural element who don't go to the theatre often" (*BB* 11.18.42: 47). *Billboard* followed up its earlier praise of country music's "naturalness and simplicity" with a recommendation in its 1942 year book of the "folk record" in general, "The richness and variety of American folk music is astounding." It gave references to Gene Autry, Ernest Tubb, Bob Wills, Roy Acuff, Jimmy Wakely, Montana Slim, and a long list mostly of white country artists. The article concluded, "It is interesting to note that the war is tending to aid the folk music field. Placing greater and greater importance upon all things that are indigenously American, it is attracting more and more attention to the great field of folk records" (*BB* 9.26.42: 86). There is a connection between the persuasions of Agnes de Mille, the work of a serious composer like Copland, his earlier commission to produce "a patriotic piece; a musical portrait of a great American," and the country and folk recordings *Billboard* was endorsing as "distinctive and down-to-earth American music—strictly American music." The national emotions provoked by the war were entering into perceptions of musical forms and traditions.

The Broadway composers Richard Rodgers and Oscar Hammerstein were also writing for a work that, allowing for the different conventions of the musical theater, had many parallels with Copland's. The idea for a musical based on the 1931 play *Green Grow the Lilacs* was suggested to Rodgers by the theater director Theresa Helburn, and Rodgers was in discussions on the project in March 1942. By July, as Copland's *Rodeo* was going into rehearsal, Rodgers had begun writing the musical with his new collaborator Hammerstein. At about the time that de Mille was working the finalized *Rodeo*, Theresa Helburn took Rodgers and Hammerstein to examine the set de Mille had designed for Copland's ballet. *Rodeo* and the new musical (which was eventually called *Oklahoma!*) were running in parallel. De Mille became choreographer for both works. According to William Hyland (1998: 143) "De Mille had written to apply for the job," but by her account the company producing the Rodgers and Hammerstein musical contacted her by telegram shortly after the premiere of *Rodeo* in New York on October 16 (Copland and Perls 1984: 361).

This first performance of *Rodeo* at the Metropolitan Opera House received superb notices and twenty-two curtain calls. In the remainder of 1942 and in 1943 it had seventy-nine further performances across the country. De Mille and the Ballet Russe company joined the millions of Americans traveling the nation's overburdened transportation network. *Rodeo* was described in press notices as a "genuine American ballet" and "a brilliant skirmish with Americana." Copland did not take the work so seriously; in a letter to Benjamin Britten that fall he wrote of it as "a frothy ballet" on "the usual wildwest subject" (Copland and Perls 1984: 364). Copland was not indifferent to Americana, but he had originally wanted de Mille to do the ballet on the subject of Ellis Island.

Americanism and patriotism were still in the foreground of Copland's concerns through the last months of 1942. The suite "Music for Movies," composed at that time, was a summation of his work in the cinema in which he aimed to "mirror in musical terms the American scenes" in films he had been involved in (1984: 366). In the fall, Copland was also writing a shorter work for the Cincinnati Symphony, as a "contribution to the war effort." "As with *Lincoln Portrait*," Copland commented, "I was gratified to participate in a patriotic activity" (1984: 368). This piece, "Fanfare for the Common Man," was to become one of Copland's most popular works.

As Ethan Mordden wrote of the American theater at this period, it was a time of "seeking cultural truths in the idea of homeland" (1981: 191). This was the departure time for the journeys that John Dos Passos took across the United States for *The State of the Nation* and of Preston Sturges's satirical movie *Sullivan's Travels*, in which a jaded film director takes off on a journey across the United States to put himself back in touch with "real people." The expression of a desire for open space and an affirmative sense of the nation and the land is delivered in a song Rodgers and Hammerstein had written by August 1942 for their Western musical, *Oh, What a Beautiful Morning*, in which "the sounds of the earth are like music." The closing number of the show contained the couplet, "We know we belong to the land/And the land we belong to is grand." About a year into the war, this was an expression of a positive national identity. The impulse for the song came from Theresa Helburn, who one evening during a taxi-ride in New York said to Oscar Hammerstein, "I wish you and Dick would write a song about the earth" (Fordin 1995: 197).

On the night *Rodeo* received its premiere at the Metropolitan Opera, the bands of Cootie Williams and Eddie Vinson were opening their engagements at the Apollo Theatre on 125th Street. The following evening the annual dance for the Independent Progressive Club of Subway Employees took place, featuring the big band of Earl Hines. Twelve blocks southeast of the Metropolitan Opera, the clubs and bars of 52nd Street, mostly between Fifth and Sixth Avenues, were featuring the kinds of musical entertainment that they had been providing for some years. By 1942, 52nd Street was the focus of jazz-based entertainment in New York City. Clubs tended to shift and migrate; some Harlem clubs had relocated to the more profitable midtown hub, and some of the longer-lasting clubs changed addresses within 52nd Street more than once. At this time, going westward from Fifth Avenue, one passed on the south side of 52nd Street Club 18 at numbers 18–20, Club Samoa at 62, The Famous Door at 66, the Hickory House at 144, and the

Yacht Club at 150. On the north side, the first celebrated venue was Jimmy Ryan's at 53, followed by the Onyx at 57. A block away, Kelly's Stables was at 141 West 51st Street.

Clubs had differing policies and stylistic preferences. Jimmy Ryan's continued to be more allied to older styles than, say, the Onyx, which in 1942 was featuring a modern-oriented small band including Dizzy Gillespie, Oscar Pettiford, and Max Roach, all of whom would later be classified as bebop players. Most clubs had house bands to which would be added special attractions and freelancers sitting in. The clubs also differed in the degree of informality. The outright jamming system was the province of the fringe clubs and Harlem locations such as Monroe's and Minton's. Though it was associated with a culture of jazz playing, 52nd Street was also, indeed primarily, an entertainment district. The addresses between jazz clubs were occupied by bars, other musical establishments, and, increasingly in wartime, strip joints and burlesque venues. The Club Samoa became a strip club in 1943, and a "skin policy" had begun to take over in a number of 52nd Street addresses by the spring of 1942, for instance, the Famous Door had the act of Zorita the Snake Charmer on the same bill as the Red Norvo group.

Small bands were the staple of 52nd Street, as big bands were impracticable both physically and financially for the small clubs' premises. The war made an immediate and positive difference to the 52nd Street economy but changed its face in some ways that were troubling. There was a lot of money around and many service personnel from out of town. In Arnold Shaw's words, the war brought a welcome influx of soldiers and sailors, but also "a rash of striptease joints, tab padding and other sharp practices, fistfights and sluggings, racial conflict, and even attacks on the music" (1977: 251). Some servicemen from the South did not take kindly to the comparatively easy interracial mixing that occurred on 52nd Street.

By this time, many musicians were in the services and posted near or passing through New York. The drummer Shelly Manne was serving in the Coast Guard and was stationed at Manhattan Beach, within range of 52nd Street, "Used to travel by subway to 52nd St., every night—it was a ride—and sit in until the last minute. Had to check in at six in the morning. I stayed up night after night—who needed sleep then?—to play the drums"

(Shaw 1977: 160). Until late in the fall of 1942, Artie Shaw's recruitment center for his navy band was still the ship moored in the Hudson River. Some players were having a more musical experience of service life than they might have expected. Bill Reinhardt, Musician 1st Class at Camp Allen, near Norfolk, Virginia, wrote an article for *Down Beat* entitled "How the Navy Musicians Live and Work," "Reveille is at 5:50. Chow is served and the full band plays colors at 8. Rehearsal lasts from 9 until 11. Chow is served again and the dance band plays in the recreation hall at noon. Liberty cards are then served if there are no parades or other afternoon work. Chow is served for the third time at 4:30 and taps is sounded at 9:30. There are other duties such as sweeping, window washing and G.I. details" (12.15.42: 18). Some musicians found places in camps and training bases, some with excellent bands that functioned like big bands in peacetime and, alternating with touring professionals, provided entertainment for the troops. *Amsterdam News* reported on a remarkable band that was "tooting for the US," the 371st Rhythm Boys, based at Camp Robinson and led by Dave Bartholomew, later a major player on the postwar New Orleans scene (2.6.43: 17). Few musicians in the armed services found a *modus vivendi* as enviable as that of the Lionel Hampton saxophonist Marshall Royal, who was based at St. Mary's College in Orinda, California, "No regular commercial band could stand the competition of coming near us when we were appearing," Royal said of his navy band. "We spent the entire duration of the war on the campus there, and never had any contact with the enemy." After the daily musical and other duties, Royal would "get into my car and drive back over the Bay Bridge to where I was staying in San Francisco, 26 miles away. I had my own car there and a gas allowance" (Royal and Gordon 1996: 78).

The trumpeter Max Kaminsky, who had been in the Artie Shaw band at the time of the attack on Pearl Harbor, was inducted into the navy in November. The band of service musicians he was assigned to, again under Shaw's direction, was stationed at Pier 92, West 52nd Street. "Pier 92 didn't sound so good," Kaminsky wrote, "But the Fifty-second Street part of it was reassuring" (Kaminsky and Hughes 1965: 132). According to Kaminsky's memoirs, one night the band was "herded into an open truck and driven to Penn Station," transported by train to San Francisco, and then shipped out to Honolulu, arriving there on Christmas Day, 1942. This was the prelude to a traumatic spell for Kaminsky and the other Shaw musicians. Working as musicians for the entertainment of the troops, they nevertheless experienced bombing raids and other hazards at Guadalcanal and other Pacific islands. At the end of a tour of duty, recuperating in Australia, "we were suffering so badly from shell shock and were so worn out and weary that one by one we started to get sick. I could hardly play and I began having nightmares and would wake up screaming night after night" (1965: 151).

Many of the 52nd Street clubs stayed in business throughout the war and despite the absence of players like Kaminsky. The period of operation that most interested jazz historians occurred a few years later. In many cases, the clubs were downscale and unprepossessing; in Leonard Feather's description, "shaped like shoe boxes. The drinks were probably watered. They were miserable places" (Shaw 1977: 280).[1] There were other well-known clubs in Greenwich Village, including the Village Vanguard, Nick's, and Café Society Downtown, which in the fall of 1942 had Lester Young playing in its resident band.

At higher levels of the market, New York had its hotels, like the Pennsylvania, and its theaters, the Apollo, the Strand, and preeminently, the Paramount, a palatial building on Times Square. An engagement at the Paramount signified the highest level of recognition for any popular performer, musician or band. It was at the Paramount, for instance, that the sensational appearance of the Benny Goodman band following its 1935 breakthrough signaled full recognition of the new wave of enthusiasm for swing and the big bands. There were other lesser, but still important, venues across Greater New York. Brooklyn had its own large and opulent Strand and Paramount Theaters. Newark had two venues, the Adams Theatre and the cavernous Mosque, which, according to a November *Billboard* item, "has been a white elephant, having made unsuccessful tries at a number of policies" (11.14.42: 11). Later that month, the Mosque would be trying out a "two-a-day vaude policy" in an attempt to recoup recent losses.

The Ellington orchestra played a performance at the army base of Fort Dix, New Jersey, on November 19. A new singer, Jimmy Britton, sang the ballad "Just As Though You Were Here," but most of the program consisted of material written by Ellington. *Metronome's* review of the radio broadcast mentioned, "The soldiers, as always, screamed, howled, broke their hands with tumultuous applause" (12.42: 16). *Variety* caught the band at their next engagement, at the Earle Theatre in Philadelphia. The pop-ular songs included Jerome Kern's "Dearly Beloved" and a new Johnny Mercer piece, "Arthur Murray Taught Me Dancing in a Hurry," sung by Lilian Fitzgerald. "Duke Ellington and his troupe of jivesters carry the entire entertainment burden on their shoulders, getting scant assistance from the film entry [a Western called *Omaha Trail*]. The Duke's minions and the surrounding acts more than fill the bill in giving the customers their money's worth" (*Var.* 11.25.42: 22). Among others, the bill included the dancer Jigsaw Jackson, who had performed with Ellington throughout this fall tour of the East.

At about this time, according to the memoirs of Leonard Feather, who had been working as press agent to Ellington since their meeting in Chicago in the summer, "William Morris, Jr., a booking agent whose con-cern for Ellington went well beyond grosses and commissions, told him: 'I want you to write a long work, and let's do it in Carnegie Hall'" (1986: 64). The idea of a major concert performance of this kind, the resurgence of the image of Carnegie Hall as well as the reality, must have taken shape around the end of November, because Feather mentioned "trips to Baltimore and Philadelphia to discuss plans [and] dream up public relations ideas." In early December, stories trailing a Carnegie Hall concert began to appear in the music press. The work Ellington would present on that occasion, however, was still in skeletal form. Ellington himself had in mind a finished version of a work called *Boola*, already in existence as a prose manuscript and a project that he had begun as long ago as 1931. Some early press stories claimed this work would be the centerpiece of the Carnegie Hall perfor-mance. The *Amsterdam News* anticipated "new works including excerpts from the composer's new opera *Boola*" (12.19.42: 12).

One story in *Billboard* read like a bland press release, telling the reader that Ellington had "huddled with" a writer, Maurice Zolotow, briefing him for an article to appear in *Reader's Digest*, "All in line with the maestro's January 23 concert at New York's Carnegie Hall" (*BB* 12.12.42: 23). Even by the Christmas issue of *Variety*, "Ellington's music program is not definitely set, but will be made up of representative music written by the leader." The story also alluded to a possible "special symphony" written for the concert (12.23.42: 3). Even by the time these articles appeared, four weeks before the concert, Ellington had barely begun the new work that the concert was to be built around. The nature of the important new composition remained undecided, and no specific writing was done on it while the Ellington band performed throughout a week in December at the Howard Theatre in Washington, D.C. Among his other concerns, Ellington was still uncertain about his status for the draft. A story in November had merely stated that he was "not going into the armed services for the present" (*BB* 11.14.42: 22).

The band went on to Hartford, Connecticut, to open on December 11 for three days at the State Theatre. In addition to the orchestra and its singers, the theater bill consisted of the dancers Baby Lawrence; Pot, Pan, and Skillet; and Jigsaw Jackson, as well as a "special added attraction," Frank Sinatra. The months since Sinatra had left Dorsey had not been a complete failure: he had secured a CBS radio program and done the spot in the *Reveille with Beverley* movie. His affairs were being handled by the GAC agency, but bookings like the Hartford engagement with Ellington, with his name well down the bill, did not represent the progress he had anticipated. A few weeks before Hartford, Sinatra was engaged as one of the performers in the new vaudeville policy at the ailing Mosque Theatre in Newark. This, too, did not seem an engagement to celebrate. To Sinatra, out of the national spotlight, living in Jersey City and playing a minor theater gig a few miles from his birthplace in Hoboken, it must have seemed as if he had never left New Jersey.

But Sinatra's agent at GAC, Harry Romm, had persuaded Bob Weitman, manager of the Times Square Paramount, to venture out to Newark one night to see Sinatra's act at the Mosque. Sinatra was not an unknown—he had spent two years with Tommy Dorsey and had been a *Down Beat* poll winner a year before. Weitman was not expecting to see anything exceptional, and the atmosphere in the Newark venue was not at first encouraging, "When Weitman and Romm entered the Mosque Theatre, the cavernous hall was more than half empty" (Shaw 1968: 45). At the moment of Sinatra coming out onto the stage, however, the reaction of the young audience was surprising and extreme. Intrigued, Weitman decided to book him to open at the Paramount on December 30. In case there was any mistake about Sinatra's potential, the bill in which he would appear was strong enough without him: the film was the premiere of *Star Spangled Rhythm*, featuring Bing Crosby and many other stars, and the band was Benny Goodman's, featuring the new young singer Peggy Lee. As he was at the Hartford State, Sinatra would be billed as a "special added attraction."

When Sinatra's and Ellington's paths crossed at the State Theatre in mid-December, for the third time since midsummer, both were at a critical moment. Sinatra was preparing for the Paramount engagement, and Ellington was facing a major Carnegie Hall presentation in six weeks' time, with as yet no music composed for it. Ellington wrote later of his impression of the young singer, "He was young, crispy-crunch fresh, and the girls were squealing then. He was very easy to get along with, and there were no hassles about his music" (Ellington 1974: 238). It was during those three days in Hartford that Ellington finally began to write the extended musical work that was to be presented at his Carnegie Hall debut. He later wrote of the setting in which the writing began, "It was in December 1942, and between stage shows I would get my paper and pencil and go to the piano on stage and experiment and write. The light was not too good, and the movie they were showing was *The Cat Woman* . . . since I could not see what was going on behind the screen, it sometimes got pretty scary back there in the dark" (1974: 181).

It was in this environment that Ellington embarked on the composition of a work which, *Amsterdam News* announced on December 26, was entitled "Black, Brown, and Beige" and "would run to 25 minutes." The new composition was begun and completed in the six weeks between the Hartford gig and the Carnegie Hall premiere in January. Of necessity and as usual for traveling musicians like Ellington, the work was done on the road, among a run of dates in New England, the Midwest, and into Canada (Tucker 1993b).

The press reactions in the first week of 1943 did not fully reflect what happened at Frank Sinatra's opening Paramount appearance on December 30 or guess at its importance for the history of American popular music. For *Variety*, it was "Sock New Year's Biz on Broadway," with Goodman and the feature film credited for the biggest takings of any week in the history of the Paramount (1.6.43: 21). The review in the same edition merely rated Sinatra as "the outstanding click of the bill," who "sells tunes easily" and "possesses a wealth of smooth salesmanship in his voice" (*Var.* 1.6.43: 208).

An eyewitness account by Neil McCaffrey described the reactions of a hip fan of the big bands to the show: registering changes in the personnel of the Goodman band, enjoying the performance of Peggy Lee, all as might be expected. According to McCaffrey, the day was "raw with sleet," and "a crowd was winding down Eighth Avenue" (Petkov and Mustazza 1995: 52). McCaffrey then described himself as "dumbstruck" by the noise that met Sinatra's appearance before he had even sung a note. Benny Goodman had the task of announcing him, and in Sinatra's words, "The sound that greeted me was absolutely deafening. It was a tremendous roar" (Shaw 1968: 45). Donald Clarke gave this account, "When Sinatra came through the curtain, a wall of screaming crashed over everybody on stage, so that Goodman, frozen in the act of giving the downbeat for the next tune, looked over his shoulder and blurted out, "What the fuck is that?" (1997: 75). The four encores that Sinatra took after the songs he performed in what McCaffrey called his "bedroom style" were unprecedented in the Paramount. The nature of the audience reaction he produced was unprecedented anywhere.

What was most striking was the reaction of the girls in the Paramount audience, as in the Newark Mosque a few weeks earlier. The excitement exhibited by Sinatra audiences, which consisted overwhelmingly of young women, has been well documented. Within a short time after the Paramount events, many analyses and diagnoses of what appeared to be a significant mass phenomenon were offered in the media. But what is also of interest, indicating an important pattern of change in American popular music, was the reaction of the men in the Paramount audience and the general listening public to Sinatra's music and his persona.

A perhaps surprising witness to an earlier Sinatra performance was the novelist Jack Kerouac, as recounted in his memoir *Vanity of Duluoz*. Kerouac was an enthusiast of jazz and popular music. He interviewed Glenn Miller for his college newspaper. While employed on construction work for the new Pentagon in April 1942, Kerouac heard "A Negro with a shovel over his back singing 'St. James Infirmary' so beautiful I follow him across the entire 5-mile construction field so I can hear every note." On his journey down from Massachusetts to Washington, "that spring, 1942, I stopped off in New York just so I could hear Frank Sinatra, and see, Frank Sinatra, sing in the Paramount Theater, waiting there in line with two thousand screaming Brooklyn Jewish and Italian girls. I'm just about, in fact, AM the only guy in line, and when we get in the theater and skinny old Frank comes out and grabs the mike, with glamorous rings on his fingers and wearing gray sports coat, black tie, gray shirt, sings 'Mighty Like a Rose,' and 'Without a Song . . . the road would never end,' oww" (Kerouac 1973: 85).

Writers on Sinatra's singing at this time describe it in terms that do not commonly relate with ideas of masculinity. Gene Lees described his voice during the Dorsey period as "a pure sweet tenor" (1987: 106). Nelson Riddle is said to have compared it to a violin. A feminine quality in Sinatra's voice and style seemed to make some male writers uncomfortable. Derek Jewell, for instance, was at pains to point out that, though he loved Sinatra's early recordings, "I was neither a girl nor a homosexual" (Petkov and Mustazza 1995: 53). The songs Sinatra had in his repertoire also placed his music in a lyrical field that did not connote masculinity. In the Paramount shows he sang "For Me and My Gal," a 1916 song expressing such sentiments as "Someday we're going to build a little home for two." Another of Sinatra's choices was "I Had the Craziest Dream," a recent hit for Helen Forrest. He sang Rodgers and Hart's intensely romantic "Where or When," best known at the time in a lovely, dead-slow version by Peggy Lee. He sang his own hit song "There Are Such Things," in another slow tempo, "A heart that's true, there are such things,/A dream for two, there are such things." The other number he is known to have performed at the Paramount was Jerome Kern's "The Song Is You," which at the time Sinatra was singing with a falsetto high F as the last note.

None of this material, vocally or lyrically, projected machismo or, by the standards of more recent popular music, even an acceptable degree of masculinity. Sinatra was delivering sentimental love lyrics in songs sometimes associated with female performers in lingering tempos and in rich orchestrations. Descriptions of Sinatra's physical presence in these performances also emphasize his thinness, even frailty. "He used to make jokes," as one female fan recalled, "about hanging on to the microphone for support" (Petkov and Mustazza 1995: 47). This was a male presented as passive, lyrical, and vulnerable. Even then, the reactions of a male audience could be expected to be ambivalent. Early Sinatra, the one that thrilled audiences at the Paramount at the end of 1942, is not favored by modern writers. The critical consensus prefers the Sinatra of the 1950s Capitol recordings and thereafter. The reasons behind this preference are significant. They tell us about the ways in which popular musical forms are theorized and written about, and they provide a measure of changes that have taken place since 1942 within popular music and the wider culture.

The historiography of popular music has the habit of being teleological, that is, it conceives of change within musical culture as having a purpose or a goal. The narrative of jazz is particularly wedded to this assumption. An example was discussed in chapter 5, the view that the bebop style was "progressive," that it moved jazz onward toward some goal. Another instance would be the "four beats good, two beats bad" theory—the straightforward assumption that the rhythmic changes that took place between the 1920s and the 1930s were an obviously good thing that had to happen in the development of jazz. Behind all of this lies a notion that somehow the longer-term destiny of jazz was being gradually unfolded—hence the idea of the historical necessity that the big-band format would decline and be replaced by something more conducive to the eventual fulfillment of the historical potential of jazz. However, it could be argued instead that the big bands went into decline because of the war and the economic factors that struck at the conditions of their existence. But jazz history has offered instead a series of teleological explanations: the demise of the big bands was required so that the next phase of jazz's journey could begin to unfold.[2]

The same teleological structuring of events is imposed on Sinatra's music.[3] His early performances and recordings were seen as having the purpose of leading to the fulfillment of his later years. The Sinatra narrative is one of youth and maturity or innocence and experience. Gene Lees's (1987) very significant distinction is "adolescence" and "manhood." Teleological explanations tend to entail a situation of lack or inadequacy: something was wrong with contemporary music for which an actor in this historical pageant had the remedy. An example would be Leonard Feather's idea of jazz "fighting its way out of a harmonic blind alley" in the early 1940s (1960: 30). Was that really what it felt like to be a jazz player in 1940 or 1941, waiting for Oscar Moore to strike that one liberating guitar chord? Was there a conscious yearning after the next great historical stride forward? Were musicians in the early 1930s aware of their need for someone to release them from the imprisonment of two-beat rhythm sections? Were Sinatra's audiences at the Paramount conscious of the gulf that separated their idol from the "artistic maturity" he had not yet achieved?

The audiences at the Paramount in 1942 and 1943 could not have this perspective on Sinatra's career. What was presented to them there and then was clearly adequate at the time. It should be the role of the writer or critic to try to understand the artist in their time and the audiences in their time. We cannot come to an appreciation of the music of Sinatra in 1942–1943 if we make no attempt at historical empathy with the interpretative community, that is, the audiences of that time, and if we do not try to suspend the teleological bias of our judgments. The story we tell ourselves about Sinatra is another narrative. Today, listeners view Sinatra in terms of the youth-maturity dichotomy, but other narratives are just as feasible.

There are other cultural shifts that separate us from Sinatra and the Paramount audience and ultimately from an understanding of the popular music of that time. Of these, the most immediately apparent are ideas of masculinity. A huge gulf of change stands between images of masculinity in 1942 and those of the present day. This is especially important because popular music has been an arena for the increasingly emphatic display of masculinity for the last several decades. From the time of the Rolling Stones, it is a convention that male popular musicians project an impression of menace or violence. At its most intense, in some varieties of metal and hip-hop, the male image in popular music is one of macho brutalism. Styles of dress and behavior and the display of heavily muscled physiques carry the notion of masculinity far outside the domain of, in Jack Kerouac's description, "skinny old Frank . . . in a gray sports coat."

There is a broader range of cultural change that correlates with this changing conception of masculinity. Shifts in aesthetic values have occurred between 1942 and now. This makes the products, the songs, and the performances created in the early 1940s to a large extent inaccessible to us. Values and qualities, in popular music and in the wider culture, which had been positive are now subject to a different valuation. In the changes of instrumental and vocal style, of musical and lyrical content in popular music in the decades since the early 1940s, one can see a movement between two sets of oppositions. Tension between the following two sets of terms has figured in many of the debates in this book.

A	B
romantic	realist
pastoral	urban
sentimental	intellectual
feminine	masculine
vocal	instrumental
melodic	rhythmic
sweet	swing
entertainment	art
popular music	jazz

For the tastes and the aesthetic values of the present and recent decades, the terms in list A represent negative qualities. Music that can be described by more than two or three of these terms is seen as lacking in or devoid of value. Music describable by a corresponding group of terms from list B will be valued much more highly and will be found aesthetically acceptable. List B is "modern," whereas list A is "dated." A twenty-first-century audience recognize list A as representing the properties of an older music, and, from today's perspective, a self-evidently inferior one. Instances of list A productions would be a 1942 piece such as "When the Roses Bloom Again" and many others within then-established song genres. Frank Sinatra's style and repertoire of late 1942 also fell in with most if not all of the values in list A; by 1960, list B would correlate better with what he was doing.

In the early 1940s the values embodied in list A were still operative. This is the principal reason for the difficulties of understanding that we experience in dealing with this music. This is especially problematic when we consider the jazz narrative, as jazz in its modern configuration correlates completely with list B. It is an antisentimental and antiromantic culture (although deeply romantic in its own narrative). Jazz is also a decidedly urban music. It is associated with intellectualism; like modernist art, jazz is "difficult," requiring special knowledge to be understood. It is instrumental rather than vocal, art rather than entertainment. As we have seen throughout this book, it is a category that is defined in opposition to popular music. Lastly, jazz is masculine, both in this general cultural sense and also, overwhelmingly, in terms of actual personnel.

In its post–World War II identity, jazz is a more or less complete embodiment of the values in list B. Because a present-day audience is comfortable with this familiar set of values and because of the teleology implicit in so many cultural histories, this is obviously a good thing. To move from "pastoral" to "urban," from "sentimental" to "intellectual," or from "entertainment" to "art" is self-evidently a progression to something more mature, more intelligent, better. Hence the "superiority" of jazz and some other forms to the popular music of the past. From a later historical perspective, it is obviously correct to find older popular music retrograde.

But in having this reaction and in making no effort to go beyond it, this perspective is blocking out a full understanding of musical culture of the past. It produces a misunderstanding of many products of American popular music and many of its musicians, including some whose work seems to be accessible in terms of later values. Individuals whom we think of as participants in the post-World War II aesthetic were in many cases completely at home in the prewar set of values.

We might think of Duke Ellington, for instance, in terms of List B: as an urban, intellectual (and hence antisentimental) figure belonging to the domain of "art" not of "entertainment." But we cannot understand Ellington fully without acknowledging him as a product of his times, and hence as being marked, like other Americans, by the values in list A. The terms *romantic* and *melodic* fit easily, but it requires an imaginative effort for a present-day audience to accept Ellington's relation to *sentimental* (one of his favorite words, as we saw earlier), to *sweet* (his music was so regarded by voters in 1940s polls), and as representing an "entertainment" rather than an "art" world. We cannot understand Duke Ellington, in the context of his times, unless we are prepared to countenance these so-called old-fashioned values as formative presences in his life and work. Born in 1899, Duke Ellington was a member of the interpretative community of that older popular culture.

The same is true of many others whose place in jazz or some other narrative effaces the fact that they participated in the older culture of the romantic/sentimental/feminine. The bebop musicians are usually represented as being at least halfway into the newer aesthetic, and the rhetoric around bebop speaks of an intellectual "revolution" in the music. But when these musicians composed ballads, they used the contemporary sentimental language of popular song, as in Dizzy Gillespie's "I Waited for You," Milt Jackson's "I've Lost Your Love," or Tadd Dameron's "If You Could See Me

Now": "If you could see me now, you'd find me being brave,/And trying awfully hard to make my tears behave."

Later suppositions about these musicians of the early 1940s represent another aspect of the illusion that Elijah Wald (2004: xiv) noted about their relation to the "mass tastes that we despise": these musicians were themselves also members of the 1940s audience, and there is no reason for us to suppose that they did not also share the taste for the romantic, sentimental, and feminine that is so problematic for later audiences. To accept this possibility about the musicians of the past makes them perhaps more alien to currently received aesthetic values, but it also allows them to be more than a projection of what later listeners would like them to be.

American popular music moved from one aesthetic to another during the 1940s. There were to be fewer sentimental songs of the types that were still current in 1942: roses, cottages, and skylarks became anachronistic symbols. Songs like "Johnny Doughboy" ceased to have currency, and songs about mothers, for some reason, ceased to be written at all. Lyrical singers like Kenny Baker, Deanna Durbin, and many others went out of fashion. Sweet bands like those of Guy Lombardo became victims of a cultural shift away from the aesthetic they represented. History is written by the winners. Because the values of "swing" bands prevailed in the discourse of jazz, the "sweet" bands were made irrelevant to the narrative and are now scarcely listened to by any sizable audience.

At the time of Frank Sinatra's first enormous success in New York at the end of 1942, *Metronome*, one of the most musician-friendly of the magazines, still had separate categories in its popularity polls for "sweet" and "hot" trombone and "pretty" and "hot" tenor. Sweetness was not necessarily an inferior range of the musical spectrum, it was simply one where a different aesthetic, still current at the time, was in force. The concept of pretty music, as well as terms like *sweet* and *mellifluous*, was soon to disappear from the vocabulary of American popular music. This was not necessarily a change to something better. Contrary to decades of received opinion, the sweet bands did not die out because they were bad but because of a complex of cultural factors. In the transfer to the aesthetic of the post–World War II period, something was lost as well as gained.

The triumph of Frank Sinatra singing to excited audiences from the stage of the Paramount in the last days of 1942 was an event occurring toward the closing of a cultural period, rather than at the opening of a new one. It marked one of the last occasions when an American artist of such importance could sing a selection of songs with romantic, sentimental lyrics in a vocal style and persona that represented the "mellifluous" and "feminine." Sinatra still seems current to a present-day audience, because he went on into later decades with a masculine, realist aesthetic that makes him accessible to the values that still prevail. But the Sinatra singing at the Paramount in December 1942 is not current to such a perspective. His music came toward the end of an era when the soldiers of a U.S. Army base could listen to and enjoy a song like "Moonlight Cocktail" without embarrassment or irony, when the word *sentimental* had a positive meaning, and when the narratives of separate "authentic" musical forms had not yet devalued the currency of the popular song.

Postscript: Black, Brown, and Beige

The band of Hal McIntyre, a former saxophonist with Glenn Miller, was booked to play a junior prom at Rhode Island State College on December 17, 1942. Shortly before the engagement, McIntyre's agency called the chairman of the prom to say that travel restrictions, which were familiar a year into the war, meant that McIntyre would not be able to keep his commitment. The agency offered the chairman, a nineteen-year-old student named David Hedison, a substitute for the same price, Duke Ellington and his orchestra. Although Hedison knew there was "a special aura" about Ellington, he was concerned, both about the fact that McIntyre had been extensively advertised and about "how my classmates were going to take this," Ellington's being a colored band (Hedison 2002, personal communication).

The prom was held in the ballroom on the fifteenth floor of the Biltmore Hotel, with a hardwood floor and long windows giving a view across the city of Providence. The *Evening Bulletin* reported that a prom queen, Miss Mary Lightbody, was selected "by the patrons and patronesses together with the members of Duke Ellington's orchestra, who provided the music for the ball." Part of the evening was broadcast on the local station WPRO. A recording exists of the band playing Jerome Kern's "Dearly Beloved" and several of Ellington's own compositions. Among details David Hedison recalled of that evening were that at the intermission "the band manager was on to me like a hawk" for the performance fee of $855 and that the singer Betty Roché was "munching on a chicken sandwich." Hedison recalled Duke Ellington himself as "a high class individual."

From Providence the Ellington band went to Bridgeport, Connecticut, to Harrisburg, Pennsylvania, to Columbus, Ohio, and then to Detroit over the Christmas holiday. At the beginning of January, publicity for the Carnegie Hall concert began to gear up again. The week of January 17 was designated "Duke Ellington Week" by the Morris agency. *Billboard* printed a page of good wishes for the event, signed by twenty-seven show business names, including Cab Calloway, Paul Whiteman, Louis Armstrong, and Chico Marx. Celebrities had been invited, and "Jimmie Lunceford, Benny Goodman, Count Basie and other distinguished contemporaries will be among the boxholders on the momentous night when Duke will present his new work" (*AN* 1.23.43: 16).

By the time the band came in to New York City to rehearse in the Nola Studios on Broadway, via one-nighters in Utica and Rochester, the new piece, "Black, Brown, and Beige," was written. The band tried it out the night before the concert, in a high-school auditorium in Rye, New York, before an audience of a thousand people. Leonard Feather was present, as were William Morris Jr.; Ellington's brother-in-law, Daniel James; and Dr. Mize of the high school's music department. Feather related that all were "stunned by the brilliance" of the piece, but they had "just one reservation: toward the end of the 'Beige' movement, Duke had written a lyric, pompously delivered by Jimmy Britton, declaring that 'We're black, brown, and beige, but we're red, white, and blue'" (1986: 64). Feather and his colleagues considered that such "simplistic flag-waving seemed redundant," but "I had already found that Duke was stubborn in clinging to his convictions. Only after Bill Morris, Dr. Mize, Dan James, and I had expressed our feelings strongly was it agreed that Duke did not need to wear his Americanism on his sleeve. The lyrics were eliminated and 'B, B&B' ran forty-eight instead of fifty minutes the next night" (1986: 64).

The January 23 concert, billed as a benefit for Russian war relief, sold out Carnegie Hall. According to John Hammond, "The whole town turned out for the event, and the auditorium itself could have been sold out many times over" (Tucker 1993a: 171). The program continued almost until midnight, with "Black, Brown, and Beige" the centerpiece, along with twenty-one other numbers, most of them by Ellington himself. At the behest of Daniel James, the concert was recorded on acetate discs, which music writers were able to listen to soon after the concert.

"Black, Brown, and Beige" itself was presented in the program notes as a "Tone Parallel to the History of the American Negro." The significance of its several movements had been spelled out by Helen Oakley in *Down Beat* a week before the concert, in the program notes, and again in Ellington's announcements from the stage. As Leonard Feather had observed the night before, Ellington was "stubborn in clinging to his convictions." In his spoken introduction to "Beige," Ellington reinserted the text that had been deleted at his colleagues' request, "The Negro is rich in education, and it develops up until we find ourselves today struggling for solidarity, but, just as we are about to get our teeth into it, our country's at war and in trouble again, and as before we of course find the black, brown, and beige right in there for the red, white, and blue."

The notices in the New York papers and the music press were generally negative. Some writers questioned whether Ellington had succeeded in making the transition from songs and small-scale portraits to a longer form. Paul Bowles, in the *Herald Tribune*, considered that "Black, Brown, and Beige" had failed to demonstrate aesthetic unity, "nothing emerged but a gaudy potpourri of tutti dance passages and solo virtuoso work" (Tucker 1993a: 166). In the *Amsterdam News*, Dan Burley found it "left no impression on the listener who was trying to connect what he was listening to with the history of the Negro in America" (1.30.43: 17). John Hammond's view was that the elements of the piece "are not woven together into a coherent whole" (Tucker 1993a: 172). Like Fats Waller a year before, Duke Ellington had "gone Carnegie Hall," but he had also not succeeded in making Carnegie Hall "go Duke Ellington."

In a liner note he wrote for the issue of the recordings in 1974, Leonard Feather saw the concert as "a giant step forward for the evolution of jazz." The narrative of jazz as a progressive music encompassed the idea that it would develop through stages that transcended or improved upon earlier stages. Jazz, once established as a separate music with its own trajectory of progression, would begin to move up the cultural hierarchy. For Feather, the Carnegie Hall concert was "the first attempt of a great Afro-American composer to break the boundaries of dance or cabaret music." This would involve a change of performance context—the abstraction of jazz, in the person of Duke Ellington, from the contexts in which it was formed and habituated.

Shortly after the concert, Feather and John Hammond had a dispute in which a main point of contention was dance. To Hammond's complaint that Ellington's new compositions moved away from the rhythms of dance, Feather riposted, "Who the hell wants to dance in Carnegie Hall anyway?" (Tucker 1993a: 175). This rhetorical question begs a number of other questions. In that case, one could ask why Carnegie Hall was a suitable place for Ellington's music. In fact, Ellington had spent the whole of his twenty-year career working with dancers: at the Cotton Club, on "Jump for Joy," in movies, in soundies, on theater stages with the dance troupe that traveled with him, and with Baby Lawrence, Jigsaw Jackson, Marie Bryant, White's Lindy Hoppers, and the rest. Even in the 1920s, Ellington's recordings were "scattered with dance references" (Fell and Wilding 1999: 120). In the 1943 Carnegie Hall concert, three of Ellington's portraits were dedicated to dancers: to Bill "Bojangles" Robinson, Bert Williams, and Florence Mills.

In the early 1940s, Duke Ellington also worked with the singers Ivie Anderson, Herb Jeffries, Jimmy Britton, Betty Roché, Al Hibbler, Joya Sherrill, Lilian Fitzgerald, and Phyllis Smiley. Ellington wrote popular songs. In performances between Pearl Harbor Sunday and the Carnegie Hall date, his band performed popular songs of the period, "Dearly Beloved," "Tangerine," "I Don't Want to Walk Without You," and "Just As Though You Were Here." To judge by this evidence, Ellington was part of the sentimental-lyrical popular song culture that Frank Sinatra also represented.

The Duke Ellington orchestra had performed in a variety of places: theaters in Los Angeles, Baltimore, Philadelphia, Kansas City; the Elms in Youngstown, "Ohio's Smartest Ballroom"; the Rink in Waukegan; the Trianon in Southgate; the Memorial Auditorium in Buffalo; the Sherman Hotel in Chicago. The supposition that Ellington's creative identity was better or more appropriately presented at Carnegie Hall than at the Howard Theatre, in Washington, D.C., at the Crystal Ballroom in Fargo, North Dakota, or at a college prom in Providence, Rhode Island, required some justification. Ellington's work had been formed in those locations, under those conditions of work, and in collaboration with those other performers, musicians, singers, dancers, actors, and comedians.

To look at the actual circumstances, the real context, of Ellington's activity or that of other artists, as opposed to the ideal circumstances into which critics such as Feather have projected them, is to confront the notion of Duke Ellington as a popular musician. Ellington wrote popular music, performed popular music composed by others, worked with popular musicians (not least Frank Sinatra) in the places that popular musicians worked in. He used the same media and the same agencies. He made recordings, appeared in movies, was on the radio, received royalties, and put together a stage musical. This is all, surely, reason for considering Ellington as a popular musician and his work an aspect of popular music.

One can see, however, in the work of criticism that had begun by 1942, the process of abstraction that takes no account of the day-to-day empirical evidence of the working life of a musician like Ellington. He is placed in a category, "jazz," which sets a single aspect of his activity apart from its entire real-life context. But Ellington was involved in many specific contacts with the culture around him, which was in no way an exclusively jazz culture. Writing on the history of jazz separates Ellington and other comparable figures from the contexts that made them who they were. This has had a long-term effect on the presentation of jazz, which in performance is now a single element presented separately. Ellington's performances in 1942, by contrast, occurred in among a rich and diverse mélange of other things.

To reinstall Ellington within the performance contexts he knew, to argue for considering him as a musician within popular music is not to lower his standing or reduce the magnitude of his achievements. Ellington was a genius, as were Charlie Parker and Louis Armstrong. The music of all of these men retains its beauty and power, whether or not we choose to think of them as serious artists. In other realms of American culture, artists working within popular forms are viewed as being the equal of anyone. Within the cinema, for instance, Frank Capra, Preston Sturges, and John Ford were "great artists" (if we must use that term), whose work has some of its greatness from its lack of separation from the popular.

Frank Sinatra is an example in another musical field. Steven Petkov wrote that Sinatra, "earned … affection and respect while working in

venues that normally would prevent a performer from being taken seriously as a great artist" (Petkov and Mustazza 1995: 74). The same could be
said of Duke Ellington in 1943. It is no disservice to Sinatra or to Ellington
to regard them as being among the greatest of popular artists, in an era
that also saw and heard Billie Holiday, Irving Berlin, Johnny Mercer,
Bing Crosby, Benny Goodman, Harry Warren, Jerome Kern, Roy Acuff,
Jimmy Durante, Jack Benny, Ella Fitzgerald, Richard Rodgers, Louis Jordan,
Charles Chaplin, Fats Waller, Orson Welles, Cole Porter, Ethel Waters,
Fred Astaire, Frank Loesser, Bob Wills, and Cab Calloway.

Notes

Chapter 1

1. Citations of periodicals use a numerical date style in which, for example, "2.1.42" represents February 1, 1942.

Chapter 2

1. Many more Pearl Harbor, anti-Japanese, and pro-MacArthur songs were produced at this time. See the material on this in the Sam DeVincent Collection in the Archives Center at the Museum of American History, Smithsonian Institution, Washington, D.C.

Chapter 3

1. See the discussion of ideas on the relation of jazz to popular music in my *Jazz in American Culture* (Townsend 2000: 70–72). The view that mainstream popular music was inferior to forms such as jazz especially in the pre-Presley period came about through the image of the years around 1950 as a particularly barren spell in popular music, and the backward extension of this to cover a much longer period. According to Palmer (1996: 16), for instance, "mainstream pop music was somnolent and squeaky-clean, despite the occasional watered-down pop-boogie hit. Perry Como crooned for suburban snoozers in his V-necked sweaters." Gillett (1971: 8) spoke of "a continuous diet of melodrama/sentiment/trivia over the major radio networks," and generalized this to a summary of popular music's range: "traditionally, popular music has used three modes of expression—sentimental, melodramatic and trivial-novelty" (1971: vi). The view that popular music was definitively an inferior product was also reinforced by the dichotomy between black music and what LeRoi Jones (1995 [1963]: 169) called "the bloodless commercialism of the white American entertainment world." For further reflections of the view of popular music taken by blues and jazz

critics, see the comments of Samuel Charters and Leonard Feather, quoted in chapters 3 and 5, respectively.

2. The Italian-American presence in American popular music has not been thoroughly examined. Italian culture has a strong orientation toward music, particularly vocal music. Other aspects worth investigating are the Italian string tradition (many jazz guitarists, for instance, have been Italian-American, from Eddie Lang [born Salvatore Massaro] to Joe Pass to Bucky Pizzarelli); the *solfeggio* method of learning; and the tendency for musical skills to be transmitted from fathers to sons.

3. However, definitions of blues have varied as much as have definitions of jazz. Modern usage implies that a blues is usually a structure of twelve bars, or sometimes eight. The structure used by Arlen is more elaborate and would be considered not "authentic" by critics who hold to such an idea. Levine's *Jazz Theory Book* (1995), for example, mentions several variants of blues forms but does not include the form used in "Blues in the Night."

Chapter 4

1. Details of the Ellington band's itinerary for 1942 come from three sources: a list given in Richard Boyer's article on Ellington in the *New Yorker* (reprinted in Tucker 1993a); the band's weekly accounts; and a document headed "Itinerary of Engagements Played by Duke Ellington and his Orchestra, January 1, 1942 to December 31, 1942." The last two items, like much of the information on Ellington used elsewhere in this book, are found in the Duke Ellington Collection in the Archives Center, Museum of American History, in the Smithsonian.

2. Boyd's comments were included in an article consulted in the cuttings section of the Duke Ellington Collection. I have no date for its publication.

3. The Mills publicity material is also available in the Duke Ellington Collection at the Smithsonian.

4. Hinton is obviously misremembering the identity of the musician he wrote with, as Chu Berry had been killed in an automobile accident in October 1941.

Chapter 5

1. The idea that jazz fragmented at a certain point, after a long untroubled continuity, was proposed by a number of other writers. Schuller (1989) and Erenberg (1998) placed it as happening in the mid-1940s and Gioia (1997) a few years later. To my knowledge, Shipton's account (2001) is the first to place this event as late as the 1970s.

2. For the fictional literature on jazz and especially the prevalence of what Vance Bourjaily called "The Story," see my *Jazz in American Culture* (Townsend 2000: ch. 4).

3. Blesh (1976: 372), for instance, wrote that "It is difficult to doubt that . . . bop unisons relate directly to the West African choral practices." More generally, full-scale jazz histories, such as those of Blesh, Stearns (1956), Collier (1978), Gioia, (1997), and Shipton

(2001), all include coverage of a long prehistoric period of jazz that links it to "folk" roots.

4. The bebop musicians were called "dissidents" in Gottlieb (1979: 113); Erenberg (1998: 227) referred to them as "avantgardists rebelling against musical convention." For Marshall Stearns (1956: 224) they were "a small gang of musical revolutionaries," and for Leonard Feather (1960: 30) "a bunch of young rebels." For Gioia (1997: 201), they "rebelled against the populist trappings of swing music." Even in a glossary in Levine's *The Jazz Theory Book*, where one might expect a technical definition, bebop is referred to as "the revolutionary style of jazz that evolved in the early 1940s" (1995: xi).

5. See, for example, Stowe (1994: 10), "the more regimented modes of swing." Harris (1952: 180) described big bands as "highly disciplined aggregations who could churn out one arranged piece after another, meticulously arranged down to the last cymbal crash." Schuller (1989: 848) called the pre-bebop bands "creatively restrictive and inflexible." Gioia (1997: 193) related the decline of swing to the same cause, "its vital core enervated by the formulaic gestures of the big-name bands."

6. A BBC radio feature on Gillespie, broadcast in June 2005, devoted several of its thirty minutes to explaining not just the spitball incident, but, for the benefit of British listeners, what a spitball is.

7. The commentary to the program on bebop in this series follows the fabricated line "I came alive" with another that appears to have been freshly minted for this film, "I could fly," attributed to Charlie Parker, whose nickname was "Bird." This formulation is even more effectively mythical than the usual one.

8. See, for example, Stearns (1956: 228), "In terms of harmony, jazz developed along the same lines as classical music (by adopting the next note in the overtone series), but more recently and rapidly." See also Collier (1978: 350).

Chapter 6

1. David Ake (2002: 42–61) wrote of the failure to recognize rhythm-and-blues artists such as Louis Jordan in relation to the jazz narrative, whereas earlier blues-based performers are linked into the narrative routinely. Collier's jazz history (1978: 449), for instance, claims that Jordan's music "owed as much to the black vaudeville tradition" as to other blues musicians. Gioia's (1997) more recent history of jazz, in a listing of recommended jazz recordings, continues the practice of citing earlier blues performers (Robert Johnson, Charlie Patton, and Bessie Smith) as part of jazz history but listing no post-1940 performers in this category.

Chapter 7

1. Feather's description of the typical squalor of a 52nd Street club was perhaps exaggerated, as he was an exponent of the view that jazz needed to elevate itself into such venues as the concert hall.

2. The decline of the big-band format is frequently put down to aesthetic or intellectual failures rather than to concrete circumstances; for example, Erenberg (1998: 225) described "the failure of swing's ecstatic promise of a modern America rooted in pluralism and individualism" as one of the causes of a shift to bebop.

3. In addition to the comments of Donald Clarke and Gene Lees, cited earlier, the following statement in a liner note to a reissue of Sinatra's famous 1956 album *Songs for Swinging Lovers* is indicative of a common view of Sinatra's progress: "Sinatra's singing on this album," noted critic John Rockwell, "has a verve and conviction that make his records from the Forties sound bland."

Works Cited

Books, Articles, and Liner Notes

Adorno, Theodor. 1941. On popular music. *Studies in Philosophy and Social Science* 9: 66–79.

Adorno, Theodor. 1989 [1937]. On jazz. *Discourse* 12: 36–69.

Ake, David. 2002. *Jazz Cultures*. Berkeley: University of California Press.

Allen, Bob, ed. 1994. *The Blackwell Guide to Recorded Country Music*. London: Blackwell.

Atkins, Cholly, and Jacqui Malone. 2001. *Class Act: The Jazz Life of Choreographer Cholly Atkins*. New York: Columbia University Press.

Baker, Dorothy. 1939. *Young Man with a Horn*. London: Gollancz.

Barker, Danny, with Alyn Shipton. 1986. *A Life in Jazz*. London: Macmillan.

Basie, Count, with Albert Murray. 1987. *Good Morning Blues*. London: Paladin.

Berendt, Joachim. 1976. *The Jazz Book*. London: Paladin.

Bigard, Barney, and Barry Martyn, eds. 1985. *With Louis and the Duke: The Autobiography of a Jazz Clarinetist*. London: Macmillan.

Blau, Dick, Angeliki Keil, and Charles Keil. 1992. *Polka Happiness*. Philadelphia: Temple University Press.

Blesh, Rudi. 1976. *Shining Trumpets: A History of Jazz*. 2nd ed. New York: Da Capo.

Blum, John Morton. 1976. *V Was for Victory: Politics and American Culture During World War II*. New York: Harcourt Brace Jovanovich.

Bryant, Clora, Buddy Collette, William Green, Steven Isoardi, Jack Kelson, Horace Tapscott, Gerald Wilson, and Marl Young. 1998. *Central Avenue Sounds: Jazz in Los Angeles*. Berkeley: University of California Press.

Carmichael, Hoagy, with Stephen Longstreet. 1966. *Sometimes I Wonder: The Story of Hoagy Carmichael*. London: Alvin Redman.

Carr, Patrick. 1980. *The Illustrated History of Country Music*. New York: Dolphin.

Chapman, James. 2002. Introduction. *Approaches to Film History*. Milton Keynes, U.K.: Open University Press.

Charters, Samuel B. 1963. *The Poetry of the Blues*. New York: Oak Publications.

Chilton, John. 1990. *The Song of the Hawk: The Life and Recordings of Coleman Hawkins*. London: Quartet.

Clarke, Donald. 1997. *All or Nothing at All: A Life of Frank Sinatra*. London: Macmillan.

Cogdell Dje Dje, Jacqueline, and Eddie S. Meadows, eds. 1998. *California Soul: Music of African Americans in the West*. Berkeley: University of California Press.

Collier, James Lincoln. 1978. *The Making of Jazz: A Comprehensive History*. New York: Delta.

Copland, Aaron. 1941. *Our New Music: Leading Composers in Europe and America*. New York: McGraw-Hill.

Copland, Aaron, and Vivian Perls. 1984. *Copland: Volume I, 1900–1942*. London: Faber and Faber.

Dance, Stanley. 1980. *The World of Count Basie*. London: Sidgwick and Jackson.

Davidoff, Nicholas. 1998. *In the Country of Country: A Journey to the Roots of American Music*. New York: Vintage.

DeVeaux, Scott. 1988. Bebop and the recording industry: the 1942 AFM recording ban reconsidered. *Journal of the American Musicological Society* 41: 126–165.

DeVeaux, Scott. 1991. Constructing the jazz tradition: jazz historiography. *Black American Literature Forum* 25(3): 525–560.

DeVeaux, Scott. 1997. *The Birth of Bebop: A Social and Musical History*. Berkeley: University of California Press.

Directory of Music, Entertainment, and Drama in Buffalo and the Niagara Frontier. 1941. Buffalo, N.Y.: Stoeckel.

Dos Passos, John. 1945. *State of the Nation*. London: Routledge.

Easton, Carol. 1973. *Straight Ahead: The Story of Stan Kenton*. New York: Morrow.

Ellington, Edward Kennedy [Duke]. 1974. *Music Is My Mistress*. London: W. H. Allen.

Erenberg, Lewis A. 1998. *Swingin' the Dream: Big Band Jazz and the Rebirth of American Culture*. Chicago: University of Chicago Press.

Escott, Colin. 2002. *Roadkill on the Three-Chord Highway*. New York: Routledge.

Ewen, David. 1977. *All the Years of American Popular Music*. Englewood Cliffs, N.J.: Prentice-Hall.

Feather, Leonard. 1960. *The Encyclopedia of Jazz*. New York: Horizon.

Feather, Leonard. 1974. Liner notes to *The Duke Ellington Carnegie Hall Concerts: January 1943*, Prestige Records LP, CD on Fantasy 34004–2.

Feather, Leonard. 1977 [1949]. *Inside Jazz*. New York: Da Capo.

Feather, Leonard. 1986. *The Jazz Years: Earwitness to an Era*. London: Quartet Books.

Fell, John L., with Thorkild Wilding. 1999. *Stride!* London: Scarecrow Press.

Fernett, Gene. 1970. *Swing Out: Great Negro Dance Bands*. Midland, Mich.: Pendell.

Flanagan, Bill. 1987. *Written in My Soul*. New York: Omnibus.

Flower, John. 1972. *Moonlight Serenade: A Bio-discography of the Glenn Miller Civilian Band*. New Rochelle, N.Y.: Arlington House.

Fordin, Hugh. 1995. *Getting to Know Him: A Biography of Oscar Hammerstein II*. New York: Da Capo.

Friedwald, Will. 1995. *Sinatra! The Song Is You: A Singer's Art.* New York: Scribner.

Gennari, John. 1991. Jazz criticism: its development and ideologies. *Black American Literature Forum* 25(3): 449–523.

Gillett, Charlie. 1971. *The Sound of the City.* London: Sphere.

Gioia, Ted. 1997. *The History of Jazz.* New York: Oxford University Press.

Gitler, Ira. 1985. *Swing to Bop: An Oral History of the Transition in Jazz in the 1940s.* New York: Oxford University Press.

Goldman, Mark. 1983. *High Hopes: The Rise and Decline of Buffalo, New York.* Albany: State University of New York Press.

Gordon, Robert. 2002. *Can't Be Satisfied: The Life and Times of Muddy Waters.* London: Jonathan Cape.

Gottlieb, William P. 1979. *The Golden Age of Jazz.* London: Quartet.

Green, Benny. 1973. *Drums in My Ears.* London: Davis-Poynter.

Gunther, John. 1997 [1947]. *Inside U.S.A.* New York: The New Press.

Hamm, Charles. 1983. *Yesterdays: Popular Song in America.* New York: Norton.

Harris, Rex. 1952. *Jazz.* Harmondsworth, U.K.: Penguin.

Hentoff, Nat, and Nat Shapiro, eds. 1962 [1955]. *Hear Me Talkin' to Ya.* Harmondsworth, U.K.: Penguin.

Hobsbaum, Eric [Francis Newton]. 1961. *The Jazz Scene.* Harmondsworth, U.K.: Penguin.

Holway, John B. 1991. *Black Diamonds: Life in the Negro Leagues from the Men Who Lived It.* New York: Stadium Books.

Hoops, Roy. 1977. *Americans Remember: The Home Front.* New York: Hawthorn.

Hyland, William G. 1998. *Richard Rodgers.* New Haven, Conn.: Yale University Press.

Jay, Martin. 1984. *Adorno.* London: Fontana.

Jones, LeRoi. 1995 [1963]. *Blues People.* Edinburgh: Payback Press.

Kaminsky, Max, with V. E. Hughes. 1965. *My Life in Jazz.* London: The Jazz Book Club.

Keillor, Garrison. 1991. *Radio Romance.* London: Faber and Faber.

Kenney, William Howland. 1993. *Chicago Jazz: A Cultural History, 1904–1930.* New York: Oxford University Press.

Kenney, William Howland. 1999. *Recorded Music in American Life: The Phonograph and Popular Memory, 1890–1945.* New York: Oxford University Press.

Kernfeld, Barry, ed. 1994. *The New Grove Dictionary of Jazz.* New York: St. Martin's Press.

Kerouac, Jack. 1973. *Vanity of Duluoz: An Adventurous Education, 1935–46.* London: Quartet.

Kirk, Andy, with Amy Lee. 1989. *Twenty Years on Wheels.* Oxford, U.K.: Bayou Press.

Klinkenborg, Verlyn. 1991. *The Last Fine Time.* London: Secker and Warburg.

Latzgo, Roger. 1995. Tom Morgan: prototype of a style. *Just Jazz Guitar* May: 32–36.

Lees, Gene. 1987. *Singers and the Song.* London: Oxford University Press.

Levine, Mark. 1995. *The Jazz Theory Book.* Petaluma, Calif.: Sher.

Levinson, Peter J. 1999. *Trumpet Blues: The Life of Harry James.* New York: Oxford University Press.

Lingeman, Richard R. 1979. *Don't You Know There's a War On? The American Home Front, 1941–1945.* New York: Capricorn.

Lomax, Alan. 1993. *The Land Where the Blues Began.* New York: The New Press.

Love, Preston. 1997. *A Thousand Honey Creeks Later: My Life in Music from Basie to Motown—and Beyond.* London: Wesleyan University Press.

Malone, Bill C. 1987. *Country Music, U.S.A.* Wellingborough, U.K.: Equation.

Mangione, Jerre, and Ben Morreale. 1993. *La Storia: Five Centuries of the Italian American Experience.* New York: Harper Perennial.

McCarthy, Albert. 1983. *Big Band Jazz.* London: Peerage.

Mezzrow, Mezz, with Bernard Wolfe. 1961 [1946]. *Really the Blues.* London: Transworld.

Mordden, Ethan. 1981. *The American Theatre.* New York: Oxford University Press.

Murray, Albert. 1978. *Stomping the Blues.* London: Quartet.

O'Day, Anita, with George Eells. 1983. *High Times, Hard Times.* London: Corgi.

Otis, Johnny. 1993. *Upside Your Head! Rhythm and Blues on Central Avenue.* London: Wesleyan University Press.

Owens, Thomas. 1995. *Bebop: The Music and Its Players.* New York: Oxford University Press.

Palmer, Robert. 1996. *Dancing in the Street: A Rock and Roll History.* London: BBC Books.

Panassié, Hugues. 1960 [1942]. *The Real Jazz.* New York: A. S. Barnes.

Peterson, Richard A. 1997. *Creating Country Music: Fabricating Authenticity.* Chicago: University of Chicago Press.

Petkov, Steven, and Leonard Mustazza, eds. 1995. *The Frank Sinatra Reader.* New York: Oxford University Press.

Porter, Lewis. 1998. *John Coltrane: His Life and Music.* Ann Arbor: University of Michigan Press.

Rampersad, Arnold, ed. 1995. *The Collected Poems of Langston Hughes.* New York: Vintage.

Ramsey, Frederick, Jr. 1960. *Been Here and Gone.* London: Cassell.

Ramsey, Frederick, Jr., and Charles Edward Smith, eds. 1958 [1946]. *Jazzmen.* London: The Jazz Book Club.

Reisner, Robert George. 1965 [1962]. *Bird: The Legend of Charlie Parker.* London: The Jazz Book Club.

Robertson, Alastair. 2000. Liner notes to CD *Evensong* by Artie Shaw, Hep Records 1073.

Rodgers, Richard. 1976. *Musical Stages.* London: W. H. Allen.

Royal, Marshall, with Claire P. Gordon. 1996. *Marshall Royal: Jazz Survivor.* London: Cassell.

Russell, Ross. 1971. *Jazz Style in Kansas City and the Southwest.* Berkeley: University of California Press.

Russell, Ross. 1973. *Bird Lives!* London: Quartet Books.

Rust, Brian. 1977. *Jazz Records, 1897–1942.* Chigwell, U.K.: Storyville.

Rust, Brian, with Allen G. Debus, eds. 1973. *The Complete Entertainment Discography, from the Mid- 1890s to 1942.* New Rochelle, N.Y.: Arlington House.

Sackett, Susan. 1995. *Hollywood Sings! An Inside Look at Sixty Years of Academy Award–Nominated Songs.* New York: Billboard.

Sanjek, Russell. 1988. *American Popular Music and Its Business: The First Four Hundred Years.* Vol. 3. *From 1900 to 1984.* New York: Oxford University Press.

Sargeant, Winthrop. 1959 [1938]. *Jazz: Hot and Hybrid.* London: The Jazz Book Club.

Schuller, Gunther. 1989. *The Swing Era: The Development of Jazz, 1930–45.* New York: Oxford University Press.

Seidel, Michael. 2002 [1988]. *Streak: Joe DiMaggio and the Summer of '41.* Lincoln: University of Nebraska Press.

Shaw, Arnold. 1968. *Sinatra: Retreat of the Romantic.* London: Coronet.

Shaw, Arnold. 1977. *52nd Street: The Street of Jazz.* New York: Da Capo.

Shipton, Alyn. 2001. *A New History of Jazz.* London: Continuum.

Simon, George T. 1974a. *The Big Bands.* New York: Collier.

Simon, George T. 1974b. *Glenn Miller and His Orchestra.* London: W. H. Allen.

Smith, Willie the Lion, with George Hoefer. 1964. *Music on My Mind: The Memoirs of an American Pianist.* London: The Jazz Book Club.

Spencer, Frederick J. 2002. *Jazz and Death.* Jackson: University Press of Mississippi.

Stearns, Marshall W. 1956. *The Story of Jazz.* London: Sidgwick and Jackson.

Stowe, David W. 1994. *Swing Changes: Big-Band Jazz in New Deal America.* Cambridge, Mass.: Harvard University Press.

Stratemann, Klaus. 1992. *Duke Ellington Day by Day and Film by Film.* Copenhagen: Jazz Media.

Terkel, Studs. 2001 [1984]. *"The Good War": An American Oral History of World War II.* London: Phoenix.

Townsend, Peter. 2000. *Jazz in American Culture.* Edinburgh: Edinburgh University Press.

Tucker, Mark, ed. 1993a. *The Duke Ellington Reader.* New York: Oxford University Press.

Tucker, Mark, ed. 1993b. The genesis of "Black, Brown and Beige." *Black Music Research Journal* 13(2): 67–86.

Vail, Ken. 1996. *Bird's Diary: The Life of Charlie Parker, 1945–1955.* Chessington, U.K.: Castle Communications.

van Rijn, Guido. 1997. *Roosevelt's Blues: African–American Blues and Gospel Songs on FDR.* Jackson: University Press of Mississippi.

Wald, Elijah. 2004. *Escaping the Delta: Robert Johnson and the Invention of the Blues.* New York: Amistad.

Welty, Eudora. 1943. *A Curtain of Green.* New York: Penguin.

Wilder, Alec. 1972. *American Popular Song: The Great Innovators, 1900–1950.* New York: Oxford University Press.

Wilk, Max. 1974. *They're Playing Our Song.* London: W. H. Allen.

Wilkinson, Christopher. 2001. *Jazz on the Road: Don Albert's Musical Life.* Berkeley: University of California Press.

Williams, Martin. 1967. *Jazz Masters of New Orleans.* New York: Macmillan.

Wright, Lawrie. 1992. *"Fats" in Fact.* Chigwell, U.K.: Storyville.

X, Malcolm, and Alex Haley. 1965. *The Autobiography of Malcolm X.* New York: Grove.

Periodicals and Newspapers

Abbreviations used to cite these publications in the main text are given in parentheses.

Amsterdam (New York) News (AN)

Billboard (BB)

Chicago Defender (CD)

Down Beat (DB)

Jazz Journal International (JJI)

Metronome (Metr.)

New York Times (NYT)

Providence (Rhode Island) Journal (PJ)

Variety (Var.)

Waukegan (Illinois) News-Sun (WNS)

Index